The *NEW* ROSE EXPERT

Dr. D.G.Hessayon

All Editions & Reprints: 3,930,000 copies

Published 1997
by Expert Books
a division of Transworld Publishers Ltd

A catalogue record for this book is available from the British Library

TRANSWORLD PUBLISHERS LTD
61–63 Uxbridge Road, London W5 5SA

Distributed in the United States
by Sterling Publishing Co. Inc.,
387 Park Avenue South,
New York, NY 10016–8810

Distributed in Canada by
Cavendish Books Inc.,
Unit 5, 801 West 1st Street,
North Vancouver, B.C. V7P 1A4

EXPERT BOOKS

Contents

Reproduction by Spot On Repro Ltd, Perivale, Middlesex
Printed and bound in Great Britain by Jarrold & Sons Ltd, Norwich

ISBN 0 903505 47 9   © D. G. HESSAYON 1997

CHAPTER 1

LOOKING AT YOUR ROSES

Looking at the roses in your neighbour's garden may suggest that nothing has changed in the world of roses during the 1990s. *Queen Elizabeth*, *Silver Jubilee* and *Peace* are still there, the climbers still stretch against the wall and the bushes are pruned as usual every spring.

In fact there have been many important changes since the previous edition of this book. New varieties have continued to appear in garden centres and catalogues, and in this edition about 150 new ones are illustrated and described. But it has not been just a matter of new varieties. Patio Roses and Ground Cover Roses have now been moved into separate Groups, Miniature Climbers with tiny leaves and small flowers have been introduced and the type of modern Shrub Roses with an old-fashioned look known as English Roses have become popular. Some of our techniques have also changed — a greatly simplified method of pruning has been introduced.

These changes which have occurred in the last couple of decades of the 20th century are only the latest chapter in the constantly changing rose story. In the first half of the 19th century roses were either large shrubs or climbers with a limited colour range and a limited flowering season. Things changed during Queen Victoria's reign — the tough European varieties were bred with repeat-flowering types from the East, and the blood of Persian roses brought in bright yellows and oranges.

Hardy, colourful, repeat-flowering and vigorous — it is not surprising that the new roses became Britain's most popular garden plants in the early years of this century. In came the Floribundas, out went the Hybrid Perpetuals — a continually unfolding story.

There are now more than a thousand varieties offered for sale. Nearly all are grown for the beauty and/or the fragrance of the flowers, but there are varieties noted for their decorative hips, colourful leaves and even for their beautiful thorns. The plant may struggle to reach a height of 10 cm or it may tower 10 m into the sky. Obviously making the right choice is not easy.

More roses are purchased from shops and garden centres than are ordered by post from nurseries, but for many people one of the joys of the gardening year is to study the rose catalogues which come through the letterbox in autumn.

New varieties get the largest photographs and the most alluring descriptions, but this does not always make them the best choice. For the ordinary gardener who just wants a few reliable bushes or climbers it is sometimes better to wait a year or two to see how the new ones have fared in other people's gardens. Before making out your order read the descriptions carefully, but do not expect to find all the faults listed.

The approach in this book is rather different. In the A–Z chapter (pages 10–90) you will find information on the important properties of many roses, together with an overall assessment of their value for garden or exhibition use. There are two important features of these 388 descriptions. First of all, there has been no attempt to list the 'best' roses. The ones selected have been chosen solely on the basis of their popularity and the probability of finding them in garden centres, stores, catalogues and in the popularity and reliability polls conducted by the Royal National Rose Society.

Secondly, catalogue-type decriptions have been avoided. Bad points as well as good ones have been listed, and in some cases the drawbacks outweigh the advantages.

Apart from information on varieties, guidance is provided on planting (Chapter 5), upkeep (Chapter 6) and the prevention and control of problems (Chapter 7). For some gardeners the rose is more than a pretty flower — it is an absorbing hobby. For them Chapter 8 provides more specialised information on such topics as propagation, exhibiting and rose gardens to visit. The display produced by these roses hobbyists is often spectacular, but remember that the bloom from a single bush in a beginner's garden will smell just as sweetly as its twin in their gardens.

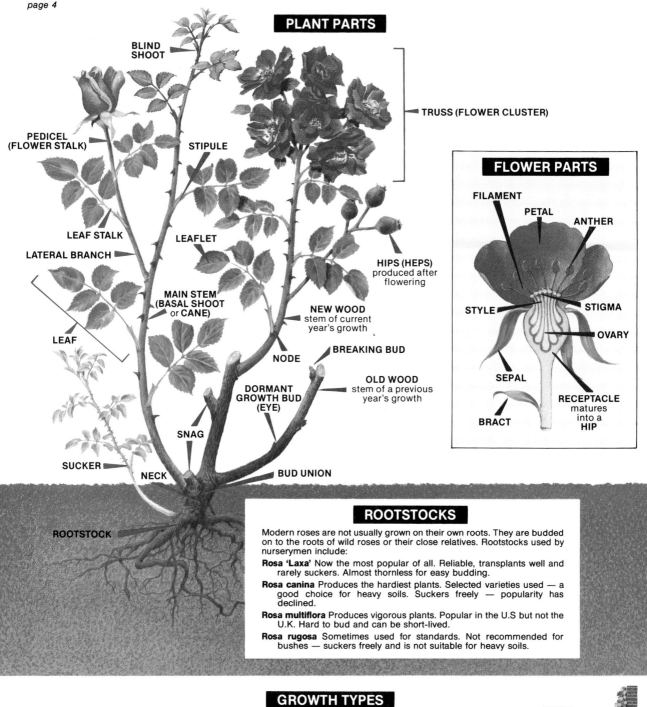

PLANT PARTS

BLIND SHOOT

TRUSS (FLOWER CLUSTER)

PEDICEL (FLOWER STALK)

STIPULE

LEAF STALK

LEAFLET

LATERAL BRANCH

HIPS (HEPS) produced after flowering

MAIN STEM (BASAL SHOOT or CANE)

NEW WOOD stem of current year's growth

LEAF

NODE

BREAKING BUD

DORMANT GROWTH BUD (EYE)

OLD WOOD stem of a previous year's growth

SNAG

SUCKER

NECK

BUD UNION

ROOTSTOCK

FLOWER PARTS

FILAMENT

PETAL

ANTHER

STYLE

STIGMA

OVARY

SEPAL

BRACT

RECEPTACLE matures into a HIP

ROOTSTOCKS

Modern roses are not usually grown on their own roots. They are budded on to the roots of wild roses or their close relatives. Rootstocks used by nurserymen include:

Rosa 'Laxa' Now the most popular of all. Reliable, transplants well and rarely suckers. Almost thornless for easy budding.

Rosa canina Produces the hardiest plants. Selected varieties used — a good choice for heavy soils. Suckers freely — popularity has declined.

Rosa multiflora Produces vigorous plants. Popular in the U.S but not the U.K. Hard to bud and can be short-lived.

Rosa rugosa Sometimes used for standards. Not recommended for bushes — suckers freely and is not suitable for heavy soils.

GROWTH TYPES

The four basic growth types are ground cover, bush, standard and climbing (see chart below). A bush may be a Hybrid Tea, Patio, Miniature, Floribunda or Shrub Rose (see page 11).

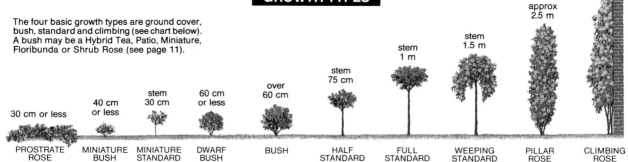

PROSTRATE ROSE	MINIATURE BUSH	MINIATURE STANDARD	DWARF BUSH	BUSH	HALF STANDARD	FULL STANDARD	WEEPING STANDARD	PILLAR ROSE	CLIMBING ROSE
30 cm or less	40 cm or less	stem 30 cm	60 cm or less	over 60 cm	stem 75 cm	stem 1 m	stem 1.5 m	approx 2.5 m	

FLOWER TYPES

Number of Petals

SINGLE	SEMI-DOUBLE	DOUBLE		

SINGLE

less than 8 petals
Examples: Ballerina
Dortmund
Fred Loads
Mermaid

SEMI-DOUBLE

8-20 petals
Examples: Boy's Brigade
Joseph's Coat
Masquerade
Sweet Magic

MODERATELY FULL
21-29 petals
Example: Pascali

FULL
30-39 petals
Example: Dearest

VERY FULL
40 petals and over
Example: Peace

Flower Colours

SINGLE COLOUR
Petals similarly coloured throughout, although some changes may occur as blooms get older.
Example: Iceberg

BI-COLOUR
Colour of the outside of each petal distinctly different from the inside hue.
Example: Piccadilly

MULTI-COLOUR
Colour of the petals changes distinctly with age. Flower trusses have several colours at the same time.
Example: Masquerade

BLEND
Two or more distinct colours merge on the inside of each petal.
Example: Peace

STRIPED
Two or more different colours on each petal, one of which is in the form of distinct bands.
Example: Rosa Mundi

HAND PAINTED
Silvery petals with red blotched and feathered over the surface, leaving a white eye at the base.
Example: Regensberg

Petal Shapes

The petals of many roses are **plain**, but those of Hybrid Teas and some Floribundas are **reflexed**. A feature of a few roses is a wavy or **ruffled** edge to the petals, and in the *Grootendorst* varieties the petals have a carnation-like **frilled** edge.

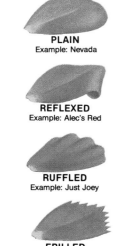

PLAIN
Example: Nevada

REFLEXED
Example: Alec's Red

RUFFLED
Example: Just Joey

FRILLED
Example: F. J. Grootendorst

Flower Shapes

HIGH-CENTRED
Classical shape of the Hybrid Tea – long inner petals forming a regular central cone.

SPLIT-CENTRED
Inner petals confused, forming an irregular central area.

BLOWN
Normally well-shaped bloom past its best – opened wide to reveal stamens.

GLOBULAR
Bloom possessing many petals forming a ball-like arrangement with a closed centre.

OPEN-CUPPED
Bloom possessing many petals forming a cup-like arrangement with an open centre.

QUARTERED
Inner petals folded into 4 distinct sections rather than forming a cone.

FLAT
Flat, low-centred bloom with a small number of petals.

ROSETTE
Flat, low-centred bloom with many short petals regularly arranged.

POMPON
Rounded bloom with many short petals regularly arranged.

FOLIAGE TYPES

Leaf Surfaces

The typical rose leaf has a smooth surface and is made up of five or seven leaflets. This standard pattern applies to nearly all garden varieties, but the shininess of the surface varies greatly. Some are highly polished as if they have been recently treated with oil — others are distinctly dull. Many varieties have leaves between these two extremes, so the three basic groups are **glossy**, **semi-glossy** and **matt**.

Not all roses have five or seven leaflets — a few such as *Canary Bird* have attractive ferny foliage composed of many small leaflets. Also the surface of the foliage is not always smooth — the Rugosa Shrubs have leaves which are deeply ribbed (**rugose**), giving them a characteristically wrinkled effect.

GLOSSY
Example: Peace

SEMI-GLOSSY
Example: Southampton

MATT
Example: Royal William

RUGOSE
Example: Rosa rugosa alba

Leaf Colours

Nearly all mature rose leaves are green, varying from the insipid pale green of *Fred Loads* to the very dark green of *Felicia*. As illustrated below, the three basic groups of rose leaf colours are **light green**, **medium green** and **dark green**. Some varieties have green foliage which is **bronze-tinted**, giving the leaves a coppery sheen. There are exceptions to this general picture, especially amongst the Shrub Roses. Young foliage is sometimes distinctly purplish or crimson, and in some varieties such as *Rosa rubrifolia* and *Buff Beauty* this red coloration persists in the mature leaves. At the other end of the colour spectrum, the leaves of the Alba type are grey-green with a bluish tinge. Several varieties have attractive autumn tints — the Rugosa type is outstanding.

LIGHT GREEN
Example: Goldstar

MEDIUM GREEN
Example: Blessings

DARK GREEN
Example: Elina

BRONZE-TINTED
Example: Pink Peace

HIPS

After the flowers have gone, the coloured and fleshy fruit cases of some Shrub Roses are an extra bonus in the autumn garden. The bottle-shaped red hips of *Rosa moyesii* and the large tomato-like fruits of *Frau Dagmar Hartopp* are well-known but there are many other varieties to choose from.

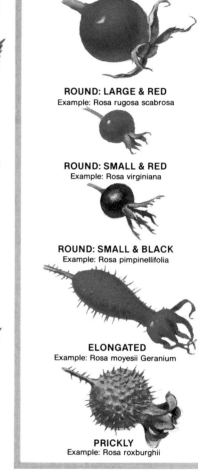

ROUND: LARGE & RED
Example: Rosa rugosa scabrosa

ROUND: SMALL & RED
Example: Rosa virginiana

ROUND: SMALL & BLACK
Example: Rosa pimpinellifolia

ELONGATED
Example: Rosa moyesii Geranium

PRICKLY
Example: Rosa roxburghii

FLOWERING PERIOD

Repeat flowering Roses produce two or more flushes of blooms during the flowering season. Modern roses generally produce blooms at intervals throughout the summer months and into the autumn — one of the main reasons for the unrivalled popularity of Hybrid Teas and Floribundas. Repeat flowering varieties, also known as recurrent and remontant varieties, may produce some flowers between the main flushes. When this feature is strongly marked the descriptions perpetual and continuous flowering are sometimes used, but they are not strictly correct.

Once flowering Roses produce a single flush of blooms which usually lasts for several weeks. Occasionally a few flowers may appear in autumn, but this flowering is far too sporadic to be considered a second flush. The once flowering varieties most frequently bloom in June/July (**summer flowering**), but there are varieties of Shrubs and Ramblers which bloom in late spring, early summer or late summer.

FRAGRANCE

People will always smell an open bloom if they are trying to decide on its merits. Because of the importance of this feature, the descriptions in the A–Z Guide (pages 12–90) include an indication of the strength of the perfume of each variety — **no fragrance**, **slightly fragrant**, **fragrant** or **very fragrant**.

These statements, however, cannot be taken as a universally agreed assessment. Fragrance depends on many factors —

- **Personal taste**: Some people like heavy sickly smells, others prefer spicy or fruity aromas.
- **Personal sensitivity**: Some people have a deficient sense of smell, which unlike poor eyesight or deafness may go unnoticed.
- **Stage of growth**: Some roses are most fragrant in early flower, others when fully open.
- **Weather**: Warmth and high air humidity enhance fragrance.

Fragrance is, of course, associated with flowers but there are a few varieties with fragrant foliage — see *Lady Penzance* (page 83).

The history of the rose

EARLY ROSES
OF THE
WESTERN WORLD

About 5000 years ago Mediterranean man created a new concept — Western civilization. Very quickly such basic features as writing, cities, the use of metals and the wheel appeared…and so did an interest in the Rose.

In Ancient Crete in 1600 BC roses were being painted on palace walls, and in Egypt a thousand years later they were portrayed on tombs. It would be wrong, however, to pretend that all ancient civilizations were fascinated by this flower — there are only two mentions of roses in the whole of the Authorized Version of the Bible … it may tell you to look at the Lilies of the Field, but it does not ask you to look at the roses!

The Greeks were perhaps the first to take the rose seriously. They had a good publicist — Sappho the poetess called it "The Queen of Flowers"; they also had a good technical adviser — Theophrastus wrote that roses should have their old wood removed to bear better flowers, that cuttings grow better than seeds and that success depends primarily on picking the right planting spot.

If the Greeks were the first to grow them in gardens and pots throughout the land, it was the Romans who first fell in love with them. They slept on the petals, carpeted their floors with them, imported early flowers from Egypt and raised their own blooms for winter in artificially-heated conservatories. They used them in food, wine, perfumes and medicines. The Legions took them to Britain and the other outposts of the Empire … and then Rome fell. The rose, now unloved and neglected, declined so that only the hardy varieties survived.

Few nations have loved the rose as much as the Romans. Thick layers of rose petals were used to carpet the floors of banqueting halls.

The early Christian Church rejected this floral symbol of Roman depravity, but it was back in favour by about 400 AD. Rosaries were made from the hips, medicines were made from the petals and circular windows in churches were designed on the pattern of the blooms.

We can take stock of the British garden roses as they existed in 1500. There was the most ancient cultivated rose of all — the Red Rose, **Rosa gallica.** A survivor from Roman times or brought over by the Crusaders, we can leave it to the experts to argue about its origin in the gardens of the Middle Ages.

Next the White Rose, **Rosa alba** — another very ancient rose brought over by the Romans. The fragrant **Damask Roses** came to Britain much later — modern research dates this introduction to just before 1500 rather than in the luggage of a returning Crusader as stated in many textbooks.

The red one, the white one and the richly fragrant one were all in the Tudor garden in 1500. One of the varieties was the *Autumn Damask* which had an unusually long flowering season. Not important in the early garden, perhaps, but as a parent of future generations it was destined to become one of the most important of all roses.

After the Wars of the Roses (1455–1485) the Red Rose of Lancaster (R. gallica Officinalis) and the White Rose of York (R. alba semi-plena) were combined in the Tudor Rose emblem.

By 1700 other varieties had arrived. The globular and fragrant **Centifolia** or Cabbage Rose appeared in about 1550 from the Continent. Others came from much further afield. The **Austrian Yellow** had come to Britain via Vienna from Persia in 1580 and the **Musk Rose** had come at the same time from the Himalayas.

A bouquet of ancient garden roses — once flowering, limited in colour, globular in bloom and spreading in growth habit, waiting for the introduction of the roses from the Orient a generation or two later. The marriage between these Western and Oriental roses led to a bewildering array of new varieties which culminated in the modern rose of our gardens.

ROSES OF THE ORIENT

Rose gardens existed in China when Western civilization was just beginning, and rose perfumes and petals were used for personal adornment and protection from evil spirits. The cultivation of roses in Japan also goes back into the mists of pre-history, but in neither country did the rose match the importance of the chrysanthemum, lotus or cherry blossom.

These ancient varieties are lost to us, but when the early 18th century traders from the East India Company arrived in China they found cultivated roses which were completely new to them. The flowers were small and without any distinct fragrance. The bushes were lanky and short of leaves, but the blooms appeared in flush after flush until the late autumn and there was a new colour — crimson. These were the **China Roses** — the first one to arrive in Europe was *Old Blush* in 1752, followed by *Slater's Crimson China*.

The introduction of Old Blush from China in 1752 brought the first repeat flowering rose to Europe, but both blooms and plants were not attractive.

The second wave of introductions from China occurred many years later. These were the **Tea Roses**, the first aristocrats of the rose world. Intolerant of frost and plagued with weak necks below the flowers, they still had outstanding properties — shapely buds, refined flowers, delicate fragrance and a repeat flowering habit. The first Tea Rose to arrive in Britain was *Hume's Blush Tea-Scented China* in 1810, followed by *Park's Yellow Tea-Scented China* in 1844.

Here were the ideal marriage partners for the western roses — the repeat flowering habit of the China Roses and the beautiful blooms of the Tea Roses to combine with the frost-hardiness and robustness of our own varieties.

The importance of these roses from China in the evolution of the modern rose is described in detail in every history of our favourite flower, and yet the role of the rose from Japan is often overlooked. In the 1860s **Rosa multiflora** was introduced from this relatively unknown country. The blooms of this wild Rambler would not win any prizes in a rose show — small and plain white flowers in large heads. Yet **R. multiflora** was the parent of some Ramblers and all our Floribundas.

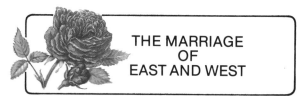

THE MARRIAGE OF EAST AND WEST

The first east-west marriage was a chance cross in Italy between *Rosa gallica Officinalis* and *Autumn Damask*. The result was *Duchess of Portland* — the first **Portland Rose**. Between 1800 and 1850 this type became moderately popular, but its decline was rapid and very few Portland Roses are now available.

Another marriage took place across the Atlantic at about the same time — this time the partners were *Old Blush* and the *Musk Rose*. South Carolina was the site of this cross and the type was named after a French immigrant — the **Noisettes**. Some Noisette hybrid Ramblers are still grown — *Madame Alfred Carrière* is described on page 67.

The big breakthrough came in 1816. A hybrid seedling was found at the base of a hedge containing *Old Blush* and *Autumn Damask*. The place was Ile de Bourbon in the Indian Ocean and the tiny new rose was the first **Bourbon Rose**. Here at last was a truly successful east-west marriage — reasonably large flowers on a bush which flowered repeatedly. France was the centre of the Bourbon craze, and thousands of varieties appeared. Their popularity lasted through much of the Victorian era, and some are still listed in the catalogues.

In 1837 a new rose appeared — *Princess Hélène*. This cross between a Bourbon Rose and a Portland Rose heralded in the **Hybrid Perpetual**, and the Bourbon lost its crown as Queen of Roses. In both Europe and the U.S rose breeders concentrated on producing more and more Hybrid Perpetuals until the end of the 19th century. Over 3,000 different varieties were introduced — in white, pink, mauve, red and purple. Some remain, led by *Frau Karl Druschki* which still keeps its place in the rose catalogues.

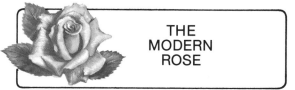

THE MODERN ROSE

The Victorian Queen of Roses, the Hybrid Perpetual, had its problems. The colour range was limited, repeat flowering was limited (a massive early flush was often followed by only sporadic summer or autumn blooming) and their garden use was restricted — the bushes were large and rampant which meant that formal bedding in a small garden was not really practical. What was needed was the introduction of some of the elegance and delicacy of the Tea Rose. Many varieties of Tea Rose were available, but none was really winter-hardy. What was wanted was a cross between the hardy Hybrid Perpetual and the dainty Tea Rose.

La France was the first Hybrid Tea. This group was created in 1880 and the honour of being the first variety was given to La France which had been introduced in 1867.

There is some argument about the identity of this first **Hybrid Tea**, but the honour generally goes to *La France*, introduced in 1867. A momentous date, as this is accepted as the birth date of the modern rose. There was no rush to buy this new rose, and the early Hybrid Teas crept in during the close of the 19th century. The acceptance of the group was accelerated by the appearance of some excellent varieties such as *Madame Caroline Testout* and *Lady Mary Fitzwilliam*, but the real breakthrough came in 1900. Pernet-Ducher in Lyons introduced *Soleil d'Or*, bred from a red Hybrid Perpetual and the *Persian Yellow* ... at last, a near-yellow flower on a bush with glossy leaves. Not truly a Hybrid Tea (it was called a Pernetiana at first), but it nevertheless enabled the Hybrid Teas to snatch the rose crown and keep it to this day.

The first pure yellow appeared in 1910 — *Rayon d'Or*. By this time the high-centred form of the Tea Rose was becoming dominant among Hybrid Teas — *Ophelia* (1912) was the first truly elegant pink. An impressive succession of trend-setting varieties were introduced up to the second World War — *Etoile de Hollande, Betty Uprichard, Shot Silk, Mrs Sam McGredy, Crimson Glory* and so on. Then just before the war a rose was bred in France which was to change the face of the Hybrid Tea. *Peace*, introduced into Britain in 1947, heralded in a new vigour and a new flower size. After the war, the steady stream of exciting advances continued. In 1960 *Super Star* came to Britain from Germany — the first of the vermilion roses. Then came *Fragrant Cloud, Alec's Red, Alexander, Silver Jubilee* ... and the quest for better Hybrid Teas goes on.

Hybrid Teas are not the only popular modern roses — the Floribundas are challenging them for the crown. Their story goes back to Guillot, the man who raised *La France*. In 1875 he introduced *Ma Paquerette*, which had *Rosa multiflora* and a China Rose as its parents. The small white blooms were borne in large clusters over a long flowering period on a small bush. This was the first

Polyantha Rose, and the introduction of *Orléans Rose* in 1909 established the popularity of this type. *The Fairy* (page 90) survives in the catalogues.

But the Polyanthas needed something more — extra height and extra flower size, and here the Poulsen family in Denmark were the originators of the Polyantha x Hybrid Tea cross. These were the **Hybrid Polyanthas** or Poulsen Roses — *Else Poulsen* came first in 1924, followed by *Kirsten Poulsen* and *Anne Poulsen*. Many other varieties followed, bred in Denmark, Britain, United States, Germany and other countries, and the Hybrid Tea influence became stronger and stronger. A new name was obviously required, and the U.S term **Floribunda** was accepted by the National Rose Society in 1952.

Else Poulsen was the first Floribunda. Introduced in 1924, it was classed first as an H.T and then a Hybrid Polyantha before the Floribunda group was invented in 1934 and generally accepted in 1952.

The milestones marking the history of the Floribundas are many, and any short list must omit numerous epoch-making roses. *Masquerade* and *Fashion* introduced new colours in the 1940s and *Queen Elizabeth* introduced a new size and elegance in the 1950s. New shapes and colours flooded in during the 1960s, and the 1970s were marked by the growing interest in dwarfs (*Topsi, Golden Slippers*, etc) and new colours such as *Picasso* (1971) and *Iced Ginger* (1971). The 1980s saw *Mountbatten* take away *Queen Elizabeth's* crown in the world of tall Floribundas.

There were several important developments during the final quarter of the 20th century. In the 1980s a number of excellent low-growing Floribundas appeared — *Gentle Touch* (1986), *Sweet Magic* (1987) and *Sweet Dream* (1988) all received the 'Rose of the Year' award. Most of these dwarf Floribundas and a few tall Miniatures were classed as a new group — the **Patio Rose**. Something similar happened in the world of Shrub Roses. A stream of excellent new varieties began to appear in the 1980s which had a spreading growth habit, and so these prostrate and arching varieties were separated as a new group — the **Ground Cover Rose**. Finally, a new type has appeared among the Climbers. Small flowers and small leaves but growing 2.5 m high — the Miniature Climber has recently appeared on the scene.

The next advance is just around the corner, but we cannot see it. The history of the rose is still being written.

CHAPTER 2

ROSES A–Z

The Seven Groups

HYBRID TEA ROSES

see pages 12–30

The most popular group, available in both bush and standard form. The flower stems are long and the blooms are shapely. The typical Hybrid Tea bears blooms which are medium-sized or large, with many petals forming a distinct central cone. The blooms are borne singly or with several side buds.

FLORIBUNDA ROSES

see pages 31–43

Second only to Hybrid Teas in popularity. The Floribunda bears its flowers in clusters or trusses, and several blooms open at one time in each truss. This group is unrivalled for providing a colourful, reliable and long-lasting bedding display, but in general the flower form is inferior to that of the Hybrid Tea.

PATIO ROSES

see pages 44–49

A group which appeared in the 1980s and now contains many popular varieties. These low-growing roses were formerly grouped with the Floribundas, and they are compact versions of this group. Patio Roses grow about 50 cm high and make excellent tub plants — they are also good for the front of the border.

MINIATURE ROSES

see pages 50–53

A group which is increasing in popularity due to its novelty and versatility. Miniatures can be used for edging beds, growing in tubs and rockeries or taking indoors as temporary pot plants. Both leaves and flowers are small, and under normal conditions the maximum height does not exceed 40 cm.

GROUND COVER ROSES

see pages 54–59

Like Patio Roses a group introduced in the 1980s. These spreading roses are repeat flowering and have good disease resistance — use these leafy mounds for covering banks or for planting between taller shrubs. Some are low-growing and quite restrained — others may spread widely and grow to a height of 1.5 m.

CLIMBERS & RAMBLERS

see pages 60–71

A group of roses which if tied to a support can be made to climb. There are two types: Ramblers with long pliable stems, bearing large trusses of small flowers as a single summer flush, and Climbers with stiff stems, bearing flowers which are larger than Rambler blooms and may be repeat flowering.

SHRUB ROSES

see pages 72–90

A large group of bush roses with only one feature in common — they are neither Hybrid Teas nor Floribundas. The typical Shrub is taller than a bedding rose, and is a Species variety (related to a wild rose), an Old-Fashioned variety (dating back to pre-Hybrid Tea days) or a Modern Shrub Rose.

HYBRID TEA ROSES
(Large-flowered Bushes)

There are seven groups of roses, as described on page 11, but when planting time comes around the average gardener looks no further than the Floribundas and the Hybrid Teas. And it is the Hybrid Tea which usually wins the day, because it is the aristocrat of roses.

Each flower on the bush or standard is a thing of beauty in itself. Here is the "classic" rose — a long, pointed bud which opens to reveal many velvety or satin-like petals, neatly reflexed and regularly arranged to form a high central cone. The range of colours is bewildering, the fragrance is usually moderate or strong. It is the prime choice for the show-bench and the flower vase. It is the flower which brings forth the comment "Now that's what I call a rose!"

But it was not always so. When Florence Nightingale tended her sick, the "classic" rose was unknown. It was a chance cross, a hybrid between a delicate Tea Rose and a Hybrid Perpetual, which gave rise to the first Hybrid Tea — *La France*. This event in 1867 is well-known to the keen rose grower — less well known is the lack of interest aroused by the discovery.

Nearly 20 years passed before the first lists appeared in catalogues, but then the popularity of the Hybrid Tea began. In 1900 the first yellow (*Soleil d'Or*) appeared and a steady stream of innovations, noted on page 9, has led to the thousands of different varieties which grace the gardens of the world.

The glowing descriptions in catalogues and the features of the H.T bloom outlined above sometimes give the impression that this group represents the **ideal** rose. This is certainly not true — many H.T bushes are upright and rigid and many H.T blooms are ruined by wet weather. In general, Hybrid Teas bloom less frequently and provide less garden colour than Floribundas. They will not put up with bad conditions like many Shrubs and Floribundas, and the number of blooms produced by some Exhibition H.Ts is disappointing.

So choose carefully. As you will see in the following pages, not all Hybrid Teas are suitable for garden display — some are designed to be cossetted for appealing to show judges rather than the neighbours. The Hybrid Tea is quite rightly regarded as the Queen of Roses — shapely blooms on long stems appearing in flushes throughout the summer and autumn ... but it is not always perfect.

KEY TO THE ROSE GUIDES

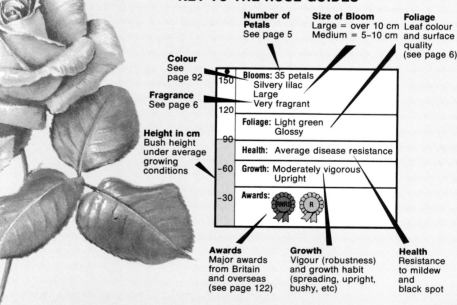

Number of Petals
See page 5

Size of Bloom
Large = over 10 cm
Medium = 5–10 cm

Foliage
Leaf colour and surface quality
(see page 6)

Colour
See page 92

Fragrance
See page 6

Height in cm
Bush height under average growing conditions

150

120

90

60

30

Blooms: 35 petals
Silvery lilac
Large
Very fragrant

Foliage: Light green
Glossy

Health: Average disease resistance

Growth: Moderately vigorous
Upright

Awards:

Awards
Major awards from Britain and overseas
(see page 122)

Growth
Vigour (robustness) and growth habit (spreading, upright, bushy, etc)

Health
Resistance to mildew and black spot

ABBEYFIELD ROSE
Other Name: COCBROSE

Blooms: 25 petals
Rosy red
Medium-sized
Slightly fragrant

Foliage: Dark green
Glossy

Health: Good disease resistance

Growth: Vigorous
Bushy

Awards: RHS, GL

This is not a variety to choose if you want to win a prize at your local horticultural show — the flowers are not very large and they are not packed with petals. It is, however, a good choice for bedding, especially for a small plot. Growth is compact and the blooms are borne in large numbers on leafy stems. These flowers have high centres and are an attractive deep pink colour. A rose of the 1980s with awards in the 1990s.

ADMIRAL RODNEY

Blooms: 45 petals
Pale rose pink
Large
Very fragrant

Foliage: Light green
Glossy

Health: Average disease resistance

Growth: Vigorous
Upright

Awards:

Unlike most of the varieties in this chapter you will have to search the catalogues for this one. It is not popular for ordinary garden display as it is not free-flowering and it is not robust. It is included here as opinion polls show that it is regarded by keen rose growers as one of the best of all varieties for exhibiting. The pale-centred pink blooms are beautifully shaped and they are exceptionally fragrant but, alas, there are too few of them for garden display.

ALEC'S RED

Blooms: 45 petals
Cherry red
Large, globular
Very fragrant

Foliage: Medium green
Glossy

Health: Good disease resistance

Growth: Vigorous
Bushy

Awards: RNRS, RNRS, RNRS, B

This daughter of *Fragrant Cloud* has been popular for many years. Choose it for bedding, cutting or exhibiting — you will have no difficulty in finding a supplier. Fragrance is an outstanding quality — very rich and sweet. It has an impressive list of virtues — vigorous healthy growth, strong flower stalks and abundant large blooms throughout the season. The flowers have good rain resistance and hold their colour well with age, but the colour does not appeal to everyone.

ALEXANDER
Other Name: ALEXANDRA

Blooms: 22 petals
Vermilion red
Medium-sized
Slightly fragrant

Foliage: Dark green
Glossy

Health: Good disease resistance

Growth: Very vigorous
Upright

Awards: RNRS, RHS, JM, B

This tall bush is ideal for a large bed or for hedging, but it is not a good choice if you like large blooms full of petals or if space is limited. Brilliant flower colour is the outstanding feature — the vermilion is much more luminous than in its illustrious parent *Super Star*. The blooms have good rain-resisting properties. Young flowers have pointed centres and the long stalks make them excellent for cutting.

ALPINE SUNSET

Blooms: 30 petals
Creamy yellow, flushed pink
Large, globular
Very fragrant

Foliage: Light green
Glossy

Health: Average disease resistance

Growth: Vigorous
Upright

Awards: RNRS, H

This English-bred rose forms a neat and compact bush with blooms which are suitable for general garden display and also the show bench. The flowers are very large and the fragrance is outstanding. It comes from a good family (*Grandpa Dickson* is one of the parents) and its sturdy upright stems bear lots of attractive blooms which are good for cutting. There is a drawback — blooms appear in distinct flushes rather than in continuous succession.

HYBRID TEA ROSES

Height in cm

APRICOT SILK

This may be one for you, but only if you are a keen flower arranger. The elegant buds are borne on long stems and they open into flowers with silky petals and an unusual shade of apricot. The leaves are purple when young and the blooms have excellent keeping qualities in water. A flower arranger's rose, but not one for garden display. The growth is distinctly upright and it is not a robust plant. It also requires regular spraying to protect it from mildew and black spot.

Blooms: 20 petals
Apricot, reverse orange-red
Large
Fragrant

Foliage: Green, tinted bronze
Glossy

Health: Prone to disease

Growth: Moderately vigorous
Upright

Awards:

BARKAROLE
Other Name: TANELORAK

Barkarole is a Tantau rose which appeared at the end of the 1980s, and without having any single outstanding feature it brings together a number of desirable features. The large blooms are a lovely rich red and the texture of the petals is velvety. The fragrance is strong, but is not as pronounced as *Alec's Red* or *Double Delight*. The branching growth is wide-spreading, so each bush covers quite a large area.

Blooms: 25 petals
Deep red
Large
Fragrant

Foliage: Dark green
Glossy

Health: Average disease resistance

Growth: Vigorous
Spreading

Awards:

BELLE EPOQUE
Other Name: FRYYABOO

This English-bred rose attracted a lot of attention when it was launched at the Chelsea Flower Show in 1994. The reason was the unusual colour of the flowers — amber or golden-bronze on the inside of the petals and a richer bronze on the outside. It comes into flower early in the season, the long buds opening into classic-shaped Hybrid Tea blooms. The fragrance is reasonably strong and it may prove to be a winner — only time will tell.

Blooms: 25 petals
Amber, reverse deep bronze
Large
Fragrant

Foliage: Medium green
Glossy

Health: Good disease resistance

Growth: Vigorous
Bushy

Awards: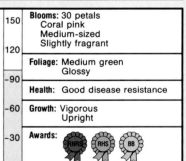

BLESSINGS

This rose has been described as the ideal bedding variety, yet it is neither strongly fragrant nor are the blooms exceptionally large or shapely. The colour is attractive, but its popularity is due to the abundance of leaves and blooms borne on the bush. From early in the season until late in the autumn the pink flowers appear in large numbers either singly or in clusters, maintaining their attraction even in rainy weather. A good choice for bed or border display.

Blooms: 30 petals
Coral pink
Medium-sized
Slightly fragrant

Foliage: Medium green
Glossy

Health: Good disease resistance

Growth: Vigorous
Upright

Awards:

BLUE MOON
Other Names: MAINZER FASTNACHT, SISSI

This variety is still the most popular of the so-called "blue" roses, but it is distinctly pale lilac and not blue. Many people dislike the washed-out appearance of the petals in the garden, but indoors the blooms make excellent cut flowers. The buds are tall and pointed, the stems are long and the fragrance is exceptionally strong. Disease resistance is not good these days and spraying against mildew is necessary.

Blooms: 35 petals
Silvery lilac
Large
Very fragrant

Foliage: Light green
Glossy

Health: Average disease resistance

Growth: Moderately vigorous
Upright

Awards: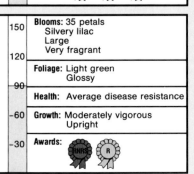

HYBRID TEA ROSES

CHESHIRE LIFE

Blooms:	35 petals Vermilion, shaded orange Large Slightly fragrant
Foliage:	Dark green Semi-glossy
Health:	Good disease resistance
Growth:	Vigorous Bushy
Awards:	

The vermilion colour of the blooms of this Fryer-bred rose will appeal to gardeners who admire *Super Star*, but this variety has the advantage of good resistance to mildew and black spot. The outstanding feature of *Cheshire Life* is its ability to put up with both cold and wet conditions — in poor weather it will still produce lots of leathery leaves and an abundance of brightly-coloured blooms. Growth is compact — its only major drawback is the absence of a strong fragrance.

CHICAGO PEACE
Other Name: JOHNAGO

Blooms:	45 petals Pink, copper and yellow Large Slightly fragrant
Foliage:	Dark green Glossy
Health:	Average disease resistance
Growth:	Very vigorous Bushy
Awards:	

This colourful sport of *Peace* was discovered in a Chicago garden and was launched in the U.S in 1962. It is still widely available and is an excellent general-purpose rose which reaches 100–150 cm, depending on pruning. It can be used for bedding, hedging or exhibiting — its blooms are more colourful than those of its famous parent. Copper and pink dominate and the reverse is coppery yellow.

CONGRATULATIONS
Other Names: KORLIFT, SYLVIA

Blooms:	40 petals Rose pink Medium-sized Slightly fragrant
Foliage:	Medium green Semi-glossy
Health:	Good disease resistance
Growth:	Vigorous Upright
Awards:	BARB

This tall variety won top honours from the British Association Representing Breeders, but it has not become a best-seller. The problem is that its upright lanky growth is not really suitable for bedding in a modest-sized garden, but it is an excellent choice for both hedging and cutting. Disease resistance is above average and the abundant clusters of well-shaped blooms are borne on long thorn-free shoots.

DAWN CHORUS
Other Name: DICQUASAR

Blooms:	24 petals Deep orange, flushed yellow Medium-sized Fragrant
Foliage:	Dark green, tinged red Glossy
Health:	Good disease resistance
Growth:	Vigorous Upright
Awards:	ROTY

Dawn Chorus is one of the group of outstanding H.Ts introduced in the 1990s. An impressive list of virtues made it Rose of the Year 1993. The high-centred flowers are often borne in clusters and may be abundant enough to cover the attractive leaves. The orange-peel colour is eye-catching, it is scented and there is a long and continuous flowering period. Try this Dickson-raised variety if you want a bright bedding rose.

DEEP SECRET
Other Name: MILDRED SCHEEL

Blooms:	40 petals Deep crimson Large Very fragrant
Foliage:	Dark green Glossy
Health:	Good disease resistance
Growth:	Vigorous Upright
Awards:	

You will find this one in most catalogues because it has two outstanding features. First of all the colour. It is perhaps the darkest of all red roses — darker even than *Josephine Bruce* or *Papa Meilland.* Secondly there is the fragrance — as rich and strong as you are likely to find these days. The bushes are about average height and the flowers are often borne in small trusses. The buds are almost black.

HYBRID TEA ROSES

Height in cm

DIE WELT
Other Names: THE WORLD, DIEKOR

Die Welt is an excellent choice if your goal is to win a prize at your local horticultural show — when well-grown the classic-shaped H.T blooms are outstanding. It is a popular selection for the show bench but you will have to search the catalogues to find a supplier. It flowers freely but it has not caught the public fancy as a bedding rose — there is little scent and spraying is necessary to prevent black spot.

Blooms: 25 petals Pink, orange and yellow Large Slightly fragrant	
Foliage: Medium green Glossy	
Health: Average disease resistance	
Growth: Vigorous Upright	
Awards:	

DORIS TYSTERMAN

An English-bred rose which was introduced in the 1970s and soon became popular as a bedding variety. Its free-flowering nature and good performance in autumn ensure a satisfactory display throughout the season, and the well-shaped orange-red blooms on long stems are good for cutting. There are some drawbacks — the blooms are only average in size, the fragrance is not strong and the leaves need protection against mildew.

Blooms: 30 petals Tangerine, darker at edges Medium-sized Slightly fragrant	
Foliage: Green, tinted bronze Glossy	
Health: Prone to disease	
Growth: Vigorous Upright	
Awards:	

DOUBLE DELIGHT

The fact that this American rose was voted one of the World's Favourite Roses by the World Federation of Rose Societies speaks for itself. It is the queen of the bi-colours, with petals "like a vanilla ice dipped in strawberry juice" — the ratio of cream to red is highly variable. Colour is not its only merit — the blooms are very large with a strong scent and they are freely produced. *Double Delight* is a good choice for cutting or exhibiting as well as for garden display.

Blooms: 40 petals Cream, rimmed red Large Very fragrant	
Foliage: Medium green Semi-glossy	
Health: Prone to disease	
Growth: Vigorous Upright	
Awards: BARB US B R	

DR McALPINE

If you like pink flowers and are looking for a bush for the front of the border then this low-growing variety is worth considering. It is usually found in the Hybrid Tea section of the catalogue — the large blooms have the classic shape associated with this group. But the flowers are usually borne in trusses with up to 10 blooms in each cluster, so some growers list it as a Floribunda. The flower colour is not exceptional but the fragrance is strong. *Dr McAlpine* has never become a star.

Blooms: 30 petals Deep pink Large Very fragrant	
Foliage: Dark green Semi-glossy	
Health: Average disease resistance	
Growth: Vigorous Spreading	
Awards:	

DUTCH GOLD

Dutch Gold quickly became popular after its launch in 1978 and has continued to be listed in many catalogues. A golden rose with very large fragrant blooms was bound to attract attention, especially as the colour did not fade with age and they were not damaged by rain as most large H.T blooms are. The flowers are well-shaped and freely produced. It differs from its parents — both *Peer Gynt* and *Whisky Mac* are more compact and their flowers are smaller.

Blooms: 35 petals Golden yellow Large Fragrant	
Foliage: Dark green Glossy	
Health: Average disease resistance	
Growth: Vigorous Upright	
Awards: H	

Blooms:	40 petals
	Ivory, pale yellow at base
	Large
	Fragrant
Foliage:	Dark green
	Glossy
Health:	Good disease resistance
Growth:	Vigorous
	Upright
Awards:	

150
120
90
60
30

ELINA
Other Name: PEAUDOUCE

In rose grower opinion polls this Dickson-bred variety is rated as one of the best garden, the best exhibition and the healthiest of all Hybrid Teas. The bush is well clothed with large leaves — the flowers are borne singly on strong stems. Pointed buds open to produce porcelain-like flowers — pale primrose at first but mainly ivory when mature. Despite the delicate appearance of the flowers, they stand up well to poor weather.

Blooms:	35 petals
	Cream, shaded buff and pink
	Large
	Fragrant
Foliage:	Dark green
	Semi-glossy
Health:	Average disease resistance
Growth:	Vigorous
	Bushy
Awards:	

150
120
90
60
30

ELIZABETH HARKNESS

One of the best cream-coloured Hybrid Teas you can buy. The colour of the large, high-centred flowers is hard to describe — the pale, creamy buff shades deepen in autumn. It is an early-blooming variety, continuing to flower freely throughout the season. The blooms are sweet smelling, although the perfume is not particularly strong, and they are excellent for cutting. *Elizabeth Harkness* does well in a good season, but it does not like rain.

Blooms:	30 petals
	Pale pink
	Large
	Very fragrant
Foliage:	Light green
	Glossy
Health:	Good disease resistance
Growth:	Vigorous
	Bushy
Awards:	

150
120
90
60
30

EMPRESS MICHIKO

This Dickson rose was introduced in 1992 and now appears in numerous catalogues. It has *Silver Jubilee* as one of its parents and there is the pink colouring, vigour and good health associated with its mother. There are, however, several differences — the colour is more delicate and the bush is more compact. In addition the leaves are much paler and the fragrance is much stronger. The most outstanding characteristic of this rose is its remarkable free-flowering habit.

Blooms:	30 petals
	Crimson
	Large
	Very fragrant
Foliage:	Medium green
	Semi-glossy
Health:	Average disease resistance
Growth:	Moderately vigorous
	Upright
Awards:	

150
120
90
60
30

ENA HARKNESS

A great old favourite — the most popular red rose planted in Britain for many years. These days its faults are often highlighted — the need for good cultivation, the lack of vigour which is found in modern varieties and above all the weak necks which cause the blooms to hang their heads. But it is still widely grown because the fragrance and the richness of its colour have few rivals. It is free-flowering, especially in autumn, and there is little or no fading of colour.

Blooms:	30 petals
	Crimson
	Large
	Very fragrant
Foliage:	Medium green
	Semi-glossy
Health:	Average disease resistance
Growth:	Vigorous
	Upright
Awards:	

150
120
90
60
30

ERNEST H. MORSE

Red roses may come and go, but *Ernest H. Morse* was introduced in 1965 and is still in the best-seller lists. It has proved to be thoroughly reliable, but it now needs some protection from mildew in a bad season. It is almost ideal as a bedding rose — large, fragrant flowers in glowing red which stand up to rain. They are borne prolifically throughout the season and the best of them can be used for exhibition and floral decoration.

HYBRID TEA ROSES

Height in cm

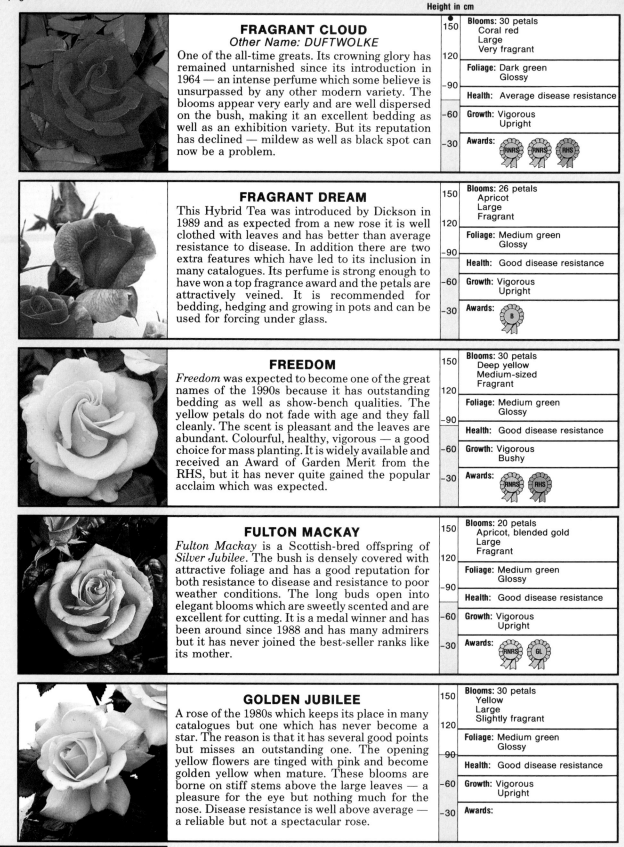

FRAGRANT CLOUD
Other Name: DUFTWOLKE

One of the all-time greats. Its crowning glory has remained untarnished since its introduction in 1964 — an intense perfume which some believe is unsurpassed by any other modern variety. The blooms appear very early and are well dispersed on the bush, making it an excellent bedding as well as an exhibition variety. But its reputation has declined — mildew as well as black spot can now be a problem.

Blooms: 30 petals
Coral red
Large
Very fragrant

Foliage: Dark green
Glossy

Health: Average disease resistance

Growth: Vigorous
Upright

Awards: RNRS RNRS RHS

150 120 90 60 30

FRAGRANT DREAM

This Hybrid Tea was introduced by Dickson in 1989 and as expected from a new rose it is well clothed with leaves and has better than average resistance to disease. In addition there are two extra features which have led to its inclusion in many catalogues. Its perfume is strong enough to have won a top fragrance award and the petals are attractively veined. It is recommended for bedding, hedging and growing in pots and can be used for forcing under glass.

Blooms: 26 petals
Apricot
Large
Fragrant

Foliage: Medium green
Glossy

Health: Good disease resistance

Growth: Vigorous
Upright

Awards: B

150 120 90 60 30

FREEDOM

Freedom was expected to become one of the great names of the 1990s because it has outstanding bedding as well as show-bench qualities. The yellow petals do not fade with age and they fall cleanly. The scent is pleasant and the leaves are abundant. Colourful, healthy, vigorous — a good choice for mass planting. It is widely available and received an Award of Garden Merit from the RHS, but it has never quite gained the popular acclaim which was expected.

Blooms: 30 petals
Deep yellow
Medium-sized
Fragrant

Foliage: Medium green
Glossy

Health: Good disease resistance

Growth: Vigorous
Bushy

Awards: RNRS RHS

150 120 90 60 30

FULTON MACKAY

Fulton Mackay is a Scottish-bred offspring of *Silver Jubilee*. The bush is densely covered with attractive foliage and has a good reputation for both resistance to disease and resistance to poor weather conditions. The long buds open into elegant blooms which are sweetly scented and are excellent for cutting. It is a medal winner and has been around since 1988 and has many admirers but it has never joined the best-seller ranks like its mother.

Blooms: 20 petals
Apricot, blended gold
Large
Fragrant

Foliage: Medium green
Glossy

Health: Good disease resistance

Growth: Vigorous
Upright

Awards: RNRS GL

150 120 90 60 30

GOLDEN JUBILEE

A rose of the 1980s which keeps its place in many catalogues but one which has never become a star. The reason is that it has several good points but misses an outstanding one. The opening yellow flowers are tinged with pink and become golden yellow when mature. These blooms are borne on stiff stems above the large leaves — a pleasure for the eye but nothing much for the nose. Disease resistance is well above average — a reliable but not a spectacular rose.

Blooms: 30 petals
Yellow
Large
Slightly fragrant

Foliage: Medium green
Glossy

Health: Good disease resistance

Growth: Vigorous
Upright

Awards:

150 120 90 60 30

HYBRID TEA ROSES

Blooms: 30 petals
Deep yellow
Medium-sized
Slightly fragrant

Foliage: Light green
Matt

Health: Good disease resistance

Growth: Vigorous
Upright

Awards:

GOLDSTAR
Other Name: CANDIDE

This Cants rose of the 1980s won top honours at the Hague. It has a special appeal for flower arrangers — the blooms are borne on long and straight stems. These flowers are carried singly or in small clusters at the top of the plant. A good garden rose, but the flowerless lower part of the bush is best hidden by planting a low-growing variety in front. The pure yellow blooms appear freely and the colour does not fade with age.

Blooms: 35 petals
Lemon yellow, edged pink
Large
Slightly fragrant

Foliage: Dark green
Glossy

Health: Good disease resistance

Growth: Vigorous
Upright

Awards:

GRANDPA DICKSON
Other Name: IRISH GOLD

Regarded by many as the best pale yellow Hybrid Tea. It appears in most catalogues and rose books sing its praises. Superbly formed blooms with long petals — the star of countless shows. In addition, its good rain resistance, freedom of flowering and late-season blooming make it an excellent bedding variety. There is a drawback or two — the bush is sometimes gaunt and good soil is necessary.

Blooms: 25 petals
Scarlet, striped yellow
Large
Slightly fragrant

Foliage: Dark green
Glossy

Health: Prone to disease

Growth: Vigorous
Bushy

Awards:

HARRY WHEATCROFT

Fittingly named after one of the great characters of the rose world, you will either love this sport of *Piccadilly* for its flamboyant novelty or you will hate it for its garishness. Each large, pointed bloom is a riot of colour, and this variety is excellent for bedding — compact, free-flowering and rain resistant. Unfortunately it has little perfume and it will need spraying against black spot. The blooms are long-lasting and recommended for flower arranging.

Blooms: 30 petals
Ivory white
Large
Fragrant

Foliage: Dark green, tinted bronze
Glossy

Health: Good disease resistance

Growth: Vigorous
Upright

Awards:

ICE CREAM

In 1993 this Kordes rose was introduced at the Chelsea Flower Show and aroused great interest. It is listed by many growers and it is an attractive bush even before the flowers appear. The plant is densely covered with leaves which are coppery red when young and dark bronzy green when mature. The broad-petalled blooms are borne in large numbers over a long period. It is recommended for both bedding and cutting but has received no British awards.

Blooms: 30 petals
Creamy orange
Large
Very fragrant

Foliage: Dark green
Glossy

Health: Good disease resistance

Growth: Vigorous
Bushy

Awards:

INDIAN SUMMER

Indian Summer is one of the newer compact Hybrid Teas which has won a lot of friends. The pale orange blooms stand out boldly against the background of dark abundant foliage. The perfume is strong — this variety won the top fragrance prize at Glasgow. Despite its name it does not need an Indian summer to flourish — its ability to succeed in a rainy season is outstanding. Another virtue is the display of hips when the flowers have faded.

HYBRID TEA ROSES

Height in cm

INGRID BERGMAN
Other Name: POULMAN

This free-flowering addition to the list of red velvety roses appeared in 1985. It is a good one to choose if you like this type of flower — it has picked up its share of awards and medals since its introduction by Poulsen of Denmark. Its dense and leathery foliage makes it a good bedding and hedging rose. The flowers are borne singly on strong stems and they last well in water — a good flower-arranger's rose.

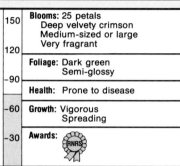

150	**Blooms:** 35 petals Deep red Medium-sized Fragrant
120	**Foliage:** Dark green Glossy
90	**Health:** Good disease resistance
60	**Growth:** Vigorous Upright
30	**Awards:** RNRS RHS B H

JOSEPHINE BRUCE

Several dark red, velvety roses have recently appeared but this old favourite still keeps its place in the catalogues. The average-sized bushes have a sprawling growth habit which can be controlled by pruning to inward-pointing buds. This variety is particularly good when grown as a standard. The early-season display is best —well-shaped blooms which are good enough for the show-bench. In late summer the petals tend to be ragged and mildew is a problem.

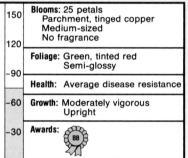

150	**Blooms:** 25 petals Deep velvety crimson Medium-sized or large Very fragrant
120	**Foliage:** Dark green Semi-glossy
90	**Health:** Prone to disease
60	**Growth:** Vigorous Spreading
30	**Awards:** RNRS

JULIA'S ROSE

Named after famous flower arranger Julia Clements, this rose is grown as a source of cut flowers. The elongated buds open slowly to produce porcelain-like flowers. The colour is hard to describe — "parchment-like" is the most frequent description. Excellent indoors, but a poor bedding variety. Growth is upright, and the long straight stems give a spindly appearance in the garden. Provide good conditions and shelter against wind. Prune lightly.

150	**Blooms:** 25 petals Parchment, tinged copper Medium-sized No fragrance
120	**Foliage:** Green, tinted red Semi-glossy
90	**Health:** Average disease resistance
60	**Growth:** Moderately vigorous Upright
30	**Awards:** BB

JUST JOEY

This English rose, bred by Cants, is quite unmistakeable with its unique colouring and ruffled petals. It has become one of the most popular of all bedding roses, combining novelty with beauty and reliability — it was voted the World's Favourite Rose in 1994. The buds are attractive and excellent for cutting, appearing with great freedom throughout the season. The open blooms are colourful and rain-resistant, and the bush blooms well into the autumn.

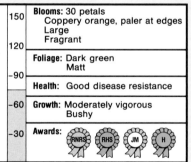

150	**Blooms:** 30 petals Coppery orange, paler at edges Large Fragrant
120	**Foliage:** Dark green Matt
90	**Health:** Good disease resistance
60	**Growth:** Moderately vigorous Bushy
30	**Awards:** RNRS RHS JM H

KEEPSAKE
Other Name: ESMERALDA

This rose of the 1980s does not appear in all the catalogues but it is included here because it is judged to be one of the top 10 varieties for exhibition. The large and well-shaped blooms in various shades of pink are quite often among the prize-winners at local shows. The stems are strong and armed with large thorns — foliage is abundant. Drawbacks include uneven growth and the absence of a strong perfume.

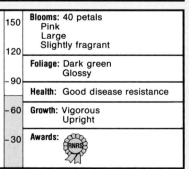

150	**Blooms:** 40 petals Pink Large Slightly fragrant
120	**Foliage:** Dark green Glossy
90	**Health:** Good disease resistance
60	**Growth:** Vigorous Upright
30	**Awards:** RNRS

HYBRID TEA ROSES

Blooms:	40 petals Rich yellow Medium-sized Fragrant
Foliage:	Dark green Glossy
Health:	Good disease resistance
Growth:	Vigorous Branching
Awards:	

KING'S RANSOM

Many roses come and go, but this American-bred variety first appeared in 1961 and is still in the catalogues, even though there are better yellow varieties these days. Growth is straggly but it has its good points — non-fading blooms which are high-centred and rain-resistant, bushes which produce stems, flowers and leaves abundantly, and buds which are beautifully shaped and excellent for cutting. Choose another rose if your soil is sandy or chalky.

Blooms:	25 petals Orange Large Slightly fragrant
Foliage:	Dark green Glossy
Health:	Good disease resistance
Growth:	Very vigorous Upright
Awards:	

L'OREAL TROPHY

A sport of *Alexander* which hoped for but did not receive the popularity and adulation given to its illustrious parent. Judges in several countries have given it their highest awards, but it is still offered by only a minority of rose growers. *L'Oréal Trophy* has all of the good points of its parent — attractive foliage, luminescent flowers and a healthy constitution. There are two differences — the flowers are orange rather than vermilion and the bushes are not quite as tall.

Blooms:	35 petals Rose pink Large Fragrant
Foliage:	Medium green Glossy
Health:	Good disease resistance
Growth:	Vigorous Bushy
Awards:	

LOVELY LADY

A pink rose which has to fight against all of the other Hybrid Tea pinks for a place among the best-sellers. It is widely offered because there is an impressive list of virtues. The flowers are large and fragrant, the stems are strong and the leaves are large and numerous. It is also a healthy plant, and so it is recommended for bedding. The flowers are shapely and high-centred, which means that *Lovely Lady* can be used for exhibition, but it is not one of the top 10 show roses.

Blooms:	30 petals Tangerine orange Medium-sized Slightly fragrant
Foliage:	Green, tinted bronze Semi-glossy
Health:	Good disease resistance
Growth:	Very vigorous Upright
Awards:	

LOVERS' MEETING

The powers that be couldn't agree at first where to place this orange star of the 1980s, but it is now placed with the Hybrid Teas rather than the Floribundas by everyone. There is no disagreement about its virtues. First of all, the colour — a new one ('clear indian orange') according to the breeder. The foliage is bronzy green and is borne on strong stems. The blooms are Hybrid Tea-shaped but are often borne in small clusters rather than singly.

Blooms:	42 petals Red Large Slightly fragrant
Foliage:	Dark green Glossy
Health:	Good disease resistance
Growth:	Vigorous Upright
Awards:	

LOVING MEMORY
Other Name: RED CEDAR

This red variety of the 1980s is regarded as one of the best Hybrid Teas by many rose growers. One large grower described it as "an ideal rose for every garden" and it certainly has a number of merits. The bush is densely covered with dark foliage and the long straight stems are excellent for cutting. The flowers are well-shaped and appear in large numbers throughout the season — they are good enough for exhibition.

HYBRID TEA ROSES

Height in cm

MISCHIEF

Introduced in 1961, *Mischief* remains a very popular bedding rose. Its great appeal lies in the remarkable profusion of rain-resistant flowers which appear throughout the season. Flower colour is 'cut strawberry' in summer but turns more orange in autumn — fragrance is sometimes strong. Flower size is variable — small blooms may appear, but disbudding can produce large blooms fit for exhibition. Not a good choice for gardens where rust is a problem.

Blooms: 30 petals	Coral salmon Medium-sized Fragrant
Foliage: Light green	Semi-glossy
Health: Prone to disease	
Growth: Vigorous	Upright
Awards:	RNRS RNRS

150 / 120 / 90 / 60 / 30

MISTER LINCOLN

A good choice if you want a velvety, deep red rose for cutting — the flowers are borne on long stems and last well in water. *Mister Lincoln* is also a fine variety for garden display in a large bed — it is less prone to mildew than the old dark reds such as *Chrysler Imperial*, and the blooms are less likely to turn purple with age. There are drawbacks — the attractive buds quickly turn into open-cupped blooms and the tall stems make it an unsuitable bush for a small bed.

Blooms: 35 petals	Dark red Large Fragrant
Foliage: Medium green	Matt
Health: Average disease resistance	
Growth: Vigorous	Upright
Awards:	US

150 / 120 / 90 / 60 / 30

MY JOY

Nearly all of the roses in this book have been chosen on the basis of their popularity for ordinary garden use. *My Joy* is different — this pink sport of *Red Devil* is available from very few suppliers. It is included here because it is rated to be one of the twelve best roses to grow for exhibiting. Apart from its colour it is very similar to its popular parent, so it is a little surprising that it is not more widely grown as an eye-catching garden rose.

Blooms: 60 petals	Deep pink Large Fragrant
Foliage: Dark green	Glossy
Health: Good disease resistance	
Growth: Vigorous	Upright
Awards:	

150 / 120 / 90 / 60 / 30

NATIONAL TRUST
Other Name: BAD NAUHEIM

You will not find it in the list of roses to grow for fragrance nor for exhibiting, yet *National Trust* is one of the outstanding red Hybrid Teas of our time. The bushes lack height and the blooms lack the size of the show varieties, but it is an excellent choice for the front of the bed or border. The blooms are held erect, their shape is impeccable and their colour unfading. The foliage is coppery red when young.

Blooms: 60 petals	Crimson Medium-sized No fragrance
Foliage: Dark green	Matt
Health: Good disease resistance	
Growth: Vigorous	Upright
Awards:	RNRS

150 / 120 / 90 / 60 / 30

NEW ZEALAND
Other Name: AOTEAROA

This McGredy rose was introduced in 1990. It is not available in most popular catalogues nor has it won any important awards, but it is included here because it is rated very highly in polls conducted among keen rose growers. It is regarded as one of the three best newer Hybrid Teas — high praise indeed. The reason for this enthusiasm is a little obscure — it is a very good all-round but not spectacular rose.

Blooms: 34 petals	Pale salmon Large Very fragrant
Foliage: Medium green	Glossy
Health: Good disease resistance	
Growth: Vigorous	Bushy
Awards:	

150 / 120 / 90 / 60 / 30

HYBRID TEA ROSES

PAPA MEILLAND

Blooms:	35 petals Dark crimson Large Very fragrant
Foliage:	Dark green Glossy
Health:	Prone to disease
Growth:	Moderately vigorous Upright
Awards:	

This variety demonstrates the need to consider both the flower *and* the plant before deciding to buy. If you were guided by the flower alone then *Papa Meilland* would be one of the finest Hybrid Teas available. Nearly black buds open into large, dark red blooms, velvety-petalled and with a scent which is unsurpassed. Unfortunately the plant does not live up to the blooms — in the garden it is unreliable, it is not a prolific bloomer and it is extremely prone to mildew.

PASCALI

Blooms:	25 petals White, shaded cream Medium-sized Slightly fragrant
Foliage:	Medium green Glossy
Health:	Average disease resistance
Growth:	Vigorous Upright
Awards:	

Introduced in 1963, *Pascali* remains a good choice. It is less prone to mildew and much more resistant to rain than most other varieties of this colour, and the blooms hold their shape longer than many roses. It is one of the best of all varieties for cutting — the stems are long and straight. Despite the bouquets it is not an ideal white rose — the bushes are spindly, the blooms are not large, the petals are not pure white and the scent is faint.

PAUL SHIRVILLE
Other Name: HEART THROB

Blooms:	30 petals Salmon pink, peach at base Large Very fragrant
Foliage:	Dark green Glossy
Health:	Average disease resistance
Growth:	Vigorous Bushy
Awards:	

This Harkness rose is widely available and has become a popular choice. The unusual flower colouring has caught the public eye — the blend of pink, salmon and peach plus outstanding fragrance are inherited from its parent *Compassion*. Growth is leafy and rather spreading — the young leaves are reddish and the elegantly-shaped blooms are high-centred. You may have to spray against black spot.

PEACE
Other Names: GLORIA DEI, GIOIA

Blooms:	45 petals Pale or dark yellow, edged pink Large Slightly fragrant
Foliage:	Dark green Glossy
Health:	Average disease resistance
Growth:	Very vigorous Bushy
Awards:	

It was for so long the world's favourite rose. Always vigorous, always reliable, the 15 cm blooms remain attractive from bud to the full-blown stage. It is not a rose for every location — it must have space. It will reach 1.2–2 m high and should never be hard pruned. There are drawbacks — the lack of fragrance, the late start to flowering, the occasional blind shoot and it is now susceptible to black spot.

PEER GYNT

Blooms:	40 petals Canary yellow, flushed pink Large Slightly fragrant
Foliage:	Medium green Matt
Health:	Prone to disease
Growth:	Vigorous Bushy
Awards:	

Peer Gynt possesses the basic ingredients of a successful bedding rose — attractive blooms which appear early in the season and continue to appear throughout the summer and autumn. The compact bush is taller than average and well-clothed with large leaves. The edges of the petals turn pink with age, providing a colourful garden display, but this variety is not really for the show-bench as the blooms are open-cupped. Weak mildew resistance is the only serious problem.

HYBRID TEA ROSES

Height in cm

PICCADILLY

Piccadilly remains the most popular of the bi-colours. To see it at its best, look at young blooms in cool weather — with age and in hot sunshine the vivid reds and yellows merge and fade. It is a splendid bedding variety — very early and remarkably free-flowering bushes which bear attractive coppery foliage. There are a few draw-backs — petals are not numerous and disease resistance, once very good, has decreased in recent years.

Blooms: 25 petals
  Scarlet, reverse yellow
  Medium-sized
  Slightly fragrant

Foliage: Green, tinted bronze
  Glossy

Health: Prone to disease

Growth: Vigorous
  Upright

Awards: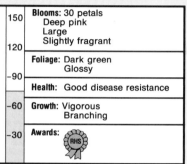

PINK FAVOURITE

This American-bred rose is high on the list of disease-resistant varieties — mildew and black spot are almost unknown. Excellent for bedding — the shiny foliage is attractive and the pink blooms appear throughout the summer on top of sturdy stems. The high-centred flowers, darker on the outside of the petals than on the inside, start to appear rather late but this is its only drawback as a bedding rose. It is also a popular exhibition variety.

Blooms: 30 petals
  Deep pink
  Large
  Slightly fragrant

Foliage: Dark green
  Glossy

Health: Good disease resistance

Growth: Vigorous
  Branching

Awards:

PINK PEACE

Like its famous parent *Peace*, this rose bears large blooms on vigorous bushes which are taller than average. However, there is no other similarity between the two varieties so the name *Pink Peace* is distinctly misleading. Growth is upright, not bushy — foliage is bronze-tinted, not dark green, and the loose, open-cupped flowers are strongly scented. The bush does not reach the height of *Peace* and the foliage is susceptible to rust, but this pink offspring is more free-flowering.

Blooms: 55 petals
  Deep pink
  Large
  Fragrant

Foliage: Green, tinted bronze
  Semi-glossy

Health: Average disease resistance

Growth: Vigorous
  Upright

Awards: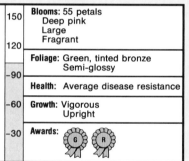

POLAR STAR
Other Name: POLARSTERN

This rose received the Certificate of Merit from the Royal National Rose Society, but its supreme award was Rose of the Year in 1985. It was considered the best white Hybrid Tea intro-duction for years, but it has lost some of its support. The high-centred blooms are exhibition quality, and are borne profusely on sturdy stems. The bushes are taller than average — rather upright but branching freely.

Blooms: 35 petals
  White
  Large
  Slightly fragrant

Foliage: Medium green
  Matt

Health: Good disease resistance

Growth: Vigorous
  Upright

Awards: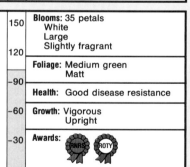

POT O' GOLD

In the 1980s several catalogues predicted that *Pot o' Gold* was destined to become the outstanding fragrant yellow Hybrid Tea of the generation. It has a number of good points — there is great freedom of flowering and weather resistance is good. The fragrance is strong and the blooms are borne in large sprays. It did not, however, become a best-seller to be found in every catalogue. In most gardens the blooms are not large and tend to be flat rather than high-centred.

Blooms: 30 petals
  Old gold
  Medium-sized
  Fragrant

Foliage: Medium green
  Semi-glossy

Health: Good disease resistance

Growth: Vigorous
  Bushy

Awards: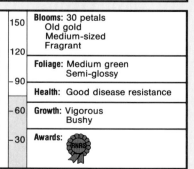

HYBRID TEA ROSES

Height in cm

Blooms:	35 petals Bright crimson Medium-sized Fragrant
Foliage:	Medium green Glossy
Health:	Good disease resistance
Growth:	Vigorous Branching
Awards:	

PRECIOUS PLATINUM
Other Names: RED STAR, OPA POTSCHKE

This rose has won no awards in Britain, has blooms which are not classic beauties and its fragrance is not strong. Despite these facts it has remained popular as a bedding rose since its introduction in 1974. The reason is its colour — dazzling red which can be seen from afar. These blooms are borne freely in small clusters and are resistant to rain. Disease resistance is above average, but you should still watch for mildew.

Blooms:	25 petals Cherry pink Large Very fragrant
Foliage:	Light green Semi-glossy
Health:	Prone to disease
Growth:	Vigorous Upright
Awards:	RNRS

PRIMA BALLERINA
Other Name: PREMIERE BALLERINE

You will find this rose in nearly all the catalogues. The glowing descriptions are justified as far as they go — *Prima Ballerina* is indeed a vigorous bedding variety, taller than average, with beautiful buds and shapely flowers which are outstandingly fragrant. Unfortunately it is now less free-flowering than it used to be and there can be quite long flowerless gaps in late summer. It is also now susceptible to mildew.

Blooms:	25 petals Ivory, shaded pink Large Fragrant
Foliage:	Dark green Glossy
Health:	Good disease resistance
Growth:	Vigorous Upright
Awards:	RNRS RNRS

PRISTINE

Not many American H.Ts have successfully crossed the Atlantic, but *Pristine* is an exception. Bushes are healthy and covered with large leaves, making it an excellent hedging plant. It is also useful for cutting and exhibiting, as the buds are long and the flowers large. Despite these points it has not reached the top 20. The shape of the bloom is good, but not as perfect as some claim. Despite its prize for fragrance, it is regarded as only moderately perfumed.

Blooms:	70 petals Scarlet, reverse pale scarlet Large Fragrant
Foliage:	Dark green Glossy
Health:	Good disease resistance
Growth:	Vigorous Upright
Awards:	RNRS B ROE

RED DEVIL
Other Name: COEUR D'AMOUR

One of the most popular and successful exhibition varieties, which deserves all the praise it has received. The form of the blooms is perhaps the closest yet achieved to the perfect Hybrid Tea shape, and by disbudding, even a beginner can produce prize-winning flowers which are extremely large and fragrant. It is also a good bedding rose but there is one serious drawback — the blooms are damaged by rain.

Blooms:	25 petals Coppery orange, blended yellow Large Slightly fragrant
Foliage:	Dark green Glossy
Health:	Good disease resistance
Growth:	Vigorous Upright
Awards:	RHS B

REMEMBER ME

Remember Me has the good health and fine foliage you would expect from an offspring of *Silver Jubilee* and *Alexander*. This rose of the mid 1980s is widely grown and has been voted one of the best 20 Hybrid Teas by keen rose growers. The flowers are well-shaped but the most outstanding feature is their arrangement on the plant. Each flower is borne in a wide-spreading truss. Large flowered *and* Cluster flowered — rose classification is difficult!

HYBRID TEA ROSES

Height in cm

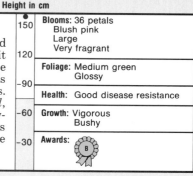

RENAISSANCE

This pale pink rose was bred by Harkness and first appeared in 1994. It is a flower to admire — it has a rounded shape and high centre, and at the heart there is a touch of cream. The perfume is both strong and sweet and the foliage is lustrous. Its parents are *Amber Queen* and *Margaret Merril*, both of which are much-loved and highly-honoured Floribundas and not Hybrid Teas. It is therefore not surprising that the blooms are borne in small clusters rather than singly.

150 / 120 / 90 / 60 / 30	**Blooms:** 36 petals / Blush pink / Large / Very fragrant
	Foliage: Medium green / Glossy
	Health: Good disease resistance
	Growth: Vigorous / Bushy
	Awards:

ROSE GAUJARD

It may seem surprising that such a well-known and well-loved rose should have its faults. The purists frown on the garishness of its colour, the tendency of its blooms to split and the absence of any worthwhile fragrance. But for the ordinary gardener it is a good choice for bedding — the bushes are vigorous, hardy, long-lasting and remarkably easy to grow in poor conditions. It stands up to rain and the blooms are borne very freely. The leaves are large and quite healthy.

150 / 120 / 90 / 60 / 30	**Blooms:** 30 petals / Rose red, silvery reverse / Large / Slightly fragrant
	Foliage: Dark green / Glossy
	Health: Good disease resistance
	Growth: Very vigorous / Branching
	Awards:

ROSEMARY HARKNESS

Another rose to bear the proud Harkness name — one for bedding rather than exhibiting. The shrubby bush is clothed with large leaves, which is just what you want from a garden rose. It also drops its petals cleanly and the flowers are an eye-catching blend of many hues. These blooms are borne singly or in clusters, and they open wide when mature. A good all-rounder with a strong fragrance but it lacks that vital spark which would put it in everybody's catalogue.

150 / 120 / 90 / 60 / 30	**Blooms:** 35 petals / Orange yellow, blended salmon / Medium-sized / Very fragrant
	Foliage: Dark green / Semi-glossy
	Health: Good disease resistance
	Growth: Vigorous / Bushy
	Awards:

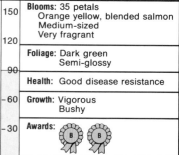

ROYAL WILLIAM

According to some experts this Kordes rose introduced in 1987 is the best of all the dark reds. The leaves are large, plentiful and healthy, and the stout branches bear a fine display of eye-catching well-formed blooms. It is recommended as a rose for flower arranging as the stalks are long and the fragrance is pleasantly spicy. Keen amateur rose growers rate it among the top 10 Hybrid Teas and it was chosen by professional rose growers as their Rose of the Year in 1987.

150 / 120 / 90 / 60 / 30	**Blooms:** 35 petals / Deep crimson / Large / Fragrant
	Foliage: Dark green / Semi-glossy
	Health: Good disease resistance
	Growth: Vigorous / Upright
	Awards:

RUBY WEDDING

Ruby Wedding proves that a variety can have popular appeal without large blooms, novel colouring nor a strong fragrance. The blooms, though nicely shaped, are rather small for a Hybrid Tea. The bush is spreading and below average height. A rose for the small garden or the front of the border — the flowers are borne on stiff stems and the growers recommend it for cutting. There are better reds to choose from, unless you have a ruby wedding to celebrate.

150 / 120 / 90 / 60 / 30	**Blooms:** 30 petals / Ruby red / Medium-sized / Slightly fragrant
	Foliage: Dark green / Glossy
	Health: Average disease resistance
	Growth: Vigorous / Bushy
	Awards:

HYBRID TEA ROSES

Height in cm

Blooms: 24 petals Cream, blended pink Small Slightly fragrant	150 120
Foliage: Dark green Glossy	90
Health: Good disease resistance	60
Growth: Moderately vigorous Bushy	
Awards:	30

SALLY'S ROSE

In this book the age-old name 'Hybrid Tea' rather than the more fashionable 'Large-flowered Bush' has been retained for this group. This Cants-bred variety introduced in 1994 illustrates one of the reasons why — it is undoubtedly an H.T but it is a *small* flowered rose. A useful variety where space is limited — the bush is both compact and neat. It is also colourful — the blooms are a blend of cream, pink and apricot, and the foliage is dark red before it changes to dark green.

Blooms: 40 petals Pink Large Slightly fragrant	150 120
Foliage: Dark green Glossy	90
Health: Good disease resistance	
Growth: Very vigorous Bushy	60
Awards: RHS	30

SAVOY HOTEL
Other Names: INTEGRITY, VERCORS

Savoy Hotel was introduced in 1989 by Harkness and within a few years became one of Britain's favourite roses. With *Silver Jubilee* and *Amber Queen* as parents it is not surprising that it has been successful, but it received no awards from the Royal National Rose Society. Its fragrance is not strong but it still caught the public fancy — it can be used for bedding, cutting, showing and forcing under glass.

Blooms: 22 petals White Large Fragrant	150 120
Foliage: Light green Semi-glossy	90
Health: Good disease resistance	
Growth: Vigorous Upright	60
Awards:	30

SILVER ANNIVERSARY

There is a *Silver Jubilee* and a *Silver Wedding*, and now there is a *Silver Anniversary* Hybrid Tea. This Poulsen variety was introduced by Cants in 1995. There is obviously a ready market for this rose for people looking for a present to mark such an event, but this strong upright bush has more than a promotion-minded name. The flowers are both pure white and fragrant, and the bush is below average height — a combination which is both unusual and desirable in an H.T rose.

Blooms: 25 petals Coppery pink, shaded peach Large Fragrant	150 120
Foliage: Medium green Glossy	90
Health: Good disease resistance	
Growth: Vigorous Bushy	60
Awards: RNRS BARB RHS JM	30

SILVER JUBILEE

The only sad note in the story of this rose was the death of its breeder shortly before its introduction in 1978 — Alec Cocker did not live to see the universal acclaim given to *Silver Jubilee*. Few newcomers have gained such instant popularity, and there are several reasons. Shapely blooms on short stems, long petals which do not lose their colour in hot weather, dense foliage and an outstandingly free-flowering habit combine to make it a splendid bedding variety.

Blooms: 35 petals Creamy white Medium-sized Slightly fragrant	150 120
Foliage: Dark green Semi-glossy	90
Health: Average disease resistance	
Growth: Moderately vigorous Bushy	60
Awards:	30

SILVER WEDDING

Silver Wedding and *Ruby Wedding* have several features in common — both were introduced by Gregory in the 1970s and both bear medium-sized flowers which are recommended for cutting. The flowers, of course, are completely different. *Silver Wedding* blooms are creamy white with a pinkish blush on the outside — the centre is a pale honey colour. These blooms are borne in clusters rather than singly and the bushes have a neat growth habit and bronze-tinted young leaves.

HYBRID TEA ROSES

Height in cm

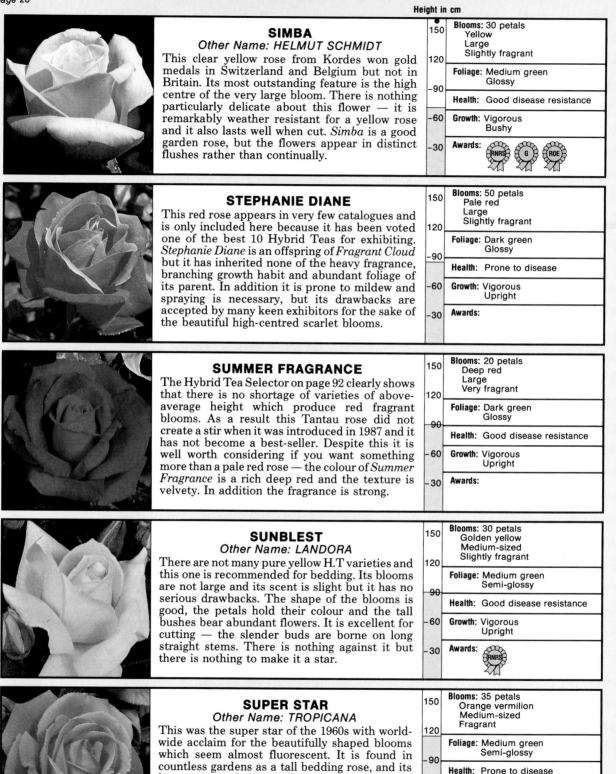

SIMBA
Other Name: HELMUT SCHMIDT

This clear yellow rose from Kordes won gold medals in Switzerland and Belgium but not in Britain. Its most outstanding feature is the high centre of the very large bloom. There is nothing particularly delicate about this flower — it is remarkably weather resistant for a yellow rose and it also lasts well when cut. *Simba* is a good garden rose, but the flowers appear in distinct flushes rather than continually.

150	**Blooms:** 30 petals Yellow Large Slightly fragrant
120	
90	**Foliage:** Medium green Glossy
	Health: Good disease resistance
60	**Growth:** Vigorous Bushy
30	**Awards:**

STEPHANIE DIANE

This red rose appears in very few catalogues and is only included here because it has been voted one of the best 10 Hybrid Teas for exhibiting. *Stephanie Diane* is an offspring of *Fragrant Cloud* but it has inherited none of the heavy fragrance, branching growth habit and abundant foliage of its parent. In addition it is prone to mildew and spraying is necessary, but its drawbacks are accepted by many keen exhibitors for the sake of the beautiful high-centred scarlet blooms.

150	**Blooms:** 50 petals Pale red Large Slightly fragrant
120	
90	**Foliage:** Dark green Glossy
	Health: Prone to disease
60	**Growth:** Vigorous Upright
30	**Awards:**

SUMMER FRAGRANCE

The Hybrid Tea Selector on page 92 clearly shows that there is no shortage of varieties of above-average height which produce red fragrant blooms. As a result this Tantau rose did not create a stir when it was introduced in 1987 and it has not become a best-seller. Despite this it is well worth considering if you want something more than a pale red rose — the colour of *Summer Fragrance* is a rich deep red and the texture is velvety. In addition the fragrance is strong.

150	**Blooms:** 20 petals Deep red Large Very fragrant
120	
90	**Foliage:** Dark green Glossy
	Health: Good disease resistance
60	**Growth:** Vigorous Upright
30	**Awards:**

SUNBLEST
Other Name: LANDORA

There are not many pure yellow H.T varieties and this one is recommended for bedding. Its blooms are not large and its scent is slight but it has no serious drawbacks. The shape of the blooms is good, the petals hold their colour and the tall bushes bear abundant flowers. It is excellent for cutting — the slender buds are borne on long straight stems. There is nothing against it but there is nothing to make it a star.

150	**Blooms:** 30 petals Golden yellow Medium-sized Slightly fragrant
120	
90	**Foliage:** Medium green Semi-glossy
	Health: Good disease resistance
60	**Growth:** Vigorous Upright
30	**Awards:**

SUPER STAR
Other Name: TROPICANA

This was the super star of the 1960s with world-wide acclaim for the beautifully shaped blooms which seem almost fluorescent. It is found in countless gardens as a tall bedding rose, and its long stems make it excellent for cutting. It was never perfect — flowering begins rather late and the petals turn purple with age. Nowadays it has distinct drawbacks — the foliage is susceptible to mildew and old bushes produce few flowers.

150	**Blooms:** 35 petals Orange vermilion Medium-sized Fragrant
120	
90	**Foliage:** Medium green Semi-glossy
	Health: Prone to disease
60	**Growth:** Vigorous Upright
30	**Awards:**

HYBRID TEA ROSES

Blooms:	40 petals
	Yellow, edged scarlet
	Large
	Slightly fragrant
Foliage:	Dark green
	Glossy
Health:	Good disease resistance
Growth:	Vigorous
	Bushy
Awards:	RNRS RHS B

TEQUILA SUNRISE

A new star, regarded as one of the best of the newer roses. The bush is of average height and is attractively clothed with dark shiny foliage, but there is no doubt that it is the catalogue description of the colour of the flowers which has created the great demand for this variety. The background colour is golden yellow and the edging of bright scarlet creates a spectacular effect. These blooms are plentiful and are borne well above the leaves.

Blooms:	35 petals
	Honey yellow, edged salmon
	Large
	Slightly fragrant
Foliage:	Medium green
	Semi-glossy
Health:	Good disease resistance
Growth:	Moderately vigorous
	Bushy
Awards:	RNRS RHS BB

THE LADY

Roses have been named after people, places and products — this one commemorated the centenary of a magazine. The flower is of classic shape and is high centred with reflexed petals which have a unique pastel colour. Despite the delicate appearance these blooms stand up to wet and cool conditions remarkably well. The flowers are of exhibition quality when well grown and are borne freely over a long period, appearing singly or in small clusters on tall branching stems.

Blooms:	20 petals
	Deep pink
	Large
	Very fragrant
Foliage:	Medium green
	Glossy
Health:	Good disease resistance
Growth:	Vigorous
	Upright
Awards:	B G P ROE

THE McCARTNEY ROSE

Meilland named this variety after one of the Beatles, and after its introduction in 1991 it quickly became one of the top 20 new roses in the Royal National Rose Society poll. The bush is tall, vigorous and well-clothed with leaves, and the large pink blooms have a true H.T shape. None of this is particularly unusual — the list of tall pinks on page 92 is a long one. *The McCartney Rose* does have two key features — long, elegant buds and an outstanding heavy perfume.

Blooms:	30 petals
	Orange bronze, shaded red
	Large
	Fragrant
Foliage:	Medium green
	Glossy
Health:	Good disease resistance
Growth:	Vigorous
	Upright
Awards:	RNRS RHS JM

TROIKA
Other Name: ROYAL DANE

If you like copper-coloured roses then this is a good one to choose. There is none of the die-back and disease which plague the older varieties in this colour group. The blooms are large enough for exhibition and the buds are long and shapely enough to make them excellent for cutting. But *Troika* is best considered as a bedding rose — the blooms appear early, rain resistance is good and the petals do not fade with age.

Blooms:	24 petals
	Amber yellow
	Large
	Very fragrant
Foliage:	Dark green
	Glossy
Health:	Good disease resistance
Growth:	Vigorous
	Bushy
Awards:	RNRS RNRS

VALENCIA

It is hard to describe the colour of this Kordes rose — some books describe it as 'amber yellow' and others as 'buff orange with golden shadings'. *Valencia* has two claims to fame — the blooms are very large and the perfume is strong. The foliage is an attractive bronze colour when young but the mature leaves are large and dark green. It is a good rose for cutting and has been voted as one of the best 20 new roses by members of the Royal National Rose Society.

HYBRID TEA ROSES

Height in cm

VELVET FRAGRANCE

This one is definitely for you if you like deep red roses with velvety petals. The many-petalled blooms are well shaped and have an outstanding fragrance — not all the offspring of *Fragrant Cloud* can match their mother's scent but this one certainly can. The heavy fragrance and velvety appearance give *Velvet Fragrance* an old-fashioned feel, but it is a rose of the late 1980s. A robust plant with flowers which are borne in large numbers all season long.

Blooms:	42 petals Deep red Large Very fragrant
Foliage:	Dark green Glossy
Health:	Good disease resistance
Growth:	Vigorous Upright
Awards:	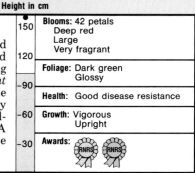

VIDAL SASSOON

And now for something different. For many years *Julia's Rose* with its parchment-brown petals has been regarded as the flower-arranger's rose because of its unique colouring. In 1994 *Vidal Sassoon* was introduced as another variety for the flower arranger. The blend of pale brown and lavender is unique and there is a touch of lemon in the strong fragrance. The blooms are borne singly or in clusters of 4 or 5 — a trifle dull outside but an eye-catcher in an indoor arrangement.

Blooms:	22 petals Tan, shaded lavender Medium-sized Very fragrant
Foliage:	Light green Semi-glossy
Health:	Good disease resistance
Growth:	Vigorous Upright
Awards:	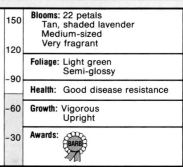

WARM WISHES

It may seem strange that a coral pink H.T with blooms which are not particularly large should have received several international awards and a spot in most popular catalogues so soon after its appearance in 1994. The reason seems to be the abundance of the blooms and their continuity throughout the season, together with the ability of the flowers to stand up to wind and rain. These blooms appear both singly and in clusters — high centred and classically shaped.

Blooms:	28 petals Peach coral Medium-sized or large Very fragrant
Foliage:	Dark green Glossy
Health:	Good disease resistance
Growth:	Vigorous Bushy
Awards:	

WENDY CUSSONS

This variety of the 1950s remains very popular and has a list of impressive qualities — outstanding perfume, large well-shaped blooms on large handsome bushes, a prolific flowering habit and above average resistance to rain. *Wendy Cussons* has an excellent reputation for longevity, but it is still not the perfect bedding rose — the strong cerise pink clashes badly with many other varieties and the outstanding resistance to disease has gone.

Blooms:	35 petals Deep reddish pink Large Very fragrant
Foliage:	Dark green Glossy
Health:	Average disease resistance
Growth:	Vigorous Branching
Awards:	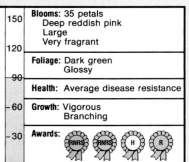

WHISKY MAC

Much has been written about the *Whisky Mac* phenomenon. Experts have often described the drawbacks of this variety — unreliability when grown in average or poor soil, susceptibility to mildew and rust, blooms which quickly become open-cupped and the loss of the free-flowering habit after a few years. Yet *Whisky Mac* has proven to be one of the most popular of all Hybrid Teas. The reason is simple — a unique colour plus an attractive and unusual scent.

Blooms:	30 petals Golden apricot Medium-sized Very fragrant
Foliage:	Green, tinted bronze Glossy
Health:	Prone to disease
Growth:	Vigorous Bushy
Awards:	

HYBRID TEA ROSES

FLORIBUNDA ROSES
(Cluster-flowered Bushes)

A Danish hybridist, Svend Poulsen, once dreamt of producing a new race of roses, with modern flowers borne in large trusses continually throughout the season. He crossed Polyanthas (pompon roses) with Hybrid Teas and his first hybrid, *Else Poulsen*, appeared in 1924 — a Hybrid Polyantha. This was followed by other Poulsen roses and the Floribundas were born, but it was not until 1952 that this term was generally adopted. In 1979 the Royal National Rose Society began to use the New Classification in which 'Floribundas' became 'Cluster-flowered Bushes' but this change has not been generally accepted by the trade.

The basic drawback of the typical Floribunda is that the blooms lack the size, beauty and fragrance of their more elegant rivals — the Hybrid Teas. But there are advantages to balance this drawback. Varieties in this group flower almost continually throughout the summer and autumn, whereas Hybrid Teas tend to bloom in distinct flushes. And it is not only frequency of blooming, it is also quantity of flowers — the Floribunda trusses generally provide a much larger splash of colour on the bush than is found on a Hybrid Tea. The benefits do not stop there. The average Floribunda is hardier, easier to care for and more reliable in wet weather than its Hybrid Tea counterpart.

The increase in popularity amongst expert and ordinary gardener alike has been due to the flood of new varieties in recent years. These have maintained the benefits, introduced new colours and have started to overcome the drawbacks listed earlier. *Shocking Blue* and *Fragrant Delight* rival the sweet-smelling Hybrid Teas for fragrance... *Melody Maker* and *Margaret Merril* rival the Hybrid Teas for elegance.

The first winner of the Rose of the Year award was *Mountbatten* in 1982, and later Floribunda winners include *Beautiful Britain*, *Amber Queen*, *Glad Tidings*, *Harvest Fayre*, *Melody Maker* and *Chatsworth*. Large Floribundas with shapely H.T blooms, such as *Queen Elizabeth*, are called Grandifloras in the U.S.

The Floribunda is the rose *par excellence* for providing colour in the garden. It can be grown as a bush or standard, in both formal and informal settings. There are tall varieties for providing hedges, and there are dwarf varieties. Nearly but not all of these 45 cm dwarfs have been moved to a separate group — the Patio Roses. These compact bushes have become great favourites and the most widely available ones are described on pages 44–49.

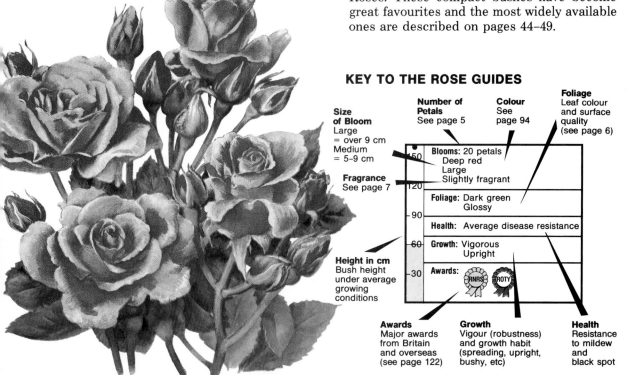

KEY TO THE ROSE GUIDES

Size of Bloom
Large = over 9 cm
Medium = 5–9 cm

Number of Petals
See page 5

Colour
See page 94

Foliage
Leaf colour and surface quality (see page 6)

Fragrance
See page 7

Height in cm
Bush height under average growing conditions

Blooms: 20 petals
Deep red
Large
Slightly fragrant

Foliage: Dark green
Glossy

Health: Average disease resistance

Growth: Vigorous
Upright

Awards: RNRS ROTY

Awards
Major awards from Britain and overseas (see page 122)

Growth
Vigour (robustness) and growth habit (spreading, upright, bushy, etc)

Health
Resistance to mildew and black spot

Height in cm

ALLGOLD

Although it won its Gold Medal in the 1950s, *Allgold* is still recommended in many catalogues. Flowering begins early, and goes on almost continually until late autumn. Even in rainy weather the colour of the blooms remains pure and unfading until the petals fall. However, there are better compact yellow Floribundas these days — the blooms are rather short of petals and the foliage may be distinctly sparse. Choose *Amber Queen*, *Baby Bio* or *Golden Years*.

150	**Blooms:** 20 petals Buttercup yellow Small Slightly fragrant
120	
-90	**Foliage:** Medium green Glossy
	Health: Good disease resistance
-60	**Growth:** Moderately vigorous Branching
-30	**Awards:**

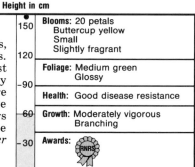

AMBER QUEEN
Other Name: PRINZ EUGEN VAN SAVOYEN

This variety won the 1984 Rose of the Year award and it's not hard to see why. The dark-leaved bush is neat and compact, and the many-petalled blooms are large and cup-shaped when fully open. The trusses bear many flowers and *Amber Queen* has got a good reputation for being free-flowering. The foliage is large and plentiful, making it a good bedding rose. It *is* fragrant, but the Hague Fragrance Medal was perhaps a surprise.

150	**Blooms:** 40 petals Amber yellow Large Fragrant
120	
-90	**Foliage:** Dark green Glossy
	Health: Good disease resistance
-60	**Growth:** Moderately vigorous Bushy
-30	**Awards:**

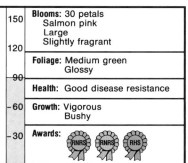

ANISLEY DICKSON
Other Name: MÜNCHNER KINDL

A bold and showy variety which won the Royal National Rose Society's top honours in 1984. The large trusses bear numerous warm-coloured flowers, and these are set off by the abundant foliage. A multi-purpose rose — grow it as a hedge or in a bed or border. In addition it is recommended for both cutting and exhibiting. *Anisley Dickson* has never quite reached the popularity which was expected.

150	**Blooms:** 30 petals Salmon pink Large Slightly fragrant
120	
90	**Foliage:** Medium green Glossy
	Health: Good disease resistance
-60	**Growth:** Vigorous Bushy
-30	**Awards:**

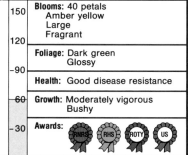

ANNA LIVIA

This rose appeared in the mid 1980s and it has many fans, but its features are good rather than outstanding. It is free flowering and the clusters are large. The bush is densely covered with leathery leaves and growth is even. However the blooms have none of the high-centred beauty of *Anisley Dickson* and the fragrance is not strong. Still, a good all-rounder for bedding, hedging and cutting but not for the show bench. Resistance to mildew and black spot is very good.

150	**Blooms:** 20 petals Pink Medium-sized Slightly fragrant
120	
-90	**Foliage:** Medium green Semi-glossy
	Health: Good disease resistance
-60	**Growth:** Vigorous Bushy
-30	**Awards:**

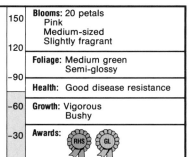

ANNE HARKNESS

August is a poor month for many roses, but this is the time when *Anne Harkness* is at its prime. Slow to come to flower, it compensates for the drawback by providing a fine mid- and late-summer display. The flowers are borne in remarkably large trusses, capable of braving both wind and rain. The flower stems are remarkably long, and the blooms last well when cut. Not surprisingly, this tall Floribunda has become a favourite flower arranger and exhibitor rose.

150	**Blooms:** 25 petals Apricot yellow Medium-sized Slightly fragrant
120	
-90	**Foliage:** Medium green Semi-glossy
	Health: Good disease resistance
-60	**Growth:** Vigorous Upright
-30	**Awards:**

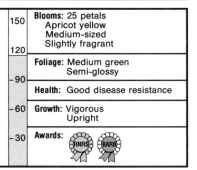

FLORIBUNDA ROSES

Blooms:	20 petals Golden yellow Large Very fragrant
Foliage:	Medium green Glossy
Health:	Good disease resistance
Growth:	Vigorous Upright
Awards:	RNRS RHS B

ARTHUR BELL

Arthur Bell deserves its reputation and popularity. The tall bush is well-clothed with an abundance of leathery leaves and the flowers are large and weather-resistant. The strength of the fragrance is rarely matched by any other Floribunda and it has a good record for mildew and black spot resistance. Flowering starts very early in the season and continues into the autumn. Its failing is well known — the golden blooms fade to pale cream as they age.

Blooms:	40 petals Golden yellow Large Slightly fragrant
Foliage:	Dark green Semi-glossy
Health:	Good disease resistance
Growth:	Vigorous Bushy
Awards:	RNRS R

BABY BIO

This dwarf Floribunda is a fairy story rose. Bred by an engine driver (Mr Smith of Sandiacre) in his small greenhouse, it was awarded a Certificate of Merit by the Royal National Rose Society in 1976. Masses of flowers are borne freely and continually throughout the season, and it is regarded as one of the best of the dwarf yellows. Its popularity has increased steadily over the years. The probable reason is the remarkable fullness and size of the blooms on such a small bush.

Blooms:	20 petals Tomato red Medium-sized Slightly fragrant
Foliage:	Medium green Semi-glossy
Health:	Good disease resistance
Growth:	Moderately vigorous Bushy
Awards:	ROTY

BEAUTIFUL BRITAIN

This 1983 Rose of the Year appears in most of the popular catalogues and has been a firm favourite for many years. The blooms are borne in large trusses — each flower is not large but it has the classic H.T shape. Unfortunately there is little fragrance and not many petals. The colour is most unusual — hence the general appeal. Other claims to fame apart from its colour have been its free-flowering habit and the abundant foliage, but *Beautiful Britain* has lost much of its strength.

Blooms:	20 petals Pale orange Medium-sized Slightly fragrant
Foliage:	Dark green, tinted red Glossy
Health:	Good disease resistance
Growth:	Vigorous Upright
Awards:	RNRS

BUCKS FIZZ

At the beginning of the 1990s this upright and rather tall Floribunda was introduced as a new colour break — a clear and soft orange. Poulsen of Denmark was the breeder, and the blooms have a classic H.T shape rather than the more open arrangement found in most varieties in this group. It can be used for hedging and cutting as well as garden display in bed or border, and it can be grown in a large container. Fragrance is variable — some catalogues describe it as strong.

Blooms:	20 petals Cream, flushed buff and pink Medium-sized, cupped Fragrant
Foliage:	Dark green Glossy
Health:	Good disease resistance
Growth:	Vigorous Branching
Awards:	RNRS RNRS M

CHANELLE

A peaches-and-cream Floribunda, much loved by gardeners who favour pastel colours in their roses. The bushes bear abundant glossy foliage which has above-average resistance to mildew. The blooms are nicely formed in bud, looking like miniature H.Ts, but they open into flat blooms. These flowers have good rain resistance, and the flowering season carries on well into autumn. *Chanelle* has a good reputation as a reliable Floribunda.

FLORIBUNDA ROSES

Height in cm

CHATSWORTH

One of a small group of roses bred by Tantau and introduced in the 1990s as the Heritage Collection. The Ground Cover *Broadlands* won the President's International Trophy — this one was voted Rose of the Year in 1995. It is low-growing but spreads out to 1 m or more — its arching stems being covered with masses of pink blooms with amber-coloured stamens. The trusses are exceptionally large and there is a reasonably strong fragrance.

150	**Blooms:** 15 petals Rich pink Medium-sized Fragrant
120	
90	**Foliage:** Dark green, tinted red Glossy
	Health: Good disease resistance
60	**Growth:** Vigorous Arching
30	**Awards:**

CITY OF LEEDS

One of the popular Floribundas, widely recommended where the gardener wants a massed planting of a single variety or the beginner requires an easy-to-grow variety. *City of Leeds* proves that a rose does not have to be perfect to be popular. The scent is hardly noticeable, the foliage is small and the flowers spot after heavy rain. These drawbacks, however, are soon forgotten when you see the trusses of rich pink flowers covering the attractive bushes.

150	**Blooms:** 20 petals Rich salmon pink Medium-sized Slightly fragrant
120	
90	**Foliage:** Dark green Semi-glossy
	Health: Average disease resistance
60	**Growth:** Vigorous Upright
30	**Awards:**

CITY OF LONDON

This excellent variety illustrates the difficulty of trying to put roses into pigeon-holes. If lightly pruned it will grow into a 1.5 m high shrub — it is listed under 'Shrubs' in a few catalogues. If pruned by the standard method it is a 90 cm bush, and most catalogues list it as a Floribunda. It is easy to grow and thoroughly reliable with an outstanding perfume — the stems are long and it is recommended for both flower arrangements and buttonholes.

150	**Blooms:** 18 petals Blush pink Medium-sized Very fragrant
120	
90	**Foliage:** Dark green Glossy
	Health: Good disease resistance
60	**Growth:** Vigorous Spreading
30	**Awards:**

DAME WENDY

A Cants variety for people who love pink. There are, of course, other pink Floribundas which grow to average height or less, but this one's claim to fame is that the warm pink petals do not fade as the flower ages, and the clusters of flowers are borne in remarkable numbers. The flowers do not fade but the foliage does — the colour of the leaves changes from reddish-green to grey-green as they get older. It is recommended for growing in containers and also for cutting.

150	**Blooms:** 22 petals Pink Medium-sized Slightly fragrant
120	
90	**Foliage:** Grey-green Glossy
	Health: Good disease resistance
60	**Growth:** Vigorous Spreading
30	**Awards:**

DEAREST

For many years *Dearest* was the top-selling pink Floribunda, but its popularity has waned. Its virtues are still there — beautiful pink blooms which are camellia-like and filled with spicy fragrance, trusses which are large and bushes which are clothed with dark and shiny foliage. As always, a good choice for bedding, cutting or exhibiting, but there are faults. This variety does not like wet weather and the foliage is susceptible to both rust and black spot.

150	**Blooms:** 30 petals Salmon pink Large Fragrant
120	
90	**Foliage:** Dark green Glossy
	Health: Prone to disease
60	**Growth:** Vigorous Branching
30	**Awards:**

FLORIBUNDA ROSES

Blooms:	35 petals Orange salmon Medium-sized Fragrant
Foliage:	Dark green Semi-glossy
Health:	Prone to disease
Growth:	Moderately vigorous Upright
Awards:	(RNRS) (RNRS)

150
120
90
60
30

ELIZABETH OF GLAMIS
Other Name: IRISH BEAUTY

It is hard to be disloyal to one of the great roses of our time and one which has been grown in countless gardens since its introduction in 1964, but it has problems these days. It is now only a sound choice for reasonably good soil — it is definitely unsuitable for cold soils or clays. When well-grown, the high-centred buds open into lovely flat blooms borne in large fragrant clusters. Spray to keep disease at bay.

Blooms:	35 petals Silver pink, edged deeper pink Medium-sized Very fragrant
Foliage:	Dark green Glossy
Health:	Good disease resistance
Growth:	Very vigorous Bushy
Awards:	(RNRS) (BARB)

150
120
90
60
30

ENGLISH MISS

An appropriate name for an English-bred rose which has petals of delicate blush pink. The classical pink Floribunda *Dearest* is one of its parents, but *English Miss* is much healthier and is less susceptible to rain. The buds open to form camellia-like flowers which possess a strong, sweet scent. The bush is densely clothed with shiny, leathery leaves which have a purplish tinge. *English Miss* is free-flowering and there is a quick repeat between flushes.

Blooms:	30 petals Vivid scarlet Medium-sized Slightly fragrant
Foliage:	Dark green Glossy
Health:	Average disease resistance
Growth:	Vigorous Branching
Awards:	(RNRS)

150
120
90
60
30

EVELYN FISON
Other Name: IRISH WONDER

One of the older bright red Floribundas but still regarded as one of the best bedding and exhibition varieties. It has an excellent reputation for reliability, and neither bright sun nor heavy rain seem to damage the blooms. The trusses are large and well-spaced, and it is extremely prolific. *Evelyn Fison* is hard to fault — perhaps the amount of foliage is sometimes inadequate and disease resistance is a little overrated.

Blooms:	22 petals Deep orange Medium-sized Slightly fragrant
Foliage:	Dark green Glossy
Health:	Good disease resistance
Growth:	Vigorous Bushy
Awards:	(RNRS) (US) (H)

150
120
90
60
30

FELLOWSHIP

Fellowship has won top honours on both sides of the Atlantic. It is a compact variety which is densely clothed with foliage — the blooms are borne in wide trusses or singly with all the brightness you would expect from a *Remember Me* x *Southampton* hybrid. Some Floribunda varieties produce their flowers in distinct flushes but not this one — flowering seems to go on and on throughout the season. It is tough and reliable, so it is a good choice if you want an 'easy' rose.

Blooms:	20 petals Coppery salmon, yellow at base Large Very fragrant
Foliage:	Medium green Glossy
Health:	Good disease resistance
Growth:	Very vigorous Upright
Awards:	(RNRS) (RNRS) (JM)

150
120
90
60
30

FRAGRANT DELIGHT

If you like Floribundas, strong fragrance and copper-coloured blooms, then *Fragrant Delight* is the rose for you. This offspring of *Chanelle* and *Whisky Mac* was introduced in the late 1970s, and the fine shape of the young blooms, together with the small size of the trusses led at least one grower to include it in the Hybrid Tea section of his catalogue. The young leaves are bronzy green, turning mid-green and remaining very shiny as they mature.

FLORIBUNDA ROSES

Height in cm

GLAD TIDINGS

This German rose bred by Tantau was voted Rose of the Year in 1989 but it has not been given the same acclaim by the public — it does not appear in the top 20 Floribunda poll. The flowers are well-shaped and they appear in profusion in large clusters which results in an attractive display. But on the drawback side there is not much fragrance and the number of petals in the flower is not high. It may be necessary to spray against black spot, but it is worth it if you love deep red.

Blooms: 20 petals	Deep red, Large, Slightly fragrant
Foliage: Dark green	Glossy
Health: Average disease resistance	
Growth: Vigorous	Upright
Awards:	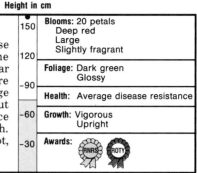

GLENFIDDICH

Glenfiddich is a popular Floribunda and is grown all over Britain, but it is truly a flower of Scotland. Raised by Cocker of Aberdeen, it was named after the Scotch Whisky which is reminiscent of its colour, and it is in Scotland and the northern counties where it is most successful. The well-formed flowers appear singly or in groups and there is good continuity throughout the season. In the south *Glenfiddich* is less reliable and the flowers are somewhat paler.

Blooms: 25 petals	Golden amber, Medium-sized, Slightly fragrant
Foliage: Dark green	Glossy
Health: Good disease resistance	
Growth: Vigorous	Upright
Awards:	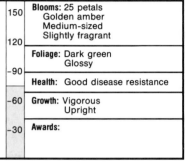

GOLDEN WEDDING

Golden yellow Floribundas continue to appear and this American one was introduced in 1990. Its special claim to fame must be its name — an excellent memento to mark 50 years of marriage. Apart from its value as a present *Golden Wedding* is a welcome addition in the garden if you like Floribundas with H.T shaped blooms and want a bush which is easy to care for. The foliage is both plentiful and attractive, but the fragrance is weak. You will find this one in most catalogues.

Blooms: 28 petals	Yellow, Large, Slightly fragrant
Foliage: Dark green	Glossy
Health: Good disease resistance	
Growth: Vigorous	Bushy
Awards:	

GOLDEN YEARS

Another 'Golden' Floribunda like the one above with dark foliage, yellow flowers and a slight fragrance. Both were introduced at the beginning of the 1990s, but there are as many differences as similarities. *Golden Years* is an English rose and the blooms open to reveal a mass of petals rather than having an H.T shape. Growth is upright rather than bushy and it is freer flowering than its rival. A good variety, which you would expect from a *Sunblest* x *Amber Queen* cross.

Blooms: 46 petals	Golden yellow, Large, Slightly fragrant
Foliage: Dark green	Glossy
Health: Good disease resistance	
Growth: Vigorous	Upright
Awards:	

GOLDFINGER

Goldfinger is small enough to be regarded by some as a Patio Rose, but the label and catalogue entry generally class it as a small Floribunda. Growth is upright and rather uneven, but it is a useful variety where space is limited, provided you do not mind the lack of strong fragrance and the tendency for the flower colour to fade. It has won no major awards and it does not appear in the popularity polls, but you will find it in the catalogues of many specialist rose growers.

Blooms: 20 petals	Golden yellow, Medium-sized, Slightly fragrant
Foliage: Dark green	Glossy
Health: Good disease resistance	
Growth: Vigorous	Upright
Awards:	

Blooms:	15 petals
	Chartreuse green
	Large
	No fragrance
Foliage:	Dark green
	Semi-glossy
Health:	Prone to disease
Growth:	Vigorous
	Upright
Awards:	

GREENSLEEVES

This Harkness rose introduced in 1980 is strictly for the flower arranger who likes to use material which is different. Cut the trusses when the buds are tinged with pink — as the blooms open the colour changes to green. Obviously a great talking point, but of little value for general garden display. The growth is unattractive and leggy, the dull blooms are flat when mature and regular spraying against disease is necessary. Still, there is nothing else like it.

Blooms:	30 petals
	White, edged dark pink
	Large
	Slightly fragrant
Foliage:	Dark green
	Glossy
Health:	Average disease resistance
Growth:	Vigorous
	Bushy
Awards:	(RNRS)

HANNAH GORDON

It is surprising that this rose has not become more popular. The Climber *Handel* became a favourite soon after its introduction because of its unusual colouring — cream blooms edged with rosy pink. *Hannah Gordon* is a Floribunda with quite similar colouring, but only a moderate number of growers have it in their catalogues. There are no obvious drawbacks — the flowers are large, the foliage is bronze-tinted when young and the growth habit is quite attractive.

Blooms:	21 petals
	Apricot orange
	Medium-sized
	Slightly fragrant
Foliage:	Medium green
	Glossy
Health:	Good disease resistance
Growth:	Vigorous
	Bushy
Awards:	(ROTY)

HARVEST FAYRE

A Rose of the Year winner in 1990. Despite this award *Harvest Fayre* is not a rose to choose if you like to see your bushes in flower before the ones next door. It starts to bloom later than most other Floribundas, but in late summer and autumn the large clusters of bright flowers show why it received the top prize. Colour is its virtue — the blooms are neither large nor filled with lots of petals. The bushes are well-clothed with attractive foliage and growth is strong.

Blooms:	25 petals
	White
	Medium-sized
	Slightly fragrant
Foliage:	Medium green
	Glossy
Health:	Prone to disease
Growth:	Vigorous
	Branching
Awards:	(RNRS) (RHS) (BB)

ICEBERG
Other Name: SCHNEEWITTCHEN

Quite simply, the most popular white Floribunda of our time. The pink-tinged buds open to flat white blooms, the quantity and continuity being quite outstanding. *Iceberg* is seen everywhere, but unfortunately it is often denied the chance to show how beautiful it can be. It needs space where it can be grown, lightly pruned, as a tall specimen bush — the blooms will then cover the whole plant and the chance of disease is reduced.

Blooms:	35 petals
	Bright yellow
	Large
	Fragrant
Foliage:	Medium green
	Glossy
Health:	Good disease resistance
Growth:	Moderately vigorous
	Bushy
Awards:	(JM) (BB)

KORRESIA
Other Names: FRIESIA, SUNSPRITE

No rose could have got off to a less promising start — unknown parentage and no early awards in Britain. Yet within a few years it became a star of the rose world — the first serious challenger to *Allgold* for its crown as the top yellow Floribunda. *Korresia* scores over its rival by having flowers which are larger, more fragrant and fully double. Continuity is very good, the trusses of unfading blooms appearing over a long period.

FLORIBUNDA ROSES

Height in cm

LILLI MARLENE

A good bedding rose, justifiably popular for more than 30 years. The bush is well-clothed with abundant foliage and the flowers are plentiful. The black buds open into velvety dark red blooms which shrug off the effects of rain or hot sun. It has a good reputation for reliability and hardiness, which makes it a suitable Floribunda for beginners. Each individual open bloom is not particularly beautiful, but the overall effect of red blooms and coppery foliage is excellent.

150	**Blooms:** 25 petals Deep crimson Medium-sized Slightly fragrant
120	
	Foliage: Green, tinted bronze Semi-glossy
90	
	Health: Prone to disease
60	**Growth:** Vigorous Bushy
30	**Awards:**

LIVERPOOL ECHO

McGredy introduced this pink Floribunda in 1971. Flowering is more or less continuous throughout the season and the flower trusses are large. It will succeed in soils which are not good enough for many other Floribundas, but it has never become popular. In fact you will have to search through many catalogues to find a supplier, and the only reason for its inclusion in this book is that it is judged to be a good exhibition variety in the RNRS polls.

150	**Blooms:** 23 petals Salmon pink Large Slightly fragrant
120	
	Foliage: Light green Glossy
90	
	Health: Average disease resistance
60	**Growth:** Vigorous Bushy
30	**Awards:**

MANY HAPPY RETURNS
Other Name: PRIMA

This Harkness rose appeared in 1991 and has become one of the newer stars of the rose world. You will find this variety in most catalogues and it has received many awards. Obviously its name makes it a good 'present' plant, but it has other merits. *Many Happy Returns* grows as a spreading shrub rather than as an upright bush and in late autumn it bears attractive hips. Best of all it is one of the first Floribundas to flower.

150	**Blooms:** 18 petals Blush pink Large Fragrant
120	
	Foliage: Medium green Glossy
90	
	Health: Good disease resistance
60	**Growth:** Vigorous Spreading
30	**Awards:**

MARGARET MERRIL

A rose to challenge *Iceberg* for the white Floribunda crown — the list of British and International awards is impressive. It does not have the height nor the abundance of flowers associated with *Iceberg*, but it beats its famous rival in two important ways — flower form and scent. The pearly flowers are high-centred beauties borne in small trusses, and the fragrance is considered by some to be the sweetest of any modern rose.

150	**Blooms:** 28 petals Pearly white Medium-sized Very fragrant
120	
	Foliage: Dark green Glossy
90	
	Health: Average disease resistance
60	**Growth:** Very vigorous Bushy
30	**Awards:**

MASQUERADE

There is a handful of roses which everybody can name, and *Masquerade* is one of them. This was the first of the multi-coloured varieties, and after 50 years it is still a popular choice for hedging or wherever a larger than average bush is required. The yellow buds quickly turn to salmon pink as they open and eventually to deep red, with each large truss bearing a medley of these colours. Flowering is profuse, but you must dead-head regularly or it will cease.

150	**Blooms:** 15 petals Yellow, then pink and red Medium-sized Slightly fragrant
120	
	Foliage: Dark green Glossy
90	
	Health: Average disease resistance
60	**Growth:** Vigorous Branching
30	**Awards:**

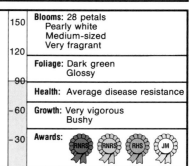

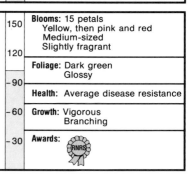

FLORIBUNDA ROSES

Blooms: 23 petals Vermilion, reverse silver Medium-sized Slightly fragrant	150 120
Foliage: Dark green Glossy	90
Health: Good disease resistance	
Growth: Vigorous Upright	60
Awards: RNRS RNRS B R	30

MATANGI

One of the group of roses bred by McGredy which is described as 'hand painted' (see page 5). Well-shaped buds open wide to reveal the unusual red and white coloration, the flowers being borne singly or in small trusses. A definite improvement on its parent *Picasso*, as its blooms appear in great profusion throughout the season and its foliage is glossy. An excellent bedding rose, healthy and rain-resistant, but unsuitable for cutting as it will not last in water.

Blooms: 30 petals Vermilion Large Fragrant	150 120
Foliage: Dark green Glossy	90
Health: Good disease resistance	
Growth: Vigorous Bushy	60
Awards: ROTY	30

MELODY MAKER

This daughter of *Anisley Dickson* took the Rose of the Year award in 1991 and is now listed in many catalogues. The large trusses of orange-red flowers set against the abundant dark foliage obviously influenced the judges in making the award. In addition the blooms have an excellent shape and appear regularly through the season. The bushes are neat and compact — a good selection for a small bed. Surprisingly it fares badly in the RNRS 'Best Floribunda' poll.

Blooms: 45 petals Mimosa yellow Large Fragrant	150 120
Foliage: Medium green Glossy	90
Health: Good disease resistance	
Growth: Vigorous Upright	60
Awards: RNRS RHS ROTY B	30

MOUNTBATTEN

In the world of the tall Floribunda *Queen Elizabeth* reigned during the 1960s and 1970s. In the 1980s the crown passed to *Mountbatten*. Both praise and awards have been heaped on it, but make sure you have enough space — it is large enough to be classed as a Modern Shrub Rose in some catalogues. Grow it as a hedge or in a border or large bed — few varieties are healthier or easier to grow. The leaves are semi-evergreen — the flowers are borne in small clusters.

Blooms: 45 petals Pink Medium-sized Fragrant	150 120
Foliage: Medium green Glossy	90
Health: Good disease resistance	
Growth: Vigorous Bushy	60
Awards:	30

OCTAVIA HILL

This rose was launched by Harkness in 1995 to mark the centenary of the National Trust. In keeping with the Victorian connection the very full blooms have a distinctly old-fashioned look but the similarity with old roses ends there. *Octavia Hill* has all the vigour, disease resistance and repeat flowering habit you would expect from a good modern variety. The bush grows about 1 m x 1 m — some books class it as a Shrub Rose rather than a Floribunda.

Blooms: 35 petals Yellow, striped orange Large Slightly fragrant	150 120
Foliage: Dark green Glossy	90
Health: Good disease resistance	
Growth: Vigorous Upright	60
Awards: RNRS BARB	30

ORANGES AND LEMONS

People either love or hate eye-catching novelties such as *Oranges and Lemons* which was introduced in 1993. The yellow blooms are boldly striped and splashed with bright orange — the ratio of yellow to orange is highly variable. On the credit side it will certainly be noticed by visitors, but there is a distinct disadvantage if you try to grow it in a bed filled with pastel-coloured varieties. Grow it instead in a mixed border and cut some of the blooms for flower arranging.

FLORIBUNDA ROSES

Height in cm

ORANGE SENSATION

Choose *Orange Sensation* if carroty vermilion appeals to you. There are many reasons why *Orange Sensation* is a good choice — the colour is vivid, the petals are numerous and the perfume is strong and sweet. The spreading growth habit means that wide spacing between plants is acceptable, and the trusses are large. The draw-backs are dull foliage and a rather late start to the flowering season. Both black spot and mildew can be problems.

150	**Blooms:** 24 petals
	Light vermilion, gold at base
120	Medium-sized
	Fragrant
	Foliage: Light green
90	Matt
	Health: Prone to disease
60	**Growth:** Vigorous
	Branching
30	**Awards:**

PICCOLO

The flower shape is good and the shade of orange red was a welcome addition to the range of low-growing Floribundas in 1984. This Tantau rose, however, has missed the attention of the judges who grant awards and it has missed the popular acclaim given to other dwarfs such as *Gentle Touch*, *Sweet Magic* etc. It is a good-enough rose — the leaves are reddish-green at first and the blooms appear freely. One drawback is the absence of scent plus a lack of compactness.

150	**Blooms:** 20 petals
	Coral red
120	Medium-sized
	Slightly fragrant
	Foliage: Dark green
90	Glossy
	Health: Good disease resistance
60	**Growth:** Moderately vigorous
	Upright
30	**Awards:**

PINK PARFAIT

Pinks and creams blend in variable amounts in this delightful American-bred Floribunda. A great favourite found in many catalogues, there seems to be little agreement on the height you can expect it to grow. However, all the books agree that it is an excellent choice for the bed or border, or grown lightly pruned as a specimen bush. Flowering is extremely prolific and it is one of the best of all Floribundas for cutting. The blooms resist rain, and the stems are almost thornless.

150	**Blooms:** 22 petals
	Pink, cream at base
120	Medium-sized
	Slightly fragrant
	Foliage: Medium green
90	Semi-glossy
	Health: Good disease resistance
60	**Growth:** Vigorous
	Branching
30	**Awards:**

PURPLE TIGER

If you are not keen on novelties or if you are not a flower arranger then read no further. The foliage on this 1993 introduction is sparse so the upright stems have a rather gaunt appearance, and both mildew and black spot can be problems. It is clearly not a rose for mass bedding, but a bush or two in a mixed border will certainly arouse interest. The blooms are striped and splashed with beetroot purple and pale cream, appearing in clusters on near-thornless stems.

150	**Blooms:** 32 petals
	Purple, striped ivory
120	Medium-sized
	Slightly fragrant
	Foliage: Medium green
90	Glossy
	Health: Average disease resistance
60	**Growth:** Moderately vigorous
	Upright
30	**Awards:**

QUEEN ELIZABETH

An American-bred rose named in the 1950s after Britain's young monarch, *Queen Elizabeth* has become one of the world's great roses. It will grow almost anywhere, but your garden might not be the right place. It is not suitable for a small bed, as it grows 1.5 m or more. Plant it as a specimen shrub or as a hedge; best of all put it at the back of the border with lower-growing roses in front. Fine foliage, lovely blooms, excellent keeping qualities in water — an outstanding rose.

150	**Blooms:** 35 petals
	Light pink
120	Large
	Slightly fragrant
	Foliage: Dark green
90	Glossy
	Health: Good disease resistance
60	**Growth:** Very vigorous
	Upright
30	**Awards:**

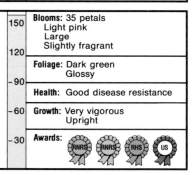

FLORIBUNDA ROSES

Blooms:	25 petals Golden yellow, edged red Medium-sized Slightly fragrant
Foliage:	Medium green Semi-glossy
Health:	Prone to disease
Growth:	Vigorous Upright
Awards:	RNRS US

150
120
90
60
30

RED GOLD

The name of this Floribunda aptly describes the young flowers — red on the petal edges and gold on the inside. The colours fade and merge with age and the mature blooms are an overall pale orange. *Red Gold* is a reliable variety which has attractive red-tinted young foliage as well as gay flowers, making it a useful rose for bedding. It is also a good exhibition variety as the flowers are exceptionally long-lasting. The blooms have good rain resistance.

Blooms:	20 petals Pale pink, white eye Large Fragrant
Foliage:	Medium green Glossy
Health:	Good disease resistance
Growth:	Moderately vigorous Bushy
Awards:	BARB BB

150
120
90
60
30

REGENSBERG
Other Name: BUFFALO BILL

A colourful dwarf Floribunda from McGredy. The bush is short and spreading — the leaves occasionally bronze-tinted. The flowers are remarkable — surprisingly large for such a small plant and opening flat to reveal the prominent white centres. *Regensberg* has a good reputation for bearing blooms all season long, but each truss bears few blooms. Like its parent *Old Master* the petals have a silvery reverse.

Blooms:	32 petals Red Medium-sized Slightly fragrant
Foliage:	Medium green Glossy
Health:	Good disease resistance
Growth:	Vigorous Bushy
Awards:	GL

150
120
90
60
30

REMEMBRANCE

Another red rose of the 1990s — this time a *Trumpeter* x *Southampton* hybrid. The colour is bright scarlet and the catalogues claim that it blooms continually until late in the season. The clusters are large and an important feature if space is limited is its compact growth habit. The cushion-like leafy mounds are about 50 cm wide but the stems are strong and the trusses are held erect. Not one for the pastel-shade lovers, but a good choice for an eye-catching display.

Blooms:	25 petals Orange scarlet Medium-sized Slightly fragrant
Foliage:	Dark green Semi-glossy
Health:	Good disease resistance
Growth:	Vigorous Upright
Awards:	RNRS H

150
120
90
60
30

SCARLET QUEEN ELIZABETH

A tall red-flowering Floribunda which is used for hedging or as a specimen shrub. It is available from many nurserymen, but its popularity is no doubt due to its famous name rather than its beauty. Unlike the blooms of its pink parent, the flowers are loose and globular, and appear later in the season than most other Floribundas. Flowering is not particularly free and the blooms are often hidden by the foliage. Not a great rose, but health and weather resistance are good.

Blooms:	35 petals Rose pink Medium-sized Slightly fragrant
Foliage:	Dark green Glossy
Health:	Good disease resistance
Growth:	Vigorous Bushy
Awards:	RNRS RHS

150
120
90
60
30

SEXY REXY

When this McGredy variety was introduced in the 1980s there were fears that the name would stop it from becoming generally popular, but by the early 1990s it was recommended by the experts as one of the best of all pink Floribundas. The reason for its success is the abundance of the floral display — the 5–7.5 cm blooms are camellia-shaped and are borne in large trusses which may almost cover the plant. Excellent for exhibition as well as for general garden display.

FLORIBUNDA ROSES

Height in cm

SHEILA'S PERFUME

There has long been a need for a strongly scented red-and-yellow rose — and it took an amateur (John Sheridan) to raise it. The flowers have a classic H.T shape and are borne singly or in small clusters. Healthy, vigorous, attractively clothed with leaves .... but *Sheila's Perfume* has never reached the top rank. Perhaps the problem is that there are not enough petals for an H.T-type flower — or perhaps contrasting blends are just too much for many people.

150	**Blooms:** 20 petals Yellow, edged red Large Very fragrant
120	
	Foliage: Dark green Semi-glossy
90	
	Health: Good disease resistance
60	**Growth:** Vigorous Bushy
30	**Awards:**

SHOCKING BLUE

Despite the name of this Kordes rose and despite the claim in some catalogues that it is the nearest yet to a blue rose this variety is lilac or mauve with a magenta background. Like all the 'blues' it can look a little washed out in the garden, but it is an excellent rose for cutting. The blooms have an attractive Hybrid Tea shape and the fragrance is quite outstanding. To enjoy this variety think of it as a pleasant pastel flower rather than a pretend blue one.

150	**Blooms:** 32 petals Lilac Large Very fragrant
120	
	Foliage: Dark green Glossy
90	
	Health: Good disease resistance
60	**Growth:** Moderately vigorous Bushy
30	**Awards:**

SOUTHAMPTON

Introduced in 1971, *Southampton* has become one of the leading Floribundas. It combines the marmalade colour beloved by flower arrangers with the robust good health desired by all gardeners. The slightly ruffled blooms are borne singly at the start of the season, but more usually they occur in trusses. Growth is taller than average, so use *Southampton* for the large bed, border or hedge. Although growth is upright the effect is not gaunt as side shoots are plentiful.

150	**Blooms:** 25 petals Apricot orange, flushed scarlet Large Slightly fragrant
120	
	Foliage: Dark green Semi-glossy
90	
	Health: Good disease resistance
60	**Growth:** Very vigorous Upright
30	**Awards:**

SUMMER DREAM

Regard this variety as a grown-up version of the popular Patio Rose *Sweet Dream*. The flowers, foliage and neat growth habit are identical in colour and shape to those of its award-winning relative but everything is larger. *Summer Dream* is a medium-sized Floribunda for areas where a Patio Rose would be too small, and on this basis it should have come close to matching the popularity of *Sweet Dream*. Somewhat surprisingly it is not a best-seller.

150	**Blooms:** 35 petals Apricot Medium-sized Fragrant
120	
	Foliage: Medium green Glossy
90	
	Health: Good disease resistance
60	**Growth:** Vigorous Bushy
30	**Awards:**

THE TIMES ROSE
Other Name: MARIANDEL

A rose needs more than a pretty face to win the President's International Trophy of the RNRS. The plant itself has to have charm — *The Times Rose* is a bushy and spreading rose with an abundance of attractive foliage which is bronze-tinted when young. The healthy bushes bear large trusses of crimson flowers which are especially attractive in sunlight. A fine bedding rose, but there is little fragrance and the petals are short.

150	**Blooms:** 30 petals Blood red Large Slightly fragrant
120	
	Foliage: Dark green Glossy
90	
	Health: Good disease resistance
60	**Growth:** Vigorous Bushy
30	**Awards:**

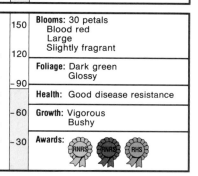

FLORIBUNDA ROSES

TOPROSE
Other Name: DANIA

Blooms:	30 petals Bright yellow Medium-sized Slightly fragrant
Foliage:	Medium green Glossy
Health:	Good disease resistance
Growth:	Vigorous Upright
Awards:	BB

There has never been a shortage of yellow Floribundas, so a new variety must have some special property if it is to become popular. This Scottish-bred rose was introduced at the start of the 1990s, and has one or two outstanding features. It is remarkably disease resistant, and the flowers remain bright and unfading even during prolonged sunny periods in summer. The leaves are large and the growth habit is upright.

TRUMPETER
Other Name: MACTRU

Blooms:	35 petals Bright vermilion Medium-sized Slightly fragrant
Foliage:	Dark green Glossy
Health:	Good disease resistance
Growth:	Vigorous Bushy
Awards:	RNRS BARB RHS JM

One of the bright red Floribundas, low-growing and compact. Introduced in 1978, *Trumpeter* has earned a high reputation as a front-of-the-border bedding rose which bears a continuous show of flowers throughout the season. Another advantage is the large number of flowers in each truss which makes it a good exhibition variety, but this is a fault in rainy weather as the heads may bow down when wet.

VALENTINE HEART

Blooms:	20 petals Pink Medium-sized Very fragrant
Foliage:	Dark green Glossy
Health:	Good disease resistance
Growth:	Vigorous Upright
Awards:	RNRS

If you believe that new varieties should look different to the old varieties then Valentine Heart could be for you. First the colour — pink with touches of cream and a pale red base to the petals. These petals have a frilled edge and the new growth is purple. The number of blooms during the season is well above average and so is the fragrance. The blooms have good resistance to both rain and disease. Impressive, but not in all recommended lists.

WISHING
Other Name: GEORGIE GIRL

Blooms:	35 petals Salmon Medium-sized Slightly fragrant
Foliage:	Medium green Semi-glossy
Health:	Good disease resistance
Growth:	Vigorous Bushy
Awards:	RNRS

A daughter of *Silver Jubilee* with the healthy, bushy and even growth you would expect. Height is a little below average and the well-shaped blooms are borne in large clusters which cover the leaves. It is the colour of the flowers which makes it stand out from the crowd. Descriptions include 'deep salmon' and 'smokey salmon' — a unique colour among Floribundas. Fragrance is unfortunately very slight.

WOBURN ABBEY

Blooms:	25 petals Coppery orange, shaded gold Medium-sized Fragrant
Foliage:	Dark green Semi-glossy
Health:	Prone to disease
Growth:	Vigorous Branching
Awards:	RNRS

A popular and long-established orange Floribunda, taller than average and pleasantly perfumed. The colour and not the beauty of the blooms is the reason for buying *Woburn Abbey*, as the flowers are rather untidy and appear crowded in the trusses. Lack of good flower shape is not the major drawback — disease is a more important problem. Mildew, black spot and rust can all be serious, and regular spraying is needed if you grow this variety.

FLORIBUNDA ROSES

PATIO ROSES

The creation of the Patio Rose group took place after the publication of the first edition of this book. Dwarf Floribundas growing 45–55 cm high have been around for a long time. *Meteor* launched in 1959 was the first one to reach the best-seller lists, and it was followed by other popular dwarfs such as *Tip Top* (1963), *Marlena* (1964), *Stargazer* (1977) and *Baby Bio* (1977). They were a little too tall and the flowers and leaves too large for the Miniature Rose group, but they were also out of place in the Floribunda group because they were much smaller than the usual modern cluster-flowering bush.

Until the 1980s they were left with the Floribundas as a collection of dwarf types which were useful where space was limited. For many years the quest had been for big and bold H.Ts and mainstream Floribundas — flowers as big as *Peace* and plants as bold as *Queen Elizabeth*. Things changed at the start of the 1980s when breeders realised that an important need for the future was a range of bushy varieties which were compact enough to be grown in small beds, the front of the border or in containers on the patio. In three successive years compact Floribundas took the prestigious Rose of the Year award — *Gentle Touch* (1986), *Sweet Magic* (1987) and *Sweet Dream* (1988). Obviously these new-style roses needed a group of their own and so the description 'Patio Rose' began to be used increasingly in catalogues and textbooks.

There is no exact or universally agreed definition for the Patio Rose. In this book they are Floribundas which do not normally exceed a height of 45–55 cm and have a bushy growth habit. In addition the size of both leaf and flower is in keeping with the size of the bush and there is an abundant display of flower clusters throughout the season. Some but not all writers leave the older dwarf Floribundas such as *Regensberg*, *Piccolo* and *Baby Bio* with the Floribundas rather than moving them to the new group.

There is much confusion in the catalogues. Some put Patio Roses and Miniatures together and a few others ignore the Patio concept and leave the dwarfs with the Floribundas. You may find a variety such as *Chatsworth* listed as a Patio Rose or Floribunda, but despite the problem the Patio Rose group is here to stay and will become increasingly popular.

KEY TO THE ROSE GUIDES

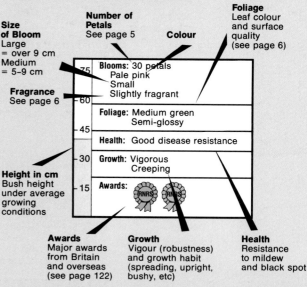

Size of Bloom
Large = over 9 cm
Medium = 5–9 cm

Fragrance
See page 6

Number of Petals
See page 5

Colour

Foliage
Leaf colour and surface quality (see page 6)

Blooms: 30 petals
Pale pink
Small
Slightly fragrant

Foliage: Medium green
Semi-glossy

Health: Good disease resistance

Growth: Vigorous
Creeping

Awards:

Height in cm
Bush height under average growing conditions

Awards
Major awards from Britain and overseas (see page 122)

Growth
Vigour (robustness) and growth habit (spreading, upright, bushy, etc)

Health
Resistance to mildew and black spot

ANNA FORD

Blooms: 20 petals
Deep orange, yellow eye
Small
Slightly fragrant

Foliage: Dark green
Glossy

Health: Good disease resistance

Growth: Moderately vigorous
Bushy

Awards:

- 75
- 60
- 45
- 30
- 15

This Floribunda x Miniature hybrid is difficult to classify — a Miniature in some catalogues and a Patio Rose in others. It forms a splendid small bush, covered with small leaves and trusses bearing many small flowers. Each yellow-eyed bloom is orange-red at first, fading slowly to orange. As an edging plant or a specimen in a pot, you can't do much better, especially if the site is in shade for part of the day — growth is dense and the leaves are dark and glossy.

BOYS' BRIGADE

Blooms: 10 petals
Red, cream eye
Small
No fragrance

Foliage: Medium green
Semi-glossy

Health: Average disease resistance

Growth: Vigorous
Bushy

Awards:

- 75
- 60
- 45
- 30
- 15

This Cocker-bred rose is neat, compact and produces trusses of flowers covering the small leaves. The number of flowers in each truss is unusually large and the bloom is unusual for a modern rose. Petals are few and there is a distinct white, cream or pale yellow eye. *Boys' Brigade* was introduced in 1984 and has never become a popular rose — it does make a change from the others but it is difficult for single and semi-double types to reach the best-seller lists.

CIDER CUP

Blooms: 20 petals
Deep apricot
Small
Slightly fragrant

Foliage: Medium green
Glossy

Health: Good disease resistance

Growth: Moderately vigorous
Bushy

Awards:

- 75
- 60
- 45
- 30
- 15

This rose first appeared in the late 1980s and is a good example of what a compact Patio Rose should feature. Both flowers and leaves are small and in keeping with the size of the bush, but the flower shape is very good and these blooms appear freely in clusters over a long period. *Cider Cup* will provide a bright splash of colour if planted over a large area and it is recommended for cutting. Choose it if you want H.T-type blooms but not if you want fragrance.

CONSERVATION

Blooms: 22 petals
Apricot pink
Medium-sized
Slightly fragrant

Foliage: Medium green
Glossy

Health: Good disease resistance

Growth: Vigorous
Bushy

Awards:

- 75
- 60
- 45
- 30
- 15

The name celebrates the 50th anniversary of The World Wildlife Fund. Like the two previous varieties this is a Patio Rose of the 1980s, bred in Scotland and a prize winner in both Glasgow and Dublin. The growth habit is spreading rather than upright so a mound of small leaves is produced. This mound is studded with large trusses of semi-double blooms which are quite large for a 45 cm Patio Rose. The colour is rather variable — the dominant colour may be either pink or orange.

FESTIVAL

Blooms: 18 petals
Scarlet, reverse silvery
Large
Slightly fragrant

Foliage: Dark green
Glossy

Health: Good disease resistance

Growth: Vigorous
Bushy

Awards:

- 75
- 60
- 45
- 30
- 15

Festival received the 1994 Rose of the Year award. To gain this prize there must be something different and eye-catching — the two novel features with this rose are the silvery shading at the back and at the base of the bright red petals, and the Holly-like shape of the dark and luxuriant leaves. This Kordes variety received a Breeders Choice award as well as the coveted ROTY prize — a Patio Rose of the mid 1990s which should become a best-seller but only time will tell.

Height in cm

GENTLE TOUCH

The outstanding feature of this Patio Rose is the beautiful form of the blooms — high-centred with a classic Hybrid Tea shape. With age, however, these flowers open flat. The trusses are strong and sturdy with a score of pink flowers — these clusters appear all season long. It was judged to be the Rose of the Year for 1986 and it is rated very highly in the Best Patio Rose poll. *Gentle Touch* can be used anywhere in the garden where you need a compact variety.

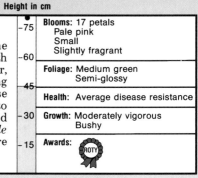

Blooms: 17 petals
Pale pink
Small
Slightly fragrant

Foliage: Medium green
Semi-glossy

Health: Average disease resistance

Growth: Moderately vigorous
Bushy

Awards:

GINGERNUT

A colourful variety which appeared in 1989 and is recommended for bedding or growing in a container. The blooms are quite widely spaced in each cluster and the colour is eye-catching and unusual — a mixture of glowing orange, pink and red. The growth habit is compact and cushion-like and in the Royal National Rose Society poll it keeps its place among the top 12 Patio Roses. For some gardeners it has a drawback — the shapely buds soon open into flat blooms.

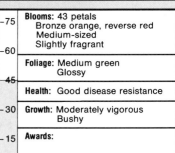

Blooms: 43 petals
Bronze orange, reverse red
Medium-sized
Slightly fragrant

Foliage: Medium green
Glossy

Health: Good disease resistance

Growth: Moderately vigorous
Bushy

Awards:

HAKUUN

Hakuun was introduced from Denmark in 1962 and so was one of the early Patio Roses. You may have to search through a few catalogues to find a supplier and it does have its limitations — there are not many petals and there is no fragrance. It is listed here because it is the only 'oldie' (pre 1970) to feature in the Best Patio Rose poll, and the mass of pale blooms (its name means 'White Cloud') makes it one of the best of all edgings for brightly-coloured beds.

Blooms: 15 petals
Creamy white
Small
No fragrance

Foliage: Medium green
Glossy

Health: Average disease resistance

Growth: Vigorous
Bushy

Awards:

HONEYBUNCH

Do think about buying this one if you are looking for a sweet-smelling bright Patio Rose for growing in a container. The perfume is strong enough for a 'fragrant' label and the petals are a warm honey colour. Each bloom is filled with petals and the trusses are freely borne throughout the season. It has a good reputation as a long-lasting cut flower and is quite widely available in the popular catalogues. Rather surprisingly it does not figure in the popularity polls.

Blooms: 45 petals
Yellow, blended salmon
Small
Fragrant

Foliage: Medium green
Semi-glossy

Health: Good disease resistance

Growth: Moderately vigorous
Bushy

Awards:

LITTLE BO-PEEP

In 1991 this cushion-like rose was given the highest award from the Royal National Rose Society. Its value in the garden cannot be questioned but its classification can — it is small enough to be put with the Miniatures and it is wide-spreading enough to be classed as a Ground Cover Rose ..... but you will find it with the Patio Roses. It looks like a tiny Shrub — lots of small leaves and dense clusters of open near-white flowers. Grow it in pots or use it as an edging.

Blooms: 30 petals
Pale pink
Small
Slightly fragrant

Foliage: Medium green
Semi-glossy

Health: Good disease resistance

Growth: Vigorous
Creeping

Awards:

Blooms: 20 petals Apricot Small Slightly fragrant	– 75 – 60
Foliage: Dark green Semi-glossy	–45
Health: Average disease resistance	
Growth: Moderately vigorous Bushy	– 30
Awards:	– 15

PEEK A BOO
Other Name: BRASS RING

Peek a Boo appeared in 1980 and was one of the earliest of the modern Patio Roses. Despite having been around for a long time it still remains one of the best for rockery and tub use and is listed in many catalogues. The bush is neat and rounded, and the clusters bear many flowers — you may find this variety in the Miniature section of the catalogues. As the flowers mature the petals change from coppery apricot to pink.

Blooms: 42 petals Yellow Small Slightly fragrant	– 75 – 60
Foliage: Dark green Glossy	–45
Health: Good disease resistance	
Growth: Vigorous Bushy	– 30
Awards:	– 15

PERESTROIKA
Other Name: SONNENKIND

This 1990 variety from Kordes is worth looking for. The blooms are bright golden yellow and have a distinctly spiky appearance as the edges of the petals are reflexed. The clusters are large and the foliage is dense. There are no obvious drawbacks — the growth habit is neat, the foliage is attractive and the bush is free-flowering, but it is not placed highly in the Best Patio Rose poll conducted by the RNRS.

Blooms: 32 petals Pale pink Medium-sized Slightly fragrant	– 75 – 60
Foliage: Medium green Glossy	–45
Health: Good disease resistance	
Growth: Vigorous Bushy	– 30
Awards:	– 15

PRETTY POLLY
Other Name: PINK SYMPHONY

Pretty Polly is a bushy Patio Rose with pink flowers which open flat when mature and emit little fragrance. From this description it may seem strange that this Meilland variety should have received the Royal National Rose Society's top award in 1989. It is, however, more than just another pink dwarf. The young blooms are extremely attractive and the dense bush is remarkably free-flowering. Highly recommended.

Blooms: 14 petals Pink Medium-sized Slightly fragrant	– 75 – 60
Foliage: Dark green Glossy	–45
Health: Good disease resistance	
Growth: Vigorous Spreading	– 30
Awards:	– 15

QUEEN MOTHER

Named to celebrate the 90th birthday of the Queen Mother, this Kordes rose looks more like a small Shrub Rose than a Patio Rose. The pure pink semi-double blooms have an open old-fashioned look and the small leaves are dark and shiny. It is thoroughly reliable — it has an excellent reputation for black spot and mildew resistance, and there is little delay between one flush of flowers and the next. A good choice for a gap in the border or for growing in a pot.

Blooms: 15 petals Yellow Small Slightly fragrant	– 75 – 60
Foliage: Dark green Glossy	–45
Health: Good disease resistance	
Growth: Vigorous Bushy	– 30
Awards:	– 15

RAY OF SUNSHINE

Ray of Sunshine is a typical Patio Rose — the growth habit is bushy and the stems are covered with small shiny leaves. The popular yellow Floribunda *Korresia* is one of its parents, so it is not surprising that its blooms are bright yellow and the colour does not fade as the flower matures. The flower shape is good but unlike *Korresia* there are not many petals. Though the blooms are small they are borne sufficiently freely to give a colourful display.

Height in cm

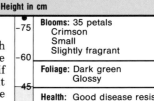

RED RASCAL

This American variety has won no major British awards and does not often appear on the recommended lists, but it is worth considering if you like red dwarfs. The colour is bright and it does not fade as the bloom ages nor are the flowers spoilt by rain. The fully double flowers are cupped and the texture is silky. The bushes are noted for their neat and even growth habit. Flowering continues until late autumn — colourful but almost odourless.

Blooms:	35 petals Crimson Small Slightly fragrant
Foliage:	Dark green Glossy
Health:	Good disease resistance
Growth:	Moderately vigorous Bushy
Awards:	

-75, -60, 45, -30, -15

ROSY FUTURE

A taller than average Patio Rose which was launched by Harkness in 1991. The deep pink colour is not particularly unusual for this group, but the fragrance is — the sweet aroma makes it stand out from nearly all other Patio varieties. Growth is upright and there is a dense cover of shiny leaves. The blooms have an attractive shape and are borne in large clusters — grow it as a low hedge or plant it in a bed or pot where its fragrance can be enjoyed.

Blooms:	30 petals Rose red Small Fragrant
Foliage:	Dark green Glossy
Health:	Good disease resistance
Growth:	Vigorous Upright
Awards:	

-75, -60, -45, -30, -15

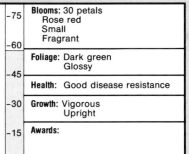

SHINE ON

This variety was bred by Dickson and introduced in 1994 — according to the breeder it 'stands out in any crowd'. A Breeders Choice winner — it obviously caught the eye of the professional growers. The bush is neat and cushiony and the continuity of flowering is excellent. The blooms have high centres and hold their shape well but as with so many other Patio Roses the aroma is only slight. A daughter of the popular variety *Sweet Magic* which it rivals for brightness.

Blooms:	30 petals Orange, blended pink Small Slightly fragrant
Foliage:	Medium green Glossy
Health:	Good disease resistance
Growth:	Vigorous Bushy
Awards:	BARB

-75, -60, 45, -30, -15

STRAWBERRY FAYRE

An eye-catching variety which came from America at the start of the 1990s. It is either white heavily edged with red, or red striped and flecked with white and with silvery white on the reverse of the petals. Either way, each bloom is a red and white cocktail and the neat bushes bear heavy clusters of blooms from June until the first frosts. There is some fragrance but it is not strong. Grow it in a pot or as a specimen plant in a mixed border.

Blooms:	22 petals Red, striped white Medium-sized Slightly fragrant
Foliage:	Dark green Glossy
Health:	Good disease resistance
Growth:	Vigorous Bushy
Awards:	

-75, -60, -45, -30, -15

SUNSEEKER
Other Name: DUCHESS OF YORK

An easy variety to identify — the open semi-double blooms have petals which are an attractive mandarin red with a sulphur yellow base. *Sunseeker* is a larger than average Patio Rose and it is not one for hiding away. It is very bright and nearly always in flower, so put it in a large container or in a bed near the house — it can also be grown as a low hedge or in the front of a shrub border.

Blooms:	14 petals Orange red, yellow eye Medium-sized Slightly fragrant
Foliage:	Medium green Semi-glossy
Health:	Good disease resistance
Growth:	Vigorous Bushy
Awards:	RNRS

-75, -60, -45, -30, -15

Blooms: 35 petals 　　Apricot 　　Medium-sized 　　Fragrant	−75 −60 −45
Foliage: Medium green 　　Glossy	
Health: Good disease resistance	
Growth: Moderately vigorous 　　Bushy	−30
Awards: ROTY	−15

SWEET DREAM

Quite simply, the best-selling and most popular Patio Rose. It won the Rose of the Year award in 1988 and now tops the Royal National Rose Society's popularity poll. This Fryer-bred rose has a number of special qualities. The unusual peachy colour does not fade with age and the well-formed blooms stand up well to rain. Growth is neat and cushion-like — foliage is dense and attractive. It is recommended for edging, low hedging, patio planting and containers.

Blooms: 17 petals 　　Orange, blended gold 　　Small 　　Fragrant	−75 −60 45
Foliage: Medium green 　　Glossy	
Health: Good disease resistance	
Growth: Vigorous 　　Bushy	−30
Awards: RNRS ROTY	−15

SWEET MAGIC

A star in its first year when it came to the market with the Rose of the Year award. The blooms are borne in large clusters, deep orange fading to golden yellow which gives each flower a glowing effect. A pink flush appears on old petals. An excellent choice for tub planting or edging — leaves, stems and flower size are all in scale and there is an autumn hip display. Fragrance is quite pronounced — an unusual feature for a Patio Rose.

Blooms: 10 petals 　　White 　　Small 　　Slightly fragrant	−75 −60 −45
Foliage: Light green 　　Glossy	
Health: Good disease resistance	
Growth: Moderately vigorous 　　Spreading	−30
Awards:	−15

TEAR DROP

Tear Drop illustrates the difficulty of rose classification. The leaves are small enough and it is often low enough to be thought of as a Miniature Rose, and it is almost sufficiently wide-spreading to make it a Ground Cover one. In appearance it resembles a mini-Shrub — masses of open semi-double blooms with attractive yellow stamens. It has never become really popular as there is a shortage of petals, but it is a good choice for edging a bed or border.

Blooms: 20 petals 　　Salmon pink 　　Medium-sized 　　Slightly fragrant	−75 −60
Foliage: Medium green 　　Matt	
Health: Prone to disease	45
Growth: Vigorous 　　Bushy	−30
Awards:	−15

TIP TOP

Tip Top was introduced in 1963 — a small Floribunda for edging, small beds and container growing. It was for many years the first choice when a pink dwarf was required, but not any more. It blooms over a long season, and the continuity is excellent. The large trusses seem to appear in profusion whatever the weather and the fragrance, although not strong, is sweet. But disease is now a problem — susceptibility to mildew and black spot is quite high.

Blooms: 35 petals 　　Bright vermilion 　　Small 　　Slightly fragrant	−75 −60
Foliage: Medium green 　　Glossy	45
Health: Good disease resistance	
Growth: Vigorous 　　Bushy	−30
Awards: RNRS ROTY H	−15

TOP MARKS

An English-bred rose which is one of the stars among the newer Patio Roses. The stems and shiny leaves form a 45 cm x 45 cm cushion, and the abundance of small, rosette-type blooms is astonishing. So is the colour — you will see it described in the catalogues as 'brilliant' and 'sparkling'. These flowers are long-lasting and do not fade and the healthy foliage is plentiful, which helped this variety to be voted Rose of the Year for 1992 with the highest-ever score.

PATIO ROSES

MINIATURE ROSES

Miniature Roses are becoming more popular in Britain, but this slowly-awakening interest for these scaled-down versions of 'normal' roses does not begin to match the enthusiasm in the U.S. The rose has for many years been Britain's favourite flower, and it is therefore surprising that we should have lagged behind. Some people believe that the price is to blame — a tiny bush does not seem good value when it costs almost as much as a Floribunda. Others feel that we don't need Miniatures in the same way — we set out to fill our gardens whereas the Americans have apartments to decorate.

It can't be that simple. A major factor may be the way we raise our plants — in the U.S they are propagated from cuttings and so grow on their own roots. Such plants are rather slow-growing and can be somewhat tender, but they do remain truly miniature all their lives. In Britain we generally raise our Miniatures as grafted plants on rootstocks — these plants are hardier, more drought-resistant and quicker-growing. Unfortunately, they also tend to be too vigorous and the fairy-like form may be lost.

Another disappointment has been their failure as reliable house plants. So many people have bought them, put them on the sideboard and expected them to bloom quite merrily from June to November like their outdoor counterparts. Miniature Roses may not be as easy to grow indoors as some people expect, but they are not as difficult as some experts claim — just follow the rules on page 133.

Miniature Roses most certainly do have a place in our gardening scene. Buy plants in pots — they do not like root disturbance. The best time for planting outdoors is spring or early summer and they will reward you each year by coming into leaf in March, opening their first flowers in midsummer and continuing to bloom until the first frosts arrive.

Even Miniatures have their dwarfs and giants. 'Small' varieties grow up to 22.5 cm high under average conditions — 'tall' Miniatures reach 45 cm. 'Small' blooms are less than 2.5 cm across — 'large' ones are about 5 cm.

There is an impressive list of uses. Edging beds and planting in rockeries can both be recommended, but perhaps the most successful use is planting in a raised bed devoted entirely to Miniatures.

The plants you buy will probably be grafted on to a rootstock — you will be able to see the join at the base. If you want to grow Miniatures as pot plants, take cuttings as described on page 130 — the success rate is high and the resulting plants will remain compact and dwarf.

Maintenance is straightforward, but not quite as easy as some books suggest. Pruning (page 109) is no problem, but you must keep a careful watch for pests and diseases. The major nuisances are mildew, black spot, die-back and greenfly. Don't forget to water in dry weather — they don't have the root system of their big sisters. Feeding is necessary — use a liquid fertilizer on a little-and-often basis for Miniatures in pots.

The history of Miniatures is as fascinating as the plants themselves. They were popular pot plants in Victorian times — *Pompon de Paris* was a well-known variety. Then they went out of fashion and disappeared at the end of the 19th century, apparently lost for ever. In 1918 Major Roulet saw a tiny rose growing in a pot in Switzerland. This survivor became *R. roulettii* and the modern Miniature story began — hybridists have given us the wide choice available today.

ANGELA RIPPON
Other Name: *OCARU*
Bred in Holland and introduced in 1978, this rose is popular for both bedding and showing. Growth is compact and bushy, reaching about 40 cm high. The double blooms are pale carmine pink, freely borne amongst the healthy foliage. The blooms are quite fragrant.

APRICOT SUNBLAZE
Other Name: *SAVAMARK*
The blooms are small but they are crowded with petals and the orange red colour was a new one for Miniatures. The cup-shaped blooms are borne singly or in clusters and there is some fragrance. Growth is neat and bushy — stems are thin and prickly, and the foliage is matt.

BABY MASQUERADE
One of the top Miniatures in many ways — in popularity, ease of cultivation, number of blooms and length of flowering season. It is rather tall and bushy, reaching 40 cm or more. The double and slightly fragrant blooms change from yellow to pink and finally to rosy red. Dead-head regularly for repeat flowering.

BUSH BABY
The blooms on this compact Miniature are double with pale salmon petals. These flowers are borne reasonably freely, but they are not large and the fragrance is very slight. The stems grow about 25 cm high and the matt green leaves have better than average disease resistance.

COLIBRI 79
Other Name: *MEIDANOVER*
A free-flowering variety, very bushy and about 25 cm tall. The double blooms are brightly coloured — golden apricot with pinkish tones. There is some confusion over names — *Colibri* (large, straw-coloured blooms) came before *Colibri 79* (also known as *Colibri 80*).

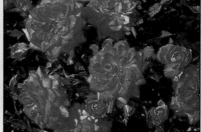

DARLING FLAME
Other Name: *MINUETTO*
Introduced in 1971, this variety has become one of the most popular Miniature Roses in Europe. It has all the requirements for success — there are beautiful double flowers, rich orange vermilion with a golden reverse, borne in profusion on a bushy plant which reaches 40 cm.

EASTER MORNING
Large ivory white flowers set amongst small shiny leaves which are dark green. The blooms have 60 petals or more, yet resistance to rain as well as to disease is excellent. This American variety is not a profuse bloomer, but it is highly recommended for edging the front of the border.

FIESTA
Miniature or Patio Rose — it depends which catalogue you read. Here it is regarded as a tall-growing Miniature, reaching 45 cm. Introduced in 1995, it received a Breeders Choice award and is set to become a star. The blooms are cherry red with a white eye — free-flowering plus excellent disease resistance.

FIRE PRINCESS
A splendid choice for edging, exhibiting or growing as a pot plant. The bushes are tall and upright with glossy, dark green foliage, but it is the flower colour which makes this an outstanding Miniature. Brilliant orange-red with a touch of gold, the hues strengthening rather than fading with age. Fragrance is slight.

MINIATURE ROSES

LITTLE BUCKAROO
A rather tall-growing variety, well-suited to the front of the border. It has a spreading growth habit, with shiny bronze-tinted leaves. The blooms are red with a white centre, small in size and pleasantly scented. There are about 25 petals. One of the early Miniatures (1956), but disease resistance is still good.

LITTLE FLIRT
A bi-coloured Miniature Rose, with small *Piccadilly*-like blooms. The petals are orange-red with a yellow reverse, and 40–50 are packed into each small fragrant bloom. The bush bears abundant foliage, light green and glossy, and the height is about 40 cm. A popular rose for more than 35 years.

MAGIC CARROUSEL
A striking and unusual Miniature, excellent for indoor decoration and the show-bench. The shapely flowers above the glossy foliage have white petals, and each petal has a clearly defined red edge. The fragrance is slight and the growth is above average, reaching about 40 cm. *Magic Carrousel* is a reliable variety.

MR BLUEBIRD
You will find *Mr Bluebird* in many catalogues, and it has its friends. Occasionally you can see why — dark green foliage studded with pale lavender flowers. In most cases it is frankly disappointing — spindly growth, poor colouring and shyness in flowering. Choose *Lavender Lace* or *Lavender Jewel* instead.

NEW PENNY
Aptly named, with shining leaves and coppery pink flowers. A most attractive Miniature — ideal for growing as a pot plant. The red buds are freely produced, opening into semi-double blooms which fade with age. There is no fragrance. The plant is well-branched and vigorous, but rarely exceeds 25 cm.

ORANGE SUNBLAZE
Other Name: SUNBLAZE
A French Miniature which appeared in 1981 and soon became a popular variety in the catalogues. The flowers are full with bright orange-red petals. The blooms last longer in water than most Miniatures. Sports in various colours (e.g *Yellow Sunblaze*) are available.

PANDORA
This Miniature was introduced in 1989 and received a Trial Ground Certificate from the RNRS. The clusters of creamy flowers are borne above the dark and shiny leaves — each small flower is fully double but there is little fragrance. The bushy growth reaches about 30 cm. A good rose for cutting.

PINK SUNBLAZE
This sport of Orange Sunblaze is a little more vigorous than its parent, reaching a height of about 45 cm. Another difference is the foliage — matt and bronze-tinted rather than glossy and light green. The salmon pink blooms are double with little scent. It is a free-flowering variety but disease resistance is only average.

POUR TOI
Other Name: PARA TI
A favourite Miniature, highly rated for the beauty of its flowers and the attractive nature of the bush. The foliage is glossy and the growth habit short (17-22 cm) and very bushy. The flowers appear profusely, white with a creamy yellow tinge at the base of the petals. Fragrance is slight.

MINIATURE ROSES

RED ACE
Other Name: AMANDA

There are, of course, a number of red Miniatures — both old and new. This De Ruiter variety of the 1980s broke new ground — the semi-double blooms are darker than other Miniatures and the surface is velvety. Good for cutting and showing — bush height is about 25 cm.

RED SUNBLAZE

There are a number of 'Sunblaze' Miniatures — Orange, Pink, Red, Snow, Yellow etc. *Red Sunblaze* is different — it was raised by Moore in the U.S and not by Meilland in France like the others. It is a compact and neat plant growing about 30 cm high with bright red flowers which repeat regularly throughout the season.

RISE 'N' SHINE
Other Name: GOLDEN SUNBLAZE

This variety is considered by many to be the best yellow Miniature. The long-pointed buds are attractive and appear abundantly under good growing conditions. The large blooms have a classic H.T form and the deep yellow colour does not fade with age.

ROSINA
Other Name: JOSEPHINE WHEATCROFT

A lovely bright yellow Miniature, with blooms which are perfectly shaped when young. The fragrance is slight and there are not many petals, but this variety has been a favourite for many years. The trusses appear freely on the upright stems.

SCARLET GEM

Scarlet Gem has the reputation for being one of the brightest of all red Miniatures. It is a popular pot plant, producing a mass of very full flowers throughout the season. The blooms keep their colour in bright sunlight and the attractive foliage is dark and glossy. Proneness to mildew is its major fault.

STACEY SUE

A neat, bushy plant from the U.S which grows about 40 cm high and with *Angela Rippon* is now regarded as the best of the pink Miniatures. The blooms are small and double — the clusters are attractive but there is little fragrance. It has a spreading growth habit and the foliage is dark green, glossy and plentiful.

STARINA

Starina remains one of the queens of the Miniature world — well-formed bright vermilion flowers cover the shiny foliage on the neat and upright stems from early summer until November. It is renowned for its vigour, and can be grown as a pot plant, dwarf bush for bedding or as a miniature standard.

STARS 'N' STRIPES

You cannot fail to recognise this one — each flower is striped with white and strawberry red. The blooms do not have an abundance of petals but they are very large. There is no scent. Rather too garish for some people, but a good bedding variety if you like your plants to be striking. Lax, bushy growth reaching about 40 cm.

YELLOW DOLL

A fine creamy yellow variety, popular on the show-bench and as a pot plant. The attractive buds are borne singly or in clusters, opening into fragrant blooms crowded with 50 or more narrow petals. The dwarf bush has a spreading growth habit and reaches about 25 cm. Keep watch for black spot.

MINIATURE ROSES

GROUND COVER ROSES

It was not until the 1980s that prostrate and spreading roses were numerous enough and important enough to warrant being moved out of the Shrub section and into a group of their own. The flood of new varieties in recent years is well illustrated by the fact that over 70 per cent of the Ground Cover Roses described on the next five pages were not in the previous edition of this book.

It did not all begin in 1980 — roses were used for ground cover long before then. *R. wichuriana* has a spread up to 6 m and has been used as a trailing plant since the last century — its much more compact offspring *Max Graf* was introduced in 1919 and *Nozomi* with tiny leaves and pink flowers on trailing stems has enjoyed some popularity as a low-growing ground-covering bush since its introduction in 1968.

The problem with these early Ground Cover Roses was their non repeat-flowering habit and in the 1970s breeders set about looking for ground-covering varieties which could become best-sellers — roses which would cover an area of soil around the stems and with a floral display which would last from early summer to autumn. By the end of the decade a new generation of Ground Cover Roses began to appear. From Meilland in France came *Swany* and *Fiona* — from Holland there were *Red Blanket* and *Rosy Cushion*.

This trickle of new varieties became a flood in the 1980s with introductions from Meilland, Harkness, Dickson, Mattock, Ilsink, McGredy etc, but the market was dominated by two major series. Kordes introduced the 'Game Bird' series — *Grouse*, *Partridge* and so on. The 'County' series (*Suffolk*, *Surrey* etc) from Kordes and Poulsen was launched by Mattock in Britain.

There are many ways of using Ground Cover Roses as described on page 99 but you must check the expected height and spread before buying. A plant may grow to anything from 20 cm to 2 m high, and there are four different size/shape patterns. **Small Creeping** ones grow 30–45 cm high with a spread of less than 150 cm and **Large Creeping** varieties grow higher than 45 cm with a spread in excess of 150 cm. These creeping varieties grow more or less horizontally, sometimes rooting as they go. The arching varieties have a different growth habit — they have spreading branches which arch downwards to cover the ground. **Small Arching** ones grow up to 95 cm high with a spread of less than 150 cm. **Large Arching** varieties grow to at least 100 cm with a spread of 150 cm or more.

The Ground Cover Roses have come of age. *Kent* received the premier award of the Royal National Rose Society in 1990 and the same award went to *Blenheim* in 1992. In the mid 1990s *Flower Carpet* in its pink container was the most heavily promoted rose of the year. Ground Cover Roses are a new group, but they have risen from near obscurity to centre stage in a remarkably short time.

KEY TO THE ROSE GUIDES

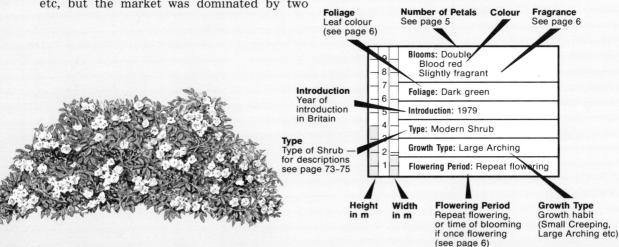

Foliage Leaf colour (see page 6)	Number of Petals See page 5	Colour	Fragrance See page 6

Blooms: Double
Blood red
Slightly fragrant

Foliage: Dark green

Introduction
Year of introduction in Britain

Introduction: 1979

Type
Type of Shrub — for descriptions see page 73–75

Type: Modern Shrub

Growth Type: Large Arching

Flowering Period: Repeat flowering

Height in m	Width in m	Flowering Period Repeat flowering, or time of blooming if once flowering (see page 6)	Growth Type Growth habit (Small Creeping, Large Arching etc)

Height
in m   Width
in m   page 55

Blooms: Semi-double Blush pink Slightly fragrant		
Foliage: Medium green		
Introduction: 1992		
Type: Modern Shrub		
Growth Type: Small Creeping		
Flowering Period: Repeat flowering		

AVON

A good choice where a small area is to be covered and you want the bush to be low-growing. This dwarf is only 30 cm high and the prostrate stems are covered with tiny leaves and 2.5 cm wide pearly white blooms. There is an abundant floral display throughout the season and the disease resistance is very good. *Avon* was a Breeders Choice in 1993 and is recommended for edging and growing in pots as well as for ground cover.

Blooms: Double White Slightly fragrant		
Foliage: Medium green		
Introduction: 1993		
Type: Modern Shrub		
Growth Type: Small Arching		
Flowering Period: Repeat flowering		

BLENHEIM

One of the 'Heritage' series raised by Tantau and launched in the 1990s. This variety was awarded the President's International Trophy by the RNRS in 1992. It is noted for the abundance of flowers borne throughout the summer. Growth is strong and the leaves have excellent resistance to both black spot and mildew. This easy-to-care-for rose will cover an area of 1–2 sq.m with roses which have a distinctly old-fashioned look.

Blooms: Semi-double Pink Slightly fragrant		
Foliage: Dark green		
Introduction: 1984		
Type: Modern Shrub		
Growth Type: Large Arching		
Flowering Period: Repeat flowering		

BONICA
Other Name: BONICA 82

There is some confusion here. The original *Bonica* was a scarlet-flowered bush — the 'Bonica' of the catalogues is really *Bonica 82*. This variety bred by Meilland is a Ground Cover Rose of the 1980s. It has been awarded top honours in the U.S and is an excellent choice where a ground-covering domed bush is required.

Blooms: Double Yellow Slightly fragrant		
Foliage: Medium green		
Introduction: 1994		
Type: Rugosa		
Growth Type: Small Arching		
Flowering Period: Repeat flowering		

BROADLANDS

British rose growers and breeders awarded this variety a Breeders Choice award in 1996. It had the necessary health and quality required for this award and there was also novelty. It is one of the few truly bright yellow Ground Cover Roses, producing its open blooms all summer long. It is another of the 'Heritage' series bred by Tantau in Germany — a Rugosa-type variety which is destined to join the best-seller lists.

Blooms: Semi-double Crimson Slightly fragrant		
Foliage: Medium green		
Introduction: 1992		
Type: Modern Shrub		
Growth Type: Large Arching		
Flowering Period: Repeat flowering		

CHILTERNS
Other Name: FIERY SUNSATION

The start of a new Ground Cover Rose series — the 'Hills of Britain' bred by Kordes. *Chilterns* is a large variety, spreading widely to produce a mounded bush densely covered with small glossy leaves. The flower clusters bear a mass of small blooms, each one with a prominent boss of yellow stamens. A good choice if you have a large bare patch of ground to cover.

Blooms: Single Deep pink, white eye Slightly fragrant		
Foliage: Medium green		
Introduction: 1989		
Type: Modern Shrub		
Growth Type: Small Creeping		
Flowering Period: Repeat flowering		

ESSEX
Other Name: PINK COVER

This prostrate Ground Cover Rose produces a dense mat of small and glossy leaves and an abundant display of small starry flowers. It will flourish in both sun and partial shade and can be grown in a large container. An offspring of *The Fairy* — this Poulsen rose has won both RNRS and Irish awards. A good choice if you like single flowers.

GROUND COVER ROSES

	Height in m	Width in m

FERDY
Other Name: FERDI

The small leaves of this Japanese-bred variety are borne in profusion and are deeply cut. The flowers are full of petals — when fully open each pink bloom reveals a creamy centre. This Ground Cover Rose has been around longer than most but it is still recommended for covering about a square metre with a dense display of arching branches and pink flowers.

Blooms: Double
Pink
No fragrance
Foliage: Light green
Introduction: 1984
Type: Modern Shrub
Growth Type: Small Arching
Flowering Period: Repeat flowering

FIONA

One of the first and still one of the largest of the Ground Cover Roses. It is described as a bush in some of the catalogues. The flowers are small and only moderately full, but the rich red colour makes up for the lack of substance. These blooms appear freely throughout the summer months, small clusters appearing amongst the small and semi-glossy leaves. Grow it in the border or plant it as a hedge.

Blooms: Double
Blood red
Slightly fragrant
Foliage: Dark green
Introduction: 1979
Type: Modern Shrub
Growth Type: Large Arching
Flowering Period: Repeat flowering

FLOWER CARPET

Few roses in recent years have received such publicity and praise. In the mid 1990s it was seen in every garden centre in its familiar bright pink pot, and in the polls of the Royal National Rose Society it features in both the 'Best New Rose' and 'Healthiest Rose' lists. The small flowers are indeed abundant and resistance to disease is truly outstanding, but some experts feel it has been somewhat overrated.

Blooms: Double
Pink
Slightly fragrant
Foliage: Light green
Introduction: 1991
Type: Modern Shrub
Growth Type: Small Creeping
Flowering Period: Repeat flowering

GROUSE
Other Name: IMMENSEE

One of the 'Game Bird' Ground Cover Roses bred by Kordes. It has two important features — the small blooms in July and August are fragrant and the prostrate branches spread over a large area. Weeds are suppressed by the abundant glossy foliage — use it to cover large banks or to drape over walls. The major drawback is the once-flowering habit.

Blooms: Single
Pale pink
Fragrant
Foliage: Medium green
Introduction: 1984
Type: Modern Shrub
Growth Type: Large Creeping
Flowering Period: Late summer

GWENT

This Gold Medal winner is well worth considering if you have a small area (about 1 sq.m) to cover or a large hanging basket to fill. The flowers are lemon yellow — an unusual colour for a Ground Cover Rose. These blooms are fragrant — another unusual feature for this group. Disease resistance is good and growth is vigorous with flowers appearing in large trusses all season long.

Blooms: Double
Yellow
Fragrant
Foliage: Dark green
Introduction: 1992
Type: Modern Shrub
Growth Type: Small Creeping
Flowering Period: Repeat flowering

HERTFORDSHIRE

Hertfordshire has a neat and compact growth habit, making it a good choice for covering patches of ground between taller shrubs and for growing in containers. Each flower has a boss of bright yellow stamens and these are borne just above the small glossy leaves. This combination of packed trusses of small flowers and abundant foliage produces an effective weed-suppressing mat after a couple of years.

Blooms: Single
Carmine pink
Slightly fragrant
Foliage: Medium green
Introduction: 1991
Type: Modern Shrub
Growth Type: Small Creeping
Flowering Period: Repeat flowering

GROUND COVER ROSES

Blooms: Semi-double, White, Slightly fragrant **Foliage:** Dark green **Introduction:** 1988 **Type:** Modern Shrub **Growth Type:** Small Arching **Flowering Period:** Repeat flowering	## KENT *Other Name:* WHITE COVER This Ground Cover Rose had to be something rather special to win the President's International Trophy in 1990. The neat bush is rounded rather than creeping and the large trusses of white flowers stand up to wet weather. Small hips are produced in autumn. The dense foliage and masses of bloom make this a good plant for the patio.

Blooms: Semi-double, Lavender, Fragrant **Foliage:** Dark green **Introduction:** 1996 **Type:** Modern Shrub **Growth Type:** Small Arching **Flowering Period:** Repeat flowering	## MAGIC CARPET It was in 1996 that a Ground Cover Rose at last won the Rose of the Year award. This *Grouse* x *Jacare* hybrid was bred by Jackson & Perkins in the U.S and introduced in Britain by Dickson. *Magic Carpet* is certainly different — the small blooms are lavender and there is a spicy fragrance. The flowers are borne all along the arching branches — use it in tubs and baskets as well as for ground cover.

Blooms: Single, Pink, white centre, Fragrant **Foliage:** Dark green **Introduction:** 1919 **Type:** Rugosa **Growth Type:** Large Creeping **Flowering Period:** Midsummer	## MAX GRAF The first and still a very useful Ground Cover Rose. The prostrate stems spread over the soil surface, rooting as they go, and quickly produce a dense green mat. The single pink flowers appear freely over a long period in June and July, but there is no repeat flowering. The flowers, borne in clusters, have an apple-like fragrance. The stems are thorny, which makes weeding a problem. *Max Graf* is recommended for growing over a wall.

Blooms: Double, Yellow, Fragrant **Foliage:** Dark green **Introduction:** 1990 **Type:** Modern Shrub **Growth Type:** Small Creeping **Flowering Period:** Repeat flowering	## NORFOLK This Poulsen-bred variety has blooms which are both yellow and fragrant — two features not often found in Ground Cover Roses. Growth is compact, the branches producing a dense mass of foliage. A good choice if you want bright flowers with scent and many petals for soil which is less than perfect. Unfortunately the bloom appears in two distinct flushes rather than continuously.

Blooms: Single, Pearly pink, No fragrance **Foliage:** Dark green **Introduction:** 1968 **Type:** Modern Shrub **Growth Type:** Small Creeping **Flowering Period:** Midsummer	## NOZOMI Technically it is a Climbing Miniature, but you will find *Nozomi* amongst the Ground Cover Roses in the catalogues. This Japanese variety was the first popular one in this group. Its trailing stems bear small glossy leaves, and in summer there are clusters of tiny pearly flowers. Not as wide-spreading as *Max Graf* or *Grouse*, but very useful for edging. Stems may be pegged down to improve the cover.

Blooms: Single, White, Fragrant **Foliage:** Medium green **Introduction:** 1984 **Type:** Modern Shrub **Growth Type:** Large Creeping **Flowering Period:** Late summer	## PARTRIDGE *Other Name:* WEISSE IMMENSEE This 'Game Bird' Ground Cover Rose from Kordes is closely related to *Grouse* — it has similar parents (*The Fairy* x seedling of *R. wichuriana*), a similar growth habit and the same-shaped single blooms which appear in July and August. There is the same fragrance but the colour is different — the blooms of Partridge are white and not pale pink.

GROUND COVER ROSES

Height in m Width in m

PHEASANT
Other Name: PALISSADE ROSE

This 'Game Bird' variety from Kordes appeared a couple of years after *Grouse* and *Partridge*. Like the other two *Pheasant* is low-growing but spreads widely, covering up to 7 sq.m, but differs by having a repeat-flowering habit rather than a single flush of flowers in late summer. This is one to think about if you have a large area to cover.

Blooms:	Double Deep pink Fragrant
Foliage:	Medium green
Introduction:	1986
Type:	Modern Shrub
Growth Type:	Large Creeping
Flowering Period:	Repeat flowering

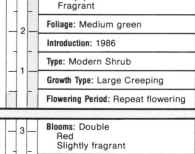

RED BELLS

The varieties in the 'Bells' series have the same parents (*Temple Bells* and *Mini-Poul*) and the same basic features. Small semi-glossy leaves cover the arching stems and in July and August there is a display of clusters of small flat flowers. They will grow in partial shade and do not demand good soil. Flower colour as denoted by the name (*Red Bells*, *White Bells* or *Pink Bells*) is the only important difference between them.

Blooms:	Double Red Slightly fragrant
Foliage:	Medium green
Introduction:	1983
Type:	Modern Shrub
Growth Type:	Small Arching
Flowering Period:	Late summer

RED BLANKET

A good name for a Ground Cover Rose, and it does live up to its name. The medium-sized flowers are produced in clusters — dull pale red against glossy dark leaves. Growth is vigorous and *Red Blanket* appears in many catalogues. Like *Rosy Cushion* it is descended from *Yesterday*, but the blooms are larger than those of its parent. It once had a good health record, but it is now susceptible to black spot.

Blooms:	Semi-double Rosy red Slightly fragrant
Foliage:	Dark green
Introduction:	1979
Type:	Modern Shrub
Growth Type:	Small Arching
Flowering Period:	Repeat flowering

REPENS MEIDILAND

This variety is one of the *Meidiland* series — others include *Alba*, *Red*, *White* and *Pride*. These Meilland-bred roses are popular with landscapers and in the U.S, but are available from only a limited number of suppliers in Britain. *Repens Meidiland* is useful for covering large bare sites as it quickly produces a dense and prostrate mat of glossy small leaves with masses of white blooms in June.

Blooms:	Single White Slightly fragrant
Foliage:	Medium green
Introduction:	1987
Type:	Modern Shrub
Growth Type:	Small Creeping
Flowering Period:	Early summer

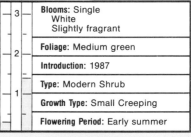

ROSY CUSHION

This Dutch rose resembles its relative *Red Blanket* in growth habit and flower form, but its flowers have a distinct white or ivory eye. Its blooms are also smaller and there are only 7–10 petals — the fragrance is occasionally quite strong. Leaf colour and form are similar — the catalogues often recommend these two varieties as partners along a path or in a border. They are also recommended for hiding unsightly objects.

Blooms:	Semi-double Pink, white eye Slightly fragrant
Foliage:	Dark green
Introduction:	1979
Type:	Modern Shrub
Growth Type:	Small Arching
Flowering Period:	Repeat flowering

SNOW CARPET
Other Name: BLANCHE NEIGE

Compare this one with *Chilterns* and you will see how different Ground Cover Roses can be. *Snow Carpet* is unusually small and is sometimes described as a Miniature Ground Cover. The creeping branches bear little shiny leaves and small multi-petalled flowers. The blooming period extends from June until October but it is technically described as non-repeat flowering.

Blooms:	Double White Slightly fragrant
Foliage:	Light green
Introduction:	1980
Type:	Modern Shrub
Growth Type:	Small Creeping
Flowering Period:	Repeat flowering

GROUND COVER ROSES

Blooms: Single Scarlet Slightly fragrant	
Foliage: Light green	
Introduction: 1988	
Type: Modern Shrub	
Growth Type: Small Creeping	
Flowering Period: Repeat flowering	

SUFFOLK
Other Name: BASSINO

Another variety in the 'County' series. This one has small red flowers with prominent yellow stamens. Foliage is plentiful and a dense mat is produced. The floral display is eye-catching and in autumn there are orange-red hips. This rose is widely available — use it in hanging baskets and other containers where you want a bright splash of colour.

Blooms: Double Ruby red No fragrance	
Foliage: Dark green	
Introduction: 1989	
Type: Modern Shrub	
Growth Type: Small Creeping	
Flowering Period: Repeat flowering	

SUMA

This Japanese variety was raised from the old favourite *Nozomi* and has kept its parent's low growing and creeping habit. The leaves are similar but the flowers and flowering habit are quite different. *Suma* bears small rosette-shaped blooms which bear many petals and these blooms appear in autumn as well as summer. More attractive than *Nozomi* — try it as a small climber or let it trail over walls.

Blooms: Double Pink Fragrant	
Foliage: Dark green	
Introduction: 1986	
Type: Modern Shrub	
Growth Type: Small Arching	
Flowering Period: Repeat flowering	

SURREY
Other Name: SOMMERWIND

One of the best of the arching varieties — the continuity of blooming is remarkable. Clusters of medium-sized blooms are borne in profusion and the perfume is stronger than most other Ground Cover types. *Surrey* received an RNRS Gold Medal in 1987 and is widely available. Use it as a weed-suppressing bush — growth is shrubby rather than prostrate.

Blooms: Double Apricot Slightly fragrant	
Foliage: Medium green	
Introduction: 1991	
Type: Modern Shrub	
Growth Type: Small Creeping	
Flowering Period: Repeat flowering	

SUSSEX

The counties of Surrey and Sussex are next to each other, but their rose namesakes are far apart. *Sussex* has a low-growing creeping habit and its flowers have an unusual colour for a Ground Cover Rose — the apricot-coloured petals fade to pale buff with age. The leafy branches form an effective weed-suppressing mat — a good choice if you want a compact dense carpet with warm-coloured blooms.

Blooms: Double White Slightly fragrant	
Foliage: Green, tinted bronze	
Introduction: 1978	
Type: Modern Shrub	
Growth Type: Small Arching	
Flowering Period: Repeat flowering	

SWANY

Swany is bushy rather than prostrate and its branches cover up to 2 sq.m with glossy leaves and small trusses of flowers. Each bloom is cupped and bears scores of petals. This Meilland-bred variety has been around for many years but it still remains popular and is widely available in the catalogues. A good choice if you want a shrubby Ground Cover Rose with lots of old-fashioned blooms.

Blooms: Double Deep pink Slightly fragrant	
Foliage: Medium green	
Introduction: 1993	
Type: Modern Shrub	
Growth Type: Small Creeping	
Flowering Period: Repeat flowering	

WILTSHIRE

This 'County' variety from Kordes has been decorated more than most Ground Cover Roses — a Certificate of Merit from the RNRS in 1991 and a Breeders Choice award in 1993. The attractive foliage is glossy and plentiful and the medium-sized blooms are borne in large trusses. However, the reason for the awards was probably the unusually long flowering period which lasts until the first frosts arrive.

GROUND COVER ROSES

CLIMBERS & RAMBLERS

About a century ago, the standard horticultural textbook described climbing roses as the most precious flowers that have ever adorned the garden. No longer true, perhaps, but they are still regarded as indispensable for some purposes. Their main use is to cover part of the house — other uses include covering arches, poles, fences, pergolas and old trees.

There are two basic types of climbing rose — Ramblers and Climbers. Ramblers have been around since Victorian times, their long pliable stems bearing huge trusses of small flowers. Growth is usually very vigorous and they can be a mass of colour in summer, but there is generally only one flush of flowers. Ramblers are no longer a popular choice — their mildew-prone leaves need regular spraying and pruning to prevent a mass of tangled stems can be a tiresome chore. Blooms are borne on new wood, so that each year some old wood may need to be cut out. If you want to cover a wall or screen, it is usually better to choose a Climber, but Ramblers do have a few special uses. They make splendid weeping standards, and can also be left to trail along the soil as ground cover or to clamber up dead trees as born-again foliage and flowers. Climbers have much stiffer stems, larger flowers and smaller trusses than Ramblers.

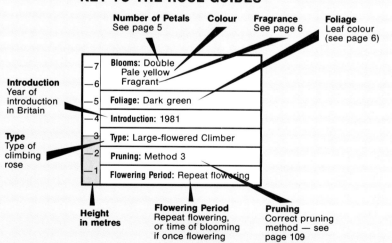

Flowers are borne on the framework of mature wood which is more or less permanent, so pruning and maintenance are much easier.

Dividing Climbers and Ramblers into various types is complex. Some catalogues lump them all together under 'Climbers and Ramblers' whereas some books split them up into numerous types such as Banksian Climbers, Wichuriana Ramblers, Climbing Hybrid Teas, Noisette Climbers and so on.

This section takes a middle course and splits them into five types. There are the Ramblers, the Large-flowered Climbers with flowers borne singly or with several side buds, the Cluster-flowered Climbers with Floribunda-like trusses, the Species Climbers which are wild roses and their close relatives, and finally the Miniature Climbers.

The Miniature Climbers are a new type. They are not particularly dwarf, reaching 2 m or more, but they do have the small leaves and the undersized flowers associated with Miniature Roses (see pages 50–53).

Of course it is a temptation to buy a Climbing Hybrid Tea or Floribunda — the idea of covering a wall with well-known beautiful blooms is appealing. Unfortunately, the climbing form has usually lost much of the repeat flowering nature of the bush form, and there may be little blossom after the first or second flush.

Don't guess with climbing roses — choose carefully, plant properly and don't expect too much in the first year. Train the stems to stimulate flowering and prune as directed.

KEY TO THE ROSE GUIDES

Number of Petals See page 5

Colour

Fragrance See page 6

Foliage Leaf colour (see page 6)

Introduction Year of introduction in Britain

Type Type of climbing rose

—7 Blooms: Double
Pale yellow
Fragrant

—6

—5 Foliage: Dark green

—4 Introduction: 1981

—3 Type: Large-flowered Climber

—2 Pruning: Method 3

—1 Flowering Period: Repeat flowering

Height in metres

Flowering Period Repeat flowering, or time of blooming if once flowering

Pruning Correct pruning method — see page 109

Blooms: Double
    Cream
    Slightly fragrant	

Foliage: Dark green	
Introduction: 1900	
Type: Rambler	
Pruning: Method 2	
Flowering Period: Midsummer	

ALBERIC BARBIER

A great old favourite, seen in gardens everywhere. It has a well-deserved reputation for flourishing under poor conditions and in difficult situations when there is little direct sunlight. It blooms profusely in late June or July, the small yellow buds opening into flat creamy white flowers. The foliage is dark and glossy, lasting through most of the winter. Grow it on a pillar rather than on a wall. Prune when the last flowers have faded.

Blooms: Double
    Pale pink
    Fragrant	

Foliage: Dark green	
Introduction: 1921	
Type: Rambler	
Pruning: Method 2	
Flowering Period: Early summer	

ALBERTINE

One of the great names in Rambler Roses — vigorous branching growth which stretches over walls or up old trees and then bursts into bloom in June. The coppery buds open into medium-sized flowers which scent the air, and when not in flower the reddish young foliage keeps the plant attractive. There are difficulties — mildew can be a serious problem and the blooms are often ruined by heavy rain.

Blooms: Double
    Rose pink, tinged salmon
    Fragrant	

Foliage: Medium green	
Introduction: 1949	
Type: Large-flowered Climber	
Pruning: Method 3	
Flowering Period: Repeat flowering	

ALOHA

If you want a pink Climber like *Albertine* with more beauty in the flowers but with much less vigour in the stems, then choose *Aloha*. It is recommended for pillars or walls where slow and restricted growth is required — its only fault is that occasionally it remains bushy and fails to climb at all. The foliage is attractive and healthy, the flowers are very full and sweetly scented. The Hybrid Tea-type blooms are resistant to rain.

Blooms: Single
    Blood red
    Slightly fragrant	

Foliage: Dark green	
Introduction: 1967	
Type: Cluster-flowered Climber	
Pruning: Method 3	
Flowering Period: Repeat flowering	

ALTISSIMO

A short Climber, sturdy and healthy, with eye-catching blooms. They first appear in June, and the plant stays in flower until autumn. There is no sudden flush of a myriad small flowers — instead there are large blooms here and there on the stems and each one is a thing of beauty. The petals are a rich red and at the centre of each flower is a boss of golden stamens. It is suitable for walls, posts and fences.

Blooms: Single
    Deep pink, white eye
    No fragrance	

Foliage: Dark green	
Introduction: 1902	
Type: Rambler	
Pruning: Method 1	
Flowering Period: Midsummer	

AMERICAN PILLAR

Before the War everyone agreed that *American Pillar* was an excellent choice as a climbing rose, but now the experts are divided. A few feel that its remarkable profusion of flower trusses in late June or July still earns it a place in the garden, but most feel that more modern varieties, such as *Dortmund*, should be used in its place. The faults are serious — there is no resistance to mildew and a good deal of pruning is required.

Blooms: Semi-double
    Pink
    Slightly fragrant	

Foliage: Medium green	
Introduction: 1967	
Type: Cluster-flowered Climber	
Pruning: Method 3	
Flowering Period: Repeat flowering	

BANTRY BAY

Bantry Bay can be grown against a wall, as it has good resistance against mildew, but it is usually recommended for clothing a pillar or fence. Don't expect a rampant grower which will quickly cover large areas — its growth habit has been described as 'restrained'. The shapely buds open into flat pink blooms, which are well-spaced in the truss. These fairly large flowers are borne in profusion throughout the season.

CLIMBERS & RAMBLERS

Height in m

BOBBIE JAMES

Rampant is the word to describe this modern Rambler — its thorny stems will readily hold on to trees and when mature it will reach 8 m or more. The foliage is both attractive and abundant, and the blooms are borne in large drooping clusters in June. Each flower is sweetly scented and bears a prominent boss of golden stamens. The plant in full bloom is spectacular, but you must give it ample space.

7	**Blooms:** Semi-double Creamy white Fragrant
6	
5	**Foliage:** Green, flushed copper
4	**Introduction:** 1961
3	**Type:** Rambler
2	**Pruning:** Method 3
1	**Flowering Period:** Midsummer

BREATH OF LIFE

A climber of the 1980s from Harkness — a prize winner from Munich to Tokyo and a popular choice in Britain. Both the flower colour and perfume are unusual in the world of the Climbers and the large Hybrid Tea-type blooms are most attractive. All the catalogues recommend it as a cut flower — the blooms are carried singly or in small clusters. Where there is no wall or pillar to spare you can prune the plant and grow it as a bush.

7	**Blooms:** Double Apricot Fragrant
6	
5	**Foliage:** Medium green
4	**Introduction:** 1982
3	**Type:** Large-flowered Climber
2	**Pruning:** Method 3
1	**Flowering Period:** Repeat flowering

CAROLINE TESTOUT, CLIMBING
Other Name: MADAME CAROLINE TESTOUT

A vigorous Climber which is useful for covering large areas. The thick stiff stems branch freely and bear abundant foliage. In midsummer the main flush of large flowers appears. When opening the blooms are a globular mass of petals — pale pink surrounding a deeper pink centre. It is tolerant of partial shade and less-than-perfect soil, but you should not try to grow this one where space is limited.

7	**Blooms:** Double Rose pink Fragrant
6	
5	**Foliage:** Grey-green
4	**Introduction:** 1901
3	**Type:** Large-flowered Climber
2	**Pruning:** Method 3
1	**Flowering Period:** Repeat flowering

CASINO

The catalogue description will make you want to rush out and buy one — deep yellow buds, Hybrid Tea in shape, opening to produce lovely full flowers which are soft yellow in colour and pleasantly scented. Foliage is healthy and the flowering season is prolonged. But there is a strong word of caution — *Casino* can be delicate so don't choose it if you live in the colder part of the country or if the planting site is exposed to cold winds.

7	**Blooms:** Double Primrose yellow Slightly fragrant
6	
5	**Foliage:** Dark green
4	**Introduction:** 1963
3	**Type:** Large-flowered Climber
2	**Pruning:** Method 2
1	**Flowering Period:** Repeat flowering

CECILE BRUNNER, CLIMBING

Cécile Brunner is a dainty bush, just 90 cm x 60 cm. The climbing sport is a giant, capable of growing up to 6 m x 6 m. Although technically described as repeat flowering, there is an impressive flush of small pink flowers in June but only sporadic flowering later in the season. The young blooms are beautifully shaped, but there is usually much more leaf than flower in summer. It is a good choice for growing up trees.

7	**Blooms:** Double Shell pink Slightly fragrant
6	
5	**Foliage:** Dark green
4	**Introduction:** 1894
3	**Type:** Cluster-flowered Climber
2	**Pruning:** Method 3
1	**Flowering Period:** Repeat flowering

COMPASSION

The many virtues of this fine variety bred by Harkness have made it one of Britain's favourite climbing roses. The flowers are beautifully shaped with forty petals, and the apricot pink colouring is unusual in this group. The scent is outstanding and the profusion of flowers is excellent. It produces new shoots freely from the base but it will not cover the side of the house — see it at its best on a pillar or against a white wall.

7	**Blooms:** Double Pink, shaded apricot Very fragrant
6	
5	**Foliage:** Dark green
4	**Introduction:** 1973
3	**Type:** Large-flowered Climber
2	**Pruning:** Method 3
1	**Flowering Period:** Repeat flowering

Blooms: Double Deep velvety crimson Very fragrant	—7 —6
Foliage: Medium green	—5
Introduction: 1946	—4
Type: Large-flowered Climber	—3
Pruning: Method 2	—2
Flowering Period: Repeat flowering	—1

CRIMSON GLORY, CLIMBING

Once the bush form of *Crimson Glory* was Britain's favourite red rose, but now it has been replaced by many newer reds without its faults. The faults are to be found in the climbing form — flowers which purple with age and leaves which are susceptible to mildew. But *Climbing Crimson Glory* has virtues which are still unmatched — velvety, dark red flowers borne in such profusion that the whole garden is scented.

Blooms: Double Crimson Slightly fragrant	—7 —6
Foliage: Light green	—5
Introduction: 1951	—4
Type: Rambler	—3
Pruning: Method 1	—2
Flowering Period: Late summer	—1

CRIMSON SHOWER

An excellent choice for people who like Rambler Roses but don't like mildew. It is free-flowering, the small rosette-shaped blooms appearing in large clusters when other Ramblers have passed their flowering season. From late July until early September the red flowers will clothe trellises, arches or pillars. *Crimson Shower* makes an excellent weeping standard. The fragrance is very faint.

Blooms: Double Orange scarlet Slightly fragrant	—7 —6
Foliage: Green, tinted bronze	—5
Introduction: 1954	—4
Type: Cluster-flowered Climber	—3
Pruning: Method 3	—2
Flowering Period: Repeat flowering	—1

DANSE DU FEU
Other Name: SPECTACULAR

One of the first of the modern repeat-flowering Climbers and still one of the most popular. The blooms are not large, but the colour is vivid and the freedom of flowering is outstanding. Trusses appear until well into the autumn and this variety is well-known for the ability to bloom in its first season. Its major fault is also well-known — the flowers turn purple with age.

Blooms: Double Rose pink Slightly fragrant	—7 —6
Foliage: Medium green	—5
Introduction: 1901	—4
Type: Rambler	—3
Pruning: Method 1	—2
Flowering Period: Late summer	—1

DOROTHY PERKINS

Nearly a century after its introduction you will still find the most famous name amongst Rambler Roses in some catalogues. Grow it for sentimental reasons, but it is no longer a good choice for garden display. It is extremely prone to mildew, making it unsuitable for growing against a wall. The small flowers appear in large clusters in late July, and the best use for *Dorothy Perkins* is to screen an open fence or arch.

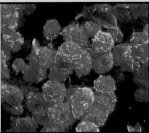

Blooms: Single Red, white eye Slightly fragrant	—7 —6
Foliage: Dark green	—5
Introduction: 1955	—4
Type: Cluster-flowered Climber	—3
Pruning: Method 3	—2
Flowering Period: Repeat flowering	—1

DORTMUND

A healthy and hardy rose, which is excellent for covering a pillar or it can be kept pruned as a large specimen bush. The big flowers have five petals, white-centred with a boss of yellow stamens. The trusses appear throughout the summer and autumn, but dead flowers should be removed or the flowering season will be shortened. The foliage is glossy and abundant, but the flowers have little scent. Growth is upright rather than spreading.

Blooms: Double Yellow Fragrant	—7 —6
Foliage: Dark green	—5
Introduction: 1973	—4
Type: Large-flowered Climber	—3
Pruning: Method 3	—2
Flowering Period: Repeat flowering	—1

DREAMING SPIRES

This climbing daughter of *Arthur Bell* has not reached the best-seller lists, but it is worth considering if you are fond of sweet-smelling yellow roses. The blooms have a high-centred shape and the colour is deep golden yellow fading to primrose yellow with age. Growth is distinctly upright rather than spreading and the stiff stems are clothed with leathery leaves. Worth considering for a sunny site.

CLIMBERS & RAMBLERS

Height in m

DUBLIN BAY

You will find this McGredy-bred rose in most catalogues, where you can read about its virtues — rich red and beautifully formed flowers borne profusely on healthy stems which are clothed with abundant glossy foliage. Unfortunately it has a drawback — at first its growth habit is inclined to be bush-like, and on some occasions it remains as an upright bush instead of a vigorous Large-flowered Climber.

7	**Blooms:** Double Deep red
6	Slightly fragrant
5	**Foliage:** Dark green
4	**Introduction:** 1976
3	**Type:** Large-flowered Climber
2	**Pruning:** Method 3
1	**Flowering Period:** Repeat flowering

EMILY GRAY

An old favourite, with two outstanding reasons for keeping its place in the catalogues. The flowers, with their unique chamois-leather colouring, and the foliage — red at first and then dark and glossy when mature. These leaves are almost evergreen — a great advantage when it is used to clothe a wall or screen. *Emily Gray* is a reasonably healthy and tolerant rose, but it is not always free-flowering. The secret is to prune very lightly.

7	**Blooms:** Double Buff yellow
6	Fragrant
5	**Foliage:** Dark green
4	**Introduction:** 1918
3	**Type:** Rambler
2	**Pruning:** Method 3
1	**Flowering Period:** Midsummer

ENA HARKNESS, CLIMBING

The drooping nature of the blooms, a disadvantage in the bush form of *Ena Harkness*, becomes a positive virtue in the climbing form. All the advantages of this old but much-loved Hybrid Tea are there — beauty of colour, form and fragrance. It flowers freely in summer but the autumn display may be disappointing. Plant it against a south-facing wall and enjoy the sweetly-scented blooms in May.

7	**Blooms:** Double Crimson
6	Fragrant
5	**Foliage:** Medium green
4	**Introduction:** 1954
3	**Type:** Large-flowered Climber
2	**Pruning:** Method 2
1	**Flowering Period:** Repeat flowering

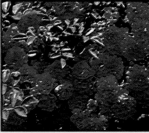

ETOILE DE HOLLANDE, CLIMBING

The bush form of *Etoile de Hollande* was the Queen of the Reds between the Wars, and its climbing sport still remains popular. In fact, it is sometimes recommended as the best of all climbing red roses for clothing the wall of a house. There the hanging flowers, velvety red and richly fragrant, can be enjoyed to the full. The summer flush of flowers is impressive, but the quantity of autumn flowering is unpredictable.

7	**Blooms:** Double Deep red
6	Very fragrant
5	**Foliage:** Dark green
4	**Introduction:** 1931
3	**Type:** Large-flowered Climber
2	**Pruning:** Method 2
1	**Flowering Period:** Repeat flowering

EXCELSA
Other Name: RED DOROTHY PERKINS

The red Rambler of yesteryear — its place has now been taken by the much healthier *Crimson Shower*. But *Excelsa* still keeps its place in many catalogues as it makes an excellent weeping standard. When grown in this way or on an arch or pillar it is festooned with small globular flowers, white-centred with crimson petals, during July. It is a rampant grower.

7	**Blooms:** Double Crimson
6	Slightly fragrant
5	**Foliage:** Dark green
4	**Introduction:** 1909
3	**Type:** Rambler
2	**Pruning:** Method 2
1	**Flowering Period:** Midsummer

FELICITE PERPETUE

In July the clusters of red-tipped buds open into small rosette-shaped blooms which stand out prominently from the background of glossy dark leaves. A vigorous climbing rose for growing up trees — the foliage is healthy and almost evergreen. *Félicité Perpétue* is renowned for its reliability — it will flourish in both cold and partly shady situations. It is recommended by the experts, but not for the big-flower enthusiast.

7	**Blooms:** Double Creamy white
6	Slightly fragrant
5	**Foliage:** Dark green
4	**Introduction:** 1827
3	**Type:** Rambler
2	**Pruning:** Method 3
1	**Flowering Period:** Midsummer

Blooms:	Double Pink Fragrant
Foliage:	Green, tinted bronze
Introduction:	1906
Type:	Rambler
Pruning:	Method 1
Flowering Period:	Early summer

FRANCOIS JURANVILLE

This old Rambler remains an excellent choice to cover a large structure such as a pergola or screen. It is a very vigorous grower capable of reaching 6 m or more. The flowers are large for a Rambler Rose, and have a heavy old-world fragrance. They appear in late June, at first deep salmon pink but soon fading to pale pink. The long flexible stems have few thorns and the leaves are small and shiny. It is tolerant of partial shade.

Blooms:	Double Pink Slightly fragrant
Foliage:	Medium green
Introduction:	1966
Type:	Cluster-flowered Climber
Pruning:	Method 3
Flowering Period:	Repeat flowering

GALWAY BAY

This offspring of *Queen Elizabeth* has the properties you would expect in a modern pillar rose — restrained growth reaching about 3 m high and leaves with good disease resistance. Although there is nothing special about the growth habit of *Galway Bay*, the flowers are noteworthy. They are large, well-formed and borne in remarkable profusion. The small clusters appear regularly during the summer and autumn.

Blooms:	Double Buff yellow Fragrant
Foliage:	Medium green
Introduction:	1853
Type:	Large-flowered Climber
Pruning:	Method 3
Flowering Period:	Repeat flowering

GLOIRE DE DIJON

Victorian rose experts wrote about the great beauty of this old climbing Tea Rose, and you can see why if you look at a mature and vigorous plant in June. The flowers are large, strikingly coloured and sweetly scented. Having started early in the season, flowering continues until the autumn. Recommended for walls, but watch out for mildew. Many modern stocks have deteriorated, so buy from a reputable supplier.

Blooms:	Double Golden yellow Fragrant
Foliage:	Dark green
Introduction:	1956
Type:	Large-flowered Climber
Pruning:	Method 3
Flowering Period:	Repeat flowering

GOLDEN SHOWERS

Golden Showers is by far the most popular yellow climbing rose — you can buy it anywhere. There are several reasons for its universal appeal — resistance to rain, bright flowers and foliage, and above all the prolonged flowering season from June until the frosts arrive. It is excellent for a small garden as it is easily kept in check. It has faults — the blooms soon become loose and growth at first is bushy rather than climbing.

Blooms:	Semi-double Yellow, blended cream Slightly fragrant
Foliage:	Medium green
Introduction:	1907
Type:	Rambler
Pruning:	Method 2
Flowering Period:	Midsummer

GOLDFINCH

This old climbing rose is much more restrained than the typical Rambler and so is suitable for the small garden. It is noted for its attractive foliage and free-flowering nature — the golden buds open into trusses of small rosette-shaped flowers. These blooms are a blend of yellow and cream with a central boss of deep golden stamens. The stems are almost thornless. You can grow this one on a north-facing wall.

Blooms:	Double Deep red, shaded black Very fragrant
Foliage:	Medium green
Introduction:	1938
Type:	Large-flowered Climber
Pruning:	Method 3
Flowering Period:	Repeat flowering

GUINEE

You will love or hate this blackest of all garden roses. Velvety deep red, the blooms may look dull on a cloudy day but can glow in full sunshine. These flowers are large, opening flat and emitting a strong perfume. Very free-flowering in June, but the later flushes are disappointing. Foliage is leathery and plentiful, but you must watch for mildew. A good variety for unshaded walls and screens — stems are stiff and quite rigid.

CLIMBERS & RAMBLERS

Height in m

HANDEL

Handel is one of the stars of the climbing rose world. The secret of its appeal lies in the unique colouring of its blooms, for it has no other unusual feature. The flowers are nicely shaped and the colour intensifies with age, but they are not full of petals. The stems are relatively thornless and the leaves are glossy, but mildew and black spot can be problems. The flowers are borne singly or in clusters over a long period, and are not spoilt by rain.

Blooms:	Double Cream, edged rosy pink Slightly fragrant
Foliage:	Green, tinted bronze
Introduction:	1965
Type:	Large-flowered Climber
Pruning:	Method 3
Flowering Period:	Repeat flowering

HIGHFIELD

Highfield is a sport of the most popular of all modern climbing roses — *Compassion*. It has many of the properties of its illustrious parent, including its free-flowering habit. The flowers are medium-sized, sometimes tinged with pink or peach. It is not a rampant grower, so it is best on a pillar, fence or arch rather than against a large wall. You will find it in a number of catalogues, but it has never matched the popularity of *Compassion*.

Blooms:	Double Pale yellow Fragrant
Foliage:	Dark green
Introduction:	1981
Type:	Large-flowered Climber
Pruning:	Method 3
Flowering Period:	Repeat flowering

HIGH HOPES

One of the new Climbers which has won high praise from the experts. This offspring of *Compassion* produces abundant clusters of medium-sized flowers with a classic H.T shape and a pleasing perfume. It is tolerant of less-than-ideal conditions and the glossy foliage is both healthy and attractive. The late season display is impressive. Growth is upright rather than spreading — a good choice for covering an arch or pergola.

Blooms:	Double Pale pink Fragrant
Foliage:	Dark green
Introduction:	1992
Type:	Large-flowered Climber
Pruning:	Method 3
Flowering Period:	Repeat flowering

ICEBERG, CLIMBING

This sport of the most successful white Floribunda of our time has not become really popular. Surprising, perhaps, because it has many admirers and is regarded as one of the most reliable climbing sports of recent years. It will clothe a wall with abundant glossy foliage studded with large trusses of flat white blooms, and this display continues until the autumn. Spraying against mildew may be necessary.

Blooms:	Double White Slightly fragrant
Foliage:	Medium green
Introduction:	1968
Type:	Cluster-flowered Climber
Pruning:	Method 3
Flowering Period:	Repeat flowering

KIFTSGATE

Other Name: ROSA FILIPES KIFTSGATE

A rambling giant of a rose, tall and wide-spreading, used for covering sheds or for growing up old trees. In July there is a cascade of bloom — enormous clusters of small fragrant flowers. These blooms are followed by bright red hips and deep golden foliage in the autumn. Treat it as an enormous bush reaching 10 m or more — don't try to keep it in bounds in a small garden by pruning.

Blooms:	Single Creamy white Fragrant
Foliage:	Medium green
Introduction:	1954
Type:	Species Climber
Pruning:	Method 3
Flowering Period:	Midsummer

LAURA FORD

This member of the new breed of Miniature Climbers has become popular. Growth is both restrained and upright, so it is suitable for clothing pillars, porches or walls between windows. The clusters of small yellow blooms cover the small shiny leaves and the pleasant perfume is an added bonus. *Laura Ford* can be grown in a container — a notable feature is the production of flowers all over the plant.

Blooms:	Semi-double Yellow, tinged pink Fragrant
Foliage:	Dark green
Introduction:	1990
Type:	Miniature Climber
Pruning:	Method 3
Flowering Period:	Repeat flowering

LAVINIA
Other Name: LAWINIA

Blooms: Double Pink Fragrant	7 6
Foliage: Medium green	5
Introduction: 1980	4
Type: Large-flowered Climber	3
Pruning: Method 3	2
Flowering Period: Repeat flowering	1

This Tantau-bred vigorous and spreading Climber has never become really popular despite the fact that everything about it is large. The big blooms are cupped and the big leaves are semi-glossy. The fragrance is questionable — some people find it strong and others quite faint. A reliable stiff-stemmed rose for either wall cover or for climbing up trees.

LEAPING SALMON

Blooms: Double Salmon pink Very fragrant	7 6
Foliage: Dark green	5
Introduction: 1986	4
Type: Large-flowered Climber	3
Pruning: Method 3	2
Flowering Period: Repeat flowering	1

The strong scent of the large bright blooms has made this a popular Climber and you will find it in many catalogues. The flowers appear freely throughout the season and the glossy foliage is abundant. The sturdy stems are stiff and upright, which makes *Leaping Salmon* an excellent pillar rose. The blooms are useful for cutting. For a modern variety it has an important drawback — disease resistance is only average.

LEVERKUSEN

Blooms: Semi-double Pale yellow Slightly fragrant	7 6
Foliage: Medium green	5
Introduction: 1955	4
Type: Cluster-flowered Climber	3
Pruning: Method 3	2
Flowering Period: Repeat flowering	1

As you would expect from a Kordesii Climber, the shiny leaves are healthy and the flowers appear freely. Even on an exposed site or in one of the colder areas of the country *Leverkusen* can be relied upon to provide an attractive display on a pillar or wall. Large clusters of medium-sized blooms appear in June and further flushes follow — the autumn show is outstanding. Can be pruned and staked to form a large bush.

MADAME ALFRED CARRIERE

Blooms: Double White, flushed pink Very fragrant	7 6
Foliage: Light green	5
Introduction: 1879	4
Type: Cluster-flowered Climber	3
Pruning: Method 3	2
Flowering Period: Repeat flowering	1

In Victorian times a wide range of Noisette Climbers were used to clothe cottages and castles — today very few remain in the catalogues. *Madame Alfred Carrière* is one, because its ability to clothe a north-facing wall of a house has not been matched by many modern varieties. It grows quickly, and the large, fragrant blooms open regularly during summer and autumn. More than a century old, but as vigorous as ever.

MADAME GREGOIRE STAECHELIN
Other Name: SPANISH BEAUTY

Blooms: Double Pink, shaded crimson Very fragrant	7 6
Foliage: Medium green	5
Introduction: 1927	4
Type: Large-flowered Climber	3
Pruning: Method 2	2
Flowering Period: Early summer	1

A sight to behold — a full-grown specimen of *Madame Grégoire Staechelin* in full flower. The H.T-type blooms are large, with frilled pink petals and a scent which is heavy and sweet. These blooms smother the abundant foliage of this very vigorous variety in June, but the flowering season lasts for only a few weeks after which the large hips begin to develop.

MAIGOLD

Blooms: Semi-double Bronze yellow Fragrant	7 6
Foliage: Dark green	5
Introduction: 1953	4
Type: Large-flowered Climber	3
Pruning: Method 3	2
Flowering Period: Early summer	1

Maigold has many virtues, and it is not surprising to find it in the best-seller lists of climbing roses. It comes to flower in May, when roses are so welcome. It also blooms early in the life of the plant — a problem with many Climbers. The foliage is healthy and attractive, and the fragrance is strong. There are drawbacks — the stems are thorny, the blooms are unshapely and flowering after the first flush is unlikely.

Height in m

MASQUERADE, CLIMBING

The visual effect of large trusses bearing yellow, pink and deep red flowers is even more spectacular on the climbing sport of *Masquerade* than on the more familiar bush form. This variety is suitable for a fence or pillar, and has a good reputation for vigour and reliability. There is a profuse flush in June, but if you fail to remove the dead flowers before the hips form then there will be few blooms later in the season.

Blooms: Semi-double Yellow, then pink and red Slightly fragrant	
Foliage: Dark green	
Introduction: 1958	
Type: Cluster-flowered Climber	
Pruning: Method 3	
Flowering Period: Repeat flowering	

MERMAID

One of the giants of the climbing rose world — a plant to cover the wall of a large house. It should, however, be a west- or south-facing wall as *Mermaid* can be killed by frost. This lack of hardiness is not the only fault of *Mermaid* — the stems are brittle and thorny, and a new plant will take a couple of years to establish. But in full flower it is supreme — the very large blooms are both eye-catching and sweetly scented.

Blooms: Single Primrose yellow Fragrant	
Foliage: Medium green	
Introduction: 1918	
Type: Large-flowered Climber	
Pruning: Method 3	
Flowering Period: Repeat flowering	

MORNING JEWEL

The pink of the large blooms has been described in many ways — "rich", "glowing" and so on. With a backcloth of shiny leaves this Scottish-bred variety gives an eye-catching display during the summer months. New shoots appear readily from the base — a useful Climber for fences or pillars. It has received an Award of Garden Merit from the RHS and the experts say it is an excellent rose to grow in an exposed or shady spot.

Blooms: Semi-double Pink Slightly fragrant	
Foliage: Medium green	
Introduction: 1969	
Type: Cluster-flowered Climber	
Pruning: Method 3	
Flowering Period: Repeat flowering	

MRS SAM McGREDY, CLIMBING

Mrs Sam McGredy has almost disappeared from the catalogues — the climbing form is the way to enjoy once again some of her former glory. Here are the bronze buds, the copper red blooms and the purple young foliage. The blooms are borne in large numbers and the flowering period lasts into the autumn. Drawbacks include the shortage of leaves, the lack of vigour and its susceptibility to black spot.

Blooms: Double Coppery orange, flushed red Fragrant	
Foliage: Green, tinted bronze	
Introduction: 1937	
Type: Large-flowered Climber	
Pruning: Method 3	
Flowering Period: Repeat flowering	

NEW DAWN

Dr W. van Fleet was once a popular Rambler, but it has now been replaced by its sport *New Dawn*. There are two distinct advantages with the newer variety — the growth is much less rampant and the flower clusters continue to appear throughout the summer. The blooms are small, but they are present in great numbers above the shiny leaves. A good multipurpose rose — use as a hedge, specimen shrub or climber.

Blooms: Semi-double Shell pink Fragrant	
Foliage: Medium green	
Introduction: 1930	
Type: Rambler	
Pruning: Method 2	
Flowering Period: Repeat flowering	

NICE DAY

A Miniature Climber which is a Breeders Choice winner. As you would expect from a variety in this new group both flowers and leaves are small — the rosette-shaped blooms have a sweet fragrance and the foliage is dense and glossy. The spread is only about 1 m so it is a good choice where the width available is limited. Flowers appear from top to bottom — put it in a pot on the patio or close to the front door so as to enjoy its fragrance.

Blooms: Double Salmon pink Fragrant	
Foliage: Dark green	
Introduction: 1993	
Type: Miniature Climber	
Pruning: Method 3	
Flowering Period: Repeat flowering	

Blooms: Double Deep yellow Slightly fragrant	
Foliage: Dark green	
Introduction: 1982	
Type: Large-flowered Climber	
Pruning: Method 3	
Flowering Period: Repeat flowering	

NIGHT LIGHT

The flowers are large and the trusses are reasonably full. The buds are orange red and the deep yellow of the blooms is often tinged with orange, but there is nothing really special about *Night Light*. The stiff and upright stems bear glossy dark leaves which form a good background for the deep orange buds and then the yellow flowers. It has good resistance to disease but the scent is quite weak and it does not do well in a shady situation.

Blooms: Semi-double Blood red Slightly fragrant	
Foliage: Dark green	
Introduction: 1957	
Type: Cluster-flowered Climber	
Pruning: Method 2	
Flowering Period: Repeat flowering	

PARKDIREKTOR RIGGERS

This variety has the profusion of flowers and the hardiness associated with Kordesii Climbers, but it does not have the family resistance to disease — both mildew and black spot can be problems. The large clusters of glowing crimson blooms are borne with remarkable freedom, and this has led to the popularity of this climbing rose. Once the flowers are dead remove them to ensure repeat flowering. It is suitable for growing on a north wall.

Blooms: Double Blush pink Slightly fragrant	
Foliage: Dark green	
Introduction: 1916	
Type: Species Climber	
Pruning: Method 2	
Flowering Period: Midsummer	

PAUL'S HIMALAYAN MUSK

A giant of a rose for covering large areas — it can reach 8 m x 8 m. In July the large drooping leaves are covered by a mass of pendent trusses, each truss bearing many small blooms. With age these flowers fade to near-white. A good choice to cover a large wall or to clamber up a tree, but not a rose to be kept in check by constant cutting back. *Paul's Himalayan Musk* is happy in partial shade. Despite its name and parentage the perfume is weak.

Blooms: Double Scarlet Slightly fragrant	
Foliage: Medium green	
Introduction: 1915	
Type: Rambler	
Pruning: Method 2	
Flowering Period: Early summer	

PAUL'S SCARLET CLIMBER

The top climbing red rose for many years, *Paul's Scarlet* is sadly past its prime. There are newer red varieties which don't dull with age, and there are varieties which have much better resistance to disease. Still, it remains an eye-catching rose in June, with masses of cupped red flowers which last for a month or more and then they are gone — there is no repeat flowering. It is less vigorous than the average old-fashioned Rambler.

Blooms: Double Pink Slightly fragrant	
Foliage: Dark green, tinted purple	
Introduction: 1965	
Type: Large-flowered Climber	
Pruning: Method 3	
Flowering Period: Repeat flowering	

PINK PERPETUE

A popular variety, due to its free-flowering nature and the ability to produce an autumn display of flower trusses which rivals the summer show. *Pink Perpetue* does not grow very tall, but it is vigorous and wide-spreading which make it a good choice for covering a fence or wall. The blooms are not large, but they have plenty of petals and an attractive globular shape. The only drawback is that rust can be a serious problem.

Blooms: Semi-double Creamy white Fragrant	
Foliage: Grey-green	
Introduction: Before 1900	
Type: Rambler	
Pruning: Method 3	
Flowering Period: Midsummer	

RAMBLING RECTOR

One of the best of all roses for covering walls, hiding unsightly buildings and scrambling up trees. The small leaves are abundant and so are the flowers in late June. These blooms fade to white with age and have a cluster of golden stamens at the centre. There are several plus points — the leaves are healthy, the flower trusses are large, it will grow on a north wall and there is a hip display. It is an excellent variety for planting in woodland.

Height in m

ROSY MANTLE

A well-bred rose — it has the reliable climbing habit of *New Dawn* and some of the floral beauty of its other parent, *Prima Ballerina*. The large and shapely blooms are borne in small clusters throughout the season, and the display is especially good in autumn. The glossy leaves are rarely troubled by disease, but the wiry stems need regular attention to ensure that they are trained properly. Suitable for a north-facing wall.

Blooms: Double Deep pink Fragrant	
Foliage: Dark green	
Introduction: 1968	
Type: Large-flowered Climber	
Pruning: Method 3	
Flowering Period: Repeat flowering	

ROYAL GOLD

A variety which sounds irresistible in the catalogue — fragrant golden blooms, high-centred like a Hybrid Tea and 10 cm in diameter. But *Royal Gold* in the garden is not as desirable as its catalogue description — it does not flower freely, vigour is distinctly lacking if the soil is not fertile and leaves are sparse. The major problem is lack of hardiness — this is a rose for a south or west wall on a sheltered site.

Blooms: Double Deep yellow Slightly fragrant	
Foliage: Medium green	
Introduction: 1967	
Type: Large-flowered Climber	
Pruning: Method 3	
Flowering Period: Repeat flowering	

SANDERS' WHITE RAMBLER

Despite its great age this fine old Rambler has kept both its health and its place in the catalogues. The rosette-shaped flowers are small but they are both sweet smelling and filled with petals. The large clusters of flowers appear in August and this variety is usually recommended for clothing arches, pillars and fences rather than walls. It is particularly good as a weeping standard where its glossy attractive leaves can be appreciated.

Blooms: Double White Fragrant	
Foliage: Light green	
Introduction: 1912	
Type: Rambler	
Pruning: Method 1	
Flowering Period: Midsummer	

SCHOOLGIRL

It is not surprising that *Schoolgirl* should have become so popular. Good orange climbing roses are rare, and the blooms of this McGredy-bred rose are large and fragrant. The leaves are glossy and abundant, and the flowers appear throughout the summer and autumn. Its main fault is the loss of the lower leaves, so that the stems appear leggy. Another drawback is the failure to produce a mass of flowers.

Blooms: Double Coppery orange Fragrant	
Foliage: Dark green	
Introduction: 1964	
Type: Large-flowered Climber	
Pruning: Method 3	
Flowering Period: Repeat flowering	

SEAGULL

Another oldie, but you should have no difficulty in locating a supplier. Its parentage is unknown — you may find it listed as a Species Climber. The small flowers bear prominent golden stamens and they appear in large numbers in summer. Growth is vigorous and the trusses are large. The continuing popularity of *Seagull* is probably due to the frequent references in the catalogues to its ability to scramble up and clothe old trees.

Blooms: Single White Fragrant	
Foliage: Grey-green	
Introduction: 1907	
Type: Rambler	
Pruning: Method 1	
Flowering Period: Midsummer	

SUMMER WINE

This Kordesii Climber received an Award of Garden Merit from the RHS. It is a vigorous plant which is well-furnished with dark semi-glossy foliage. The flowers are large and are easily recognised by the bright red stamens at the centre. The stems are upright, so it is useful for arches and pergolas. *Summer Wine* is not a fussy rose — it will grow on a north wall. It has a good reputation for growing in less-than-ideal soil.

Blooms: Semi-double Coral pink Fragrant	
Foliage: Dark green	
Introduction: 1985	
Type: Large-flowered Climber	
Pruning: Method 3	
Flowering Period: Repeat flowering	

Blooms: Double
   White, tinged pink
   Slightly fragrant
	7

Foliage: Dark green	6 5
Introduction: 1968	4
Type: Large-flowered Climber	3
Pruning: Method 3	2
Flowering Period: Repeat flowering	1

SWAN LAKE

One of the most beautiful white Climbers you can buy — the flowers are large and shapely, and the foliage is abundant. The blooms are not spoilt by wet weather — an unusual feature for a white rose. The flowers, bearing fifty petals or more, are borne freely throughout the season, but the foliage is prone to attack by mildew and black spot so spraying is necessary. Growth is stiff and branching — a good choice for an arch or pillar.

Blooms: Semi-double
   Lilac, fading to grey
   Fragrant
	7
	6

Foliage: Light green	5
Introduction: 1909	4
Type: Rambler	3
Pruning: Method 2	2
Flowering Period: Midsummer	1

VEILCHENBLAU
Other Name: VIOLET BLUE

A black and white photograph of *Veilchenblau* in bloom reveals a very ordinary rose — small, semi-double and cupped flowers. In the garden, grown against a wall shaded from the noon-day sun, it is a most unusual variety — one of the closest yet to the elusive 'blue' rose. The mature bloom is perhaps more grey than blue, but it is worth growing if you like out-of-the-ordinary roses.

Blooms: Semi-double
   Orange vermilion
   Slightly fragrant
	7
	6

Foliage: Dark green	5
Introduction: 1990	4
Type: Miniature Climber	3
Pruning: Method 3	2
Flowering Period: Repeat flowering	1

WARM WELCOME

Another Miniature Climber from Warner with all the characteristics you would expect from this group — masses of bright blooms covering the whole plant throughout the summer months and foliage which is both plentiful and healthy. The petals are bright orange with a yellow base. *Warm Welcome* differs from *Laura Ford* and *Nice Day* by spreading to about 2 m rather than having a narrow and upright growth habit.

Blooms: Single
   Creamy white
   Fragrant
	7
	6

Foliage: Medium green	5
Introduction: 1950	4
Type: Rambler	3
Pruning: Method 3	2
Flowering Period: Midsummer	1

WEDDING DAY

The only small thing about this rose is the flower — 5-petalled, cream-coloured fading to pinky white and studded with golden stamens. Everything else is on the grand scale — growth is extremely vigorous, the flower trusses in July and August are large and the rampant stems will cover 2-storey buildings or massive old trees. Good in partial shade and a rival to *Kiftsgate* for hiding unsightly objects, but a bad choice for small gardens.

Blooms: Double
   White
   Fragrant
	7
	6

Foliage: Dark green	5
Introduction: 1969	4
Type: Large-flowered Climber	3
Pruning: Method 3	2
Flowering Period: Repeat flowering	1

WHITE COCKADE

Like *Swan Lake*, this Scottish-bred variety is one of the best modern white Climbers available and is an Award of Garden Merit winner. The blooms are beautifully formed with a pleasant fragrance, and there is a prolonged flowering period. It is a short-growing Climber — obviously not a rose to cover the side of the house. Use it to clothe a low pillar or fence, or grow it as a tall bush. Disease resistance is good, and the glossy foliage is attractive.

Blooms: Semi-double
   Carmine pink
   Very fragrant
	7
	6

Foliage: Light green	5
Introduction: 1868	4
Type: Large-flowered Climber	3
Pruning: Method 3	2
Flowering Period: Repeat flowering	1

ZEPHIRINE DROUHIN
Other Name: THORNLESS ROSE

This Bourbon Rose deserves its place in the Rose Hall of Fame — after more than 100 years it still appears in nearly all the catalogues, and the praise from the experts is as loud as ever. Grow it as a Climber, or keep it pruned as a tall bush or hedge. Dead-head regularly, and there will be a succession of blooms from June onwards. Spray regularly with a fungicide.

CLIMBERS & RAMBLERS

SHRUB ROSES

You will find a large selection of Shrub Roses in most catalogues, but less than 5 per cent of the roses we buy each year belong to this class. The reason is, of course, the faults which everybody knows — Shrub Roses bloom only once, they are far too large for an average garden and they are far too old-fashioned for a modern garden.

Not one of these allegations is true. Consider the first misconception — lack of repeat flowering. Some Shrub Roses, such as the Species, the Gallicas and the Centifolias do produce only one spectacular showing, but other Shrub Roses are repeat flowering, and many examples are listed on pages 76–90. Even the once-flowering varieties should not be decried. The flowering period often lasts for many weeks and the timing, as with *Canary Bird* in May, may not be achievable with a Floribunda or Hybrid Tea. Furthermore, the sight of some of the once-flowering varieties in full bloom in June or July exceeds the display value of most of the shrubs we grow. In addition with many varieties there is the bonus of a bright display of hips in the autumn.

The second incorrect idea about Shrub Roses concerns their size. Some indeed are giants, like *William Lobb, Nevada* and *Frühlingsgold*, but there are others which could look up to an average Floribunda — there are dainty Shrubs such as *Cécile Brunner* and *The Fairy*.

Finally, the question of the old-fashioned look. Of course there are cottage-type roses — pink, overblown and full of fragrance, and that's their charm. But every flower form is available, from *Fred Loads* with its 5-petalled blooms to *Uncle Walter* with its high-centred, H.T-type flowers.

A feature of the 1980s was the marked increase in the number of Shrub Roses which could be used for ground cover. These varieties used to be grouped with all the other Shrub Roses but in this edition these varieties have been put together as a separate class — see pages 54–59.

Shrub Roses are underestimated, under-utilized and misunderstood. One of the problems is that they are not a clear-cut group — quite frankly they are a rag-bag of varieties which do not belong in any of the other classes. Included are the Species Roses (wild types and their near relatives) and Old-fashioned roses (varieties dating back to the pre-Hybrid Tea era). Finally there are the Modern ones which may have a flower form rather similar to a Floribunda or Hybrid Tea. Somewhere among this extremely varied class of roses there is a variety for nearly every garden.

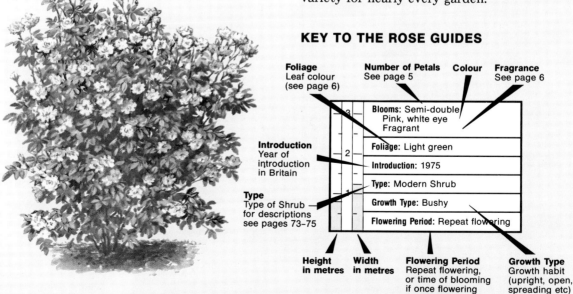

KEY TO THE ROSE GUIDES

Foliage
Leaf colour
(see page 6)

Number of Petals
See page 5

Colour

Fragrance
See page 6

Introduction
Year of introduction in Britain

Type
Type of Shrub
for descriptions
see pages 73–75

Blooms: Semi-double
Pink, white eye
Fragrant

Foliage: Light green

Introduction: 1975

Type: Modern Shrub

Growth Type: Bushy

Flowering Period: Repeat flowering

Height
in metres

Width
in metres

Flowering Period
Repeat flowering,
or time of blooming
if once flowering
(see page 6)

Growth Type
Growth habit
(upright, open,
spreading etc)

Shrub Rose Types

Shrub Roses should be regarded as extremely useful shrubs — alternatives to Lilac or Rhododendron rather than to *Silver Jubilee* or *Sweet Magic*. Unlike Lilac or Rhododendron, however, these shrubs have very few characteristics which they all share. Most are taller than Floribundas and H.Ts and most require little or no pruning, but the ranges of flowering time, flower form, cultural needs etc are extremely wide. For example the Rugosas are very easy to grow whereas the Teas need a sheltered frost-free site. It is therefore useful to know the type to which your new Shrub Rose purchase belongs, and listed below are the features of the 19 most important types. The varieties within each type generally have several shared characteristics, but the dividing line between the various types is sometimes blurred. This means that precise classification may not be as clear cut as some people believe. For instance *Ballerina* may be listed as a Hybrid Musk, Polyantha or Modern Shrub Rose depending on which catalogue or book you read.

ALBA

The Albas are an ancient group with the Dog Rose (*R. canina*) as one of the original parents. You can easily recognise an Alba Rose by its soft and drooping grey-green leaves and strong upright growth. The bush has good resistance against pests and diseases, and pruning may be necessary to keep it in check. The flowers appear in a single flush in June — usually double and pink or white with a rich fragrance. Albas can withstand partial shade better than most other roses.

Celestial

BOURBON

The Bourbon group of roses was born when a chance cross between *Autumn Damask* and a China Rose occurred in 1816. The fragrant globular flowers, large and many-petalled, became the most popular roses for a time in Victorian gardens as they had the advantage of blooming in autumn as well as June. Eventually they lost their crown to the Hybrid Perpetuals, and today you will find very few in the catalogues. They are all hardy but prone to mildew.

Madame Isaac Pereire

CENTIFOLIA   *Other Names: Cabbage Rose, Provence Rose*

Dutch flower paintings show that these multi-petalled globular flowers were flourishing in the 17th century. With their cottage garden colours and heavy fragrance the Centifolias are the epitome of old-fashioned roses. Unfortunately this group has none of the health and robustness of the Albas and Gallicas — the stems are lax and need support and the bushes need both spraying and regular feeding to ensure a satisfactory display in the garden.

Fantin-Latour

CHINA

The importance of the China Rose in the development of modern varieties is dealt with on page 8. *Old Blush*, one of the original imports from China in the 18th century, is still available from a few suppliers and so is the Victorian favourite *Cécile Brunner*. The hybrids you can buy are slender open shrubs usually less than 1.5 m high. Large clusters of small flowers in pink, red or yellow are borne throughout the summer. Choose a sunny protected site.

Cécile Brunner

DAMASK

The perfume of the white or pink flowers is the glory of the Damask Rose. Some varieties date back to the 16th century but this group has never been really popular. The arching, weak stems bear dull foliage and the weak flower stalks allow the blooms to droop. The flowers are generally borne in clusters and appear as a single flush in midsummer. Damask Roses are hardy and generally healthy, but they do need fertile soil and proper attention.

Madame Hardy

SHRUB ROSES

ENGLISH

The English group of roses is the most recent addition to the list. It was in the last quarter of the 20th century when David Austin offered his first English Roses for sale. These are hybrids of Gallicas, Damasks etc with modern H.Ts and Floribundas. They are compact bushes with a wide range of colours and the appearance of old-fashioned roses. Most are repeat flowering. They have the disease-resistance of the Floribunda or H.T parent.

The Pilgrim

GALLICA   *Other Name: French Rose*

The most ancient of all the garden roses, and over the centuries this large group has collected many common names. The hybrids grown today are usually compact with rough foliage. Flower sizes and number of petals vary widely, and the colours range from pink and red to purple. *Rosa Mundi* is the one you are most likely to see — it is almost thornless, midsummer flowering, successful in poor soil but prone to mildew.

R. gallica officinalis

HYBRID MUSK

Rev. Pemberton introduced and named this group at the beginning of the 20th century. The scent is similar to that of the old Musk Rose (*R. moschata*), but there is no close relationship. Hybrid Musks are suitable for an average-sized garden, provided that their sprawling habit is kept in check. Masses of flowers appear in large trusses in June and July — dead-head to ensure an impressive autumn display. The flowers are usually fragrant.

Penelope

HYBRID PERPETUAL

At the end of the 19th century the Hybrid Perpetual became the most popular group of garden roses in Britain. A few of the thousands of varieties are still available, but of course the Floribunda and Hybrid Tea have taken over. The H.P lost its crown because it is *not* perpetual — there is a summer flush followed by an autumn one. The bushes tend to be too vigorous for small gardens and the large blooms are usually cupped rather than high-centred like modern roses.

Frau Karl Druschki

MODERN SHRUB

This is a widely diverse group with nothing in common apart from the fact that they were bred in the 20th century and do not fit neatly into any of the eighteen specific groups described in this section. There are all sorts of colours, shapes and sizes, but most are repeat flowering and the shape of the double varieties is usually distinctly modern rather than globular or open cupped. Many such as *Nevada* and *Angelina* are single or semi-double.

Chinatown

MOSS

About 300 years ago an unknown Centifolia Rose produced a sport — the Moss Rose. All the varieties are rather similar to the parent apart from a distinctive green or brown 'moss' (sticky hairs) all over the sepals and flower stalks. The sweet-smelling double blooms have an old-fashioned look, and a few are repeat flowering. Many varieties were raised in the 19th century but they are no longer popular — the foliage display is unsightly after flowering.

William Lobb

NOISETTE

The first Noisette Roses were bred in S. Carolina by Philippe Noisette at the beginning of the 19th century. These China Rose x Musk Rose hybrids are both fragrant and repeat flowering with silky petals — colours range from blush white to deep cream. Both bushy and climbing types were once available but now the shrubs have gone from the catalogues and only a few climbers such as *Madame Alfred Carrière* remain. One problem is that most are not fully hardy.

Madame Alfred Carrière

SHRUB ROSES

POLYANTHA

A group of low-growing Shrub Roses which rarely reach more than 1 m high. The bushes are extremely hardy and produce large clusters of small blooms more or less continually throughout the summer and autumn. The first Polyantha hybrids appeared in the 1870s and were very popular in the early 1900s, but only a few remain in the catalogues. This group has been almost entirely replaced by their much showier offsprings — the Floribundas.

The Fairy

PORTLAND

The first Portland Rose was a Gallica x Damask cross and appeared at the end of the 18th century. The shrubs have rather stiff stems and short flower stalks — the white, pink, red or purple blooms are often scented and many are repeat flowering. Growth is usually compact and the Portlands are useful for low hedging — these roses are noted for the abundance of the autumn floral display. In the A–Z you will find *Comte de Chambord*.

Comte de Chambord

RUGOSA *Other Name: Japanese Rose*

R. rugosa came to Europe from Japan at the end of the 18th century and has been used as the parent for a host of distinctive hybrids — the Rugosas. They have dark green leaves with deeply impressed veins, and they are remarkably resistant to disease. They will thrive in soils and conditions where hardly any other rose would survive, and the dense and thorny stems make them excellent hedging roses. The flowers are fragrant and the hips are usually large.

Roseraie de L'Haÿ

SCOTS *Other Name: Burnet Rose*

The Scots Roses have *R. pimpinellifolia* as a parent and were widely grown in the early 1800s. The usual habit is a dense mound of prickly stems with masses of small leaves and a display of bowl-shaped blooms in early summer. Their fall from grace was due to the short flowering period, but the fine Kordesii hybrids of *R. pimpinellifolia* and Hybrid Teas in this century have brought them back to the catalogues. See *Frühlingsgold* and *Frühlingsmorgen*.

Stanwell Perpetual

SPECIES

All the so-called 'wild' roses are included here, together with varieties and hybrids which bear a very close resemblance to the parent. Many are known by their latin name (e.g *Rosa rubrifolia*) but a few have common names (e.g *Canary Bird*). There are some general characteristics but no single distinctive feature. Most, but not all, are ancient and bear single blooms with hips after flowering. There is generally a single flowering period, but this may be unusually early.

Canary Bird

SWEET BRIAR

The Sweet Briar group has been developed from *R. eglanteria* and began with *Manning's Blush* which appeared about 200 years ago. The best-known Sweet Briars are the Penzance hybrids which were raised at the end of the 19th century. The vigorous bushes have retained the sweet-smelling foliage of *R. eglanteria* — the stems are very thorny and the single flowers are followed by large hips. The more recent hybrids have lost the foliage fragrance.

Lady Penzance

TEA

The Tea Rose group was created by crossing varieties of *R. odorata* (the original Tea Rose which came from China in the early 1800s) with Noisettes, Bourbons etc. The result was a host of hybrids which were popular in Victorian times despite their lack of hardiness. This is a serious drawback and these shrubs with their refined high-centred blooms on thin stalks have almost disappeared from the catalogues. The climber *Gloire de Dijon* with quartered blooms is still widely available.

Gloire de Dijon

SHRUB ROSES

Height Width
in m   in m

ABRAHAM DARBY

You should have no trouble in finding this English Rose as it is listed in many catalogues. *Abraham Darby* is a vigorous bush with thorny stems and leathery foliage — the leaves are not particularly prone to mildew but may need protection against black spot. The large blooms are cupped and there is a strong fruity aroma. A showy rose which is suitable for all but the coldest areas of the country.

Blooms: Double
Pink, blended yellow
Fragrant

Foliage: Dark green

Introduction: 1985

Type: English

Growth Type: Arching

Flowering Period: Repeat flowering

ANGELINA

A rounded bush which is quite small for a Shrub Rose. *Angelina* is suitable for planting at the front of the shrub border or as a hedge, but despite its good points and compact size it has not become popular. The blooms are borne in trusses, appearing regularly until early autumn. There are not many petals, but the slightly cupped blooms with their prominent stamens are most attractive. Growth is vigorous and healthy.

Blooms: Semi-double
Pink, white eye
Fragrant

Foliage: Light green

Introduction: 1975

Type: Modern Shrub

Growth Type: Bushy

Flowering Period: Repeat flowering

ARMADA

This Shrub Rose is noted for the long-lasting nature of its flowers. These blooms are borne in large trusses almost continually throughout the summer and into autumn, after which there is a display of showy hips. Disease resistance is good, which is what you would expect from a rose with *Silver Jubilee* as a parent. The leaves are glossy and growth is branching and upright, making *Armada* a good choice for hedging.

Blooms: Semi-double
Rose pink
Fragrant

Foliage: Dark green

Introduction: 1988

Type: Modern Shrub

Growth Type: Upright

Flowering Period: Repeat flowering

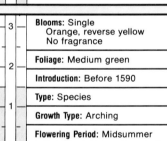

AUSTRIAN COPPER
Other Name: R. FOETIDA BICOLOR

Perhaps the brightest of all the wild roses — a superb sight in full bloom. Unfortunately the flowering season lasts for only a couple of weeks and for the rest of the summer the bush is rather dull and susceptible to black spot. The smell is neither strong nor pleasant. Some (but not all) experts believe it to be the original parent of all yellow H.Ts.

Blooms: Single
Orange, reverse yellow
No fragrance

Foliage: Medium green

Introduction: Before 1590

Type: Species

Growth Type: Arching

Flowering Period: Midsummer

BALLERINA

Masses of tiny flowers are borne in Hydrangea-like heads which appear all summer long. The bush bears an abundance of small glossy leaves, and this healthy variety is suitable for either the herbaceous border or rose bed. It can also be planted as a hedge or grown as a standard. There is a pleasant musk-like perfume and for lovers of *Ballerina* there is now a similar red variety (*Marjorie Fair*) available.

Blooms: Single
Pale pink, white eye
Slightly fragrant

Foliage: Light green

Introduction: 1937

Type: Modern Shrub

Growth Type: Bushy

Flowering Period: Repeat flowering

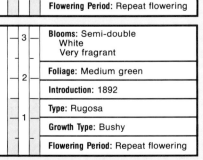

BLANC DOUBLE DE COUBERT

This old French-bred Shrub Rose remains popular. Its flowers are large and sweet-smelling, first appearing in June and continuing into the autumn. The great virtue is outstanding disease resistance, making spraying unnecessary. There are drawbacks — the papery petals are easily damaged by rain, the foliage is too sparse and the stem bases are too bare to make it either a reliable hedge or an attractive bush.

Blooms: Semi-double
White
Very fragrant

Foliage: Medium green

Introduction: 1892

Type: Rugosa

Growth Type: Bushy

Flowering Period: Repeat flowering

SHRUB ROSES

Blooms: Double / White / Fragrant	
Foliage: Dark green	
Introduction: 1880	
Type: Moss	
Growth Type: Upright	
Flowering Period: Midsummer	

BLANCHE MOREAU

Over a hundred years old and still one of the best of all Moss Roses. The white blooms are large and full with a green button centre, standing out against the dark and prickly stems. The buds are covered in brownish moss. The flowers appear in clusters in June — it is not repeat flowering but a few blooms may be produced in autumn. This Shrub Rose is suitable for use as a specimen bush or as a hedge.

Blooms: Double / Ivory / Very fragrant	
Foliage: Dark green	
Introduction: 1867	
Type: Bourbon	
Growth Type: Upright	
Flowering Period: Repeat flowering	

BOULE DE NEIGE

The English translation of the name of this French-bred Bourbon Rose is Snowball — and how appropriate it is. The red-tinged buds, borne in small clusters, open into white, ball-like blooms about 6 cm across. The petals are silky, the fragrance is strong — undoubtedly one of the best Bourbons you can buy. The main problem is balling in wet weather — black spot can also be a problem. May need support.

Blooms: Double / Pale apricot / Fragrant	
Foliage: Green, tinted purple	
Introduction: 1939	
Type: Hybrid Musk	
Growth Type: Arching	
Flowering Period: Repeat flowering	

BUFF BEAUTY

A deservedly popular Shrub Rose. The flowers are borne in large clusters, buff yellow at first then fading to a warm ivory. They are shapely in bud, but soon become confused and formless as they mature. *Buff Beauty* is a good choice for a hedge or for cutting — the perfume is pleasant and the foliage is attractive. The spreading branches will need spraying against mildew — if kept healthy, the autumn display is outstanding.

Blooms: Single / Yellow / Fragrant	
Foliage: Grey-green	
Introduction: After 1907	
Type: Species	
Growth Type: Arching	
Flowering Period: Late spring	

CANARY BIRD
Other Name: R. XANTHINA SPONTANEA

The popular choice for the rose to herald in the flowering season. In May the dainty yellow blooms appear in profusion along the arching stems. The period of flowering lasts for about a month. The ferny foliage makes an attractive bush when flowering is over. *Canary Bird* is good for hedging — grow it as a standard where space is limited. Die-back occasionally occurs.

Blooms: Double / Purple / Fragrant	
Foliage: Dark green	
Introduction: 1840	
Type: Gallica	
Growth Type: Bushy	
Flowering Period: Midsummer	

CARDINAL DE RICHELIEU

A reliable variety with an RHS Award of Garden Merit. It has an impressive list of virtues — the velvety purple blooms are borne in clusters on stems which are almost thorn-free and the foliage is both plentiful and healthy. The medium-sized flowers are sweetly fragrant and growth is compact. Grow this one in a pot, bed or as a hedge — its only fault is that like other Gallicas it only bears a single summer flush of flowers.

Blooms: Double / Shell pink / Slightly fragrant	
Foliage: Dark green	
Introduction: 1881	
Type: China	
Growth Type: Upright	
Flowering Period: Repeat flowering	

CECILE BRUNNER
Other Name: SWEETHEART ROSE

A hundred years old, but it remains a favourite in many gardens. You will still find it in some catalogues, for nothing has replaced the charm of the small bush bearing tiny pink flowers which are perfectly formed at the bud stage. Excellent for cutting or as a buttonhole rose — the clusters are large but the small leaves are sparse. Flowering is from June until October.

SHRUB ROSES

Height Width
in m in m

CELESTIAL
Other Names: CELESTE, MINDEN ROSE
Like all the Albas, *Celestial* is robust, hardy and easy to grow. It is free-flowering, the richly scented pink blooms appearing at the end of June to provide a midsummer display. The blooms have about 25 petals, opening to reveal the golden stamens within — a favourite old-fashioned variety which is excellent for hedging or as a tall specimen bush.

Blooms:	Semi-double Pale pink Very fragrant
Foliage:	Grey-green
Introduction:	Before 1800
Type:	Alba
Growth Type:	Upright
Flowering Period:	Midsummer

CHAPEAU DE NAPOLEON
Other Name: CRESTED MOSS
A Centifolia and not a true Moss Rose, despite its alternative common name. The blooms are full, globular and drooping with a pleasant old-fashioned perfume. The buds are unique — a winged extension gives the appearance of 'Napoleon's hat'. The bush is hardy and spreading. The stems may need support and protection from mildew.

Blooms:	Double Rose pink Fragrant
Foliage:	Medium green
Introduction:	1827
Type:	Centifolia
Growth Type:	Open
Flowering Period:	Midsummer

CHARLES DE MILLS
Other Name: BIZARRE TRIOMPHANT
An unusual and mysterious rose — no one knows where it came from. The blooms are large, full of wavy petals and flat when fully open. The colour is unique — wine red with white and pink blotches. The fragrance is also unique — *Charles de Mills* is a good choice if you want something different. The flower heads are heavy and the stems may need some support.

Blooms:	Double Deep red Fragrant
Foliage:	Dark green
Introduction:	Unknown
Type:	Gallica
Growth Type:	Bushy
Flowering Period:	Midsummer

CHINATOWN
Other Name: VILLE DE CHINE
A popular large bush rose — you will find it in either the Floribunda or Shrub section of the catalogue. The fragrant flowers will withstand rainy weather and the bush is healthy and tolerant of exposed situations. The flowers are borne in large trusses and appear freely throughout the season — a good choice for hedging, the back of the border or as a specimen bush.

Blooms:	Double Yellow, flushed pink Fragrant
Foliage:	Light green
Introduction:	1963
Type:	Modern Shrub
Growth Type:	Upright
Flowering Period:	Repeat flowering

CLAIRE ROSE
Claire Rose is a vigorous shrub from the David Austin stable. The shrub bears a dense cover of large leaves above which are the old-fashioned flowers. These are big blooms with many reflexed petals — cup-shaped at first and then flat rosettes when fully opened. The colour is an attractive pale pink but this fades to off-white with age. A fine sight on a sunny day, but rather bedraggled in wet weather.

Blooms:	Double Blush pink Slightly fragrant
Foliage:	Light green
Introduction:	1986
Type:	English
Growth Type:	Upright
Flowering Period:	Repeat flowering

COMMON MOSS
Other Name: R. CENTIFOLIA MUSCOSA
The original and perhaps the best of the Moss Roses, sometimes called *Old Pink Moss*. The medium-sized, globular blooms open flat when mature, appearing in June or July. Both buds and stems bear green moss and this variety has a distinctly old-fashioned look. It is suitable for the smaller garden, where it can be used as a hedge or as a specimen bush. Keep watch for mildew.

Blooms:	Double Rose pink Fragrant
Foliage:	Medium green
Introduction:	About 1700
Type:	Moss
Growth Type:	Shrubby
Flowering Period:	Midsummer

SHRUB ROSES

Blooms:	Single
	Pink, white eye
	Slightly fragrant
Foliage:	Light green
Introduction:	Unknown
Type:	Gallica
Growth Type:	Arching
Flowering Period:	Midsummer

COMPLICATA
Other Name: R. GALLICA COMPLICATA

The outstanding feature of this age-old variety is the size of the blooms which appear in June — 10 cm or more across, single and with a pleasant if not strong perfume. The stems bearing these blooms are long and lax, and this variety is best grown next to an old tree so that it can clamber upwards without artificial support. It is easily rooted from cuttings.

Blooms:	Double
	Deep pink
	Very fragrant
Foliage:	Grey-green
Introduction:	1860
Type:	Portland
Growth Type:	Bushy
Flowering Period:	Repeat flowering

COMTE DE CHAMBORD

This Portland Rose is a good advertisement for old-fashioned roses. It is reasonably compact and it flowers almost continuously all season long. The large blooms have a mass of frilly-tipped petals and they are borne in clusters well above the leaves. The fragrance of the flowers is strong and sweet and the stem growth is vigorous. The RHS Award of Garden Merit underlines its reliability as a bedding and hedging rose.

Blooms:	Double
	Pink
	Fragrant
Foliage:	Grey-green
Introduction:	1961
Type:	English
Growth Type:	Bushy
Flowering Period:	Midsummer

CONSTANCE SPRY

This is a big eye-catching rose which can be kept head-high by pruning but is perhaps better grown as a Climber when it can reach 4 m or more. The flowers are both large and full and are borne in clusters on thorny stems. The fragrance is spicy and it is more tolerant of shade and poor soil than most roses. However, there is only a single flush in June and you will need to spray to prevent the onset of mildew.

Blooms:	Double
	Pink, tinted apricot
	Fragrant
Foliage:	Dark green, tinted bronze
Introduction:	1925
Type:	Hybrid Musk
Growth Type:	Spreading
Flowering Period:	Repeat flowering

CORNELIA

Grow *Cornelia* as a hedge — if you have lots of space you can grow it as a specimen bush. It is recognised by the unusually dark appearance of its stems and leaves plus the clusters of small and fragrant pink flowers which first appear in June. These blooms are resistant to rain, and the best floral display occurs in autumn. The large trusses and free-flowering habit make *Cornelia* a popular Shrub Rose.

Blooms:	Double
	Pink
	Slightly fragrant
Foliage:	Medium green
Introduction:	1991
Type:	English
Growth Type:	Bushy
Flowering Period:	Repeat flowering

COTTAGE ROSE

This variety is listed in numerous catalogues but it has no special virtue which makes it stand out from other English Roses. It is reasonably compact and can be grown in a pot and it is well-clothed with leaves. The medium-sized blooms are open-cupped and are borne more or less continually throughout the summer. The stems branch freely and the fragrance is pleasant. A good but not outstanding rose.

Blooms:	Semi-double
	Orange red
	Slightly fragrant
Foliage:	Medium green
Introduction:	1960
Type:	Modern Shrub
Growth Type:	Upright
Flowering Period:	Repeat flowering

DOROTHY WHEATCROFT

Its glory is the profusion of large heads of bright flowers on long stems, so large that they often bow down under their own weight, so some support may be necessary. Rain resistance is good despite the size of the flowers, but spraying is essential if you live in a black spot area. Fragrance is unfortunately very slight. An RHS Gold Medal winner but it is an exhibition rose rather than a bedding one.

SHRUB ROSES

Height Width
in m in m

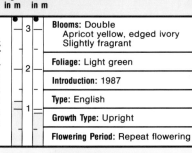

ENGLISH GARDEN

English Garden grows as a neat and compact bush. The blooms are large and are made up of many small petals which are a warm buff yellow at the centre and progressively paler towards the edges. When open the flowers are flat and quartered — a truly old-fashioned look for a modern rose. The perfume is not strong — if you like English Roses it would be better to buy one with an old-fashioned fragrance.

Blooms: Double
Apricot yellow, edged ivory
Slightly fragrant

Foliage: Light green

Introduction: 1987

Type: English

Growth Type: Upright

Flowering Period: Repeat flowering

EVELYN

An English Rose like the one above. Both have large double flowers and the basic colour is apricot, but there are several differences. *Evelyn* flowers have a richer colour and the fragrance is much more pronounced. The shape of the bloom is open-cupped and not a flat rosette like *English Garden*, and the abundant foliage is darker than its rival. A good rose which has *Graham Thomas* as a parent.

Blooms: Double
Bright apricot
Very fragrant

Foliage: Medium green

Introduction: 1991

Type: English

Growth Type: Bushy

Flowering Period: Repeat flowering

FANTIN-LATOUR

The experts sing the praises of this Centifolia and it is not surprising that it received an Award of Garden Merit from the RHS. It is abundantly clothed with glossy foliage and the clusters of flowers are borne in great profusion. There is a single flush in June when the plant is covered in large blooms packed with petals. These blooms are flat when fully open and the perfume is both sweet and strong.

Blooms: Double
Blush pink
Fragrant

Foliage: Dark green

Introduction: 1900

Type: Centifolia

Growth Type: Upright

Flowering Period: Midsummer

FELICIA

A Hybrid Musk which is noted for its long flowering season — the first sweet-smelling blooms appear in June and flowering continues throughout the summer. The best display is in the autumn and flowers are still found on the wide-spreading bushes in November. The blooms are shapely, like a Hybrid Tea, and are borne in large trusses. Excellent for cutting, *Felicia* makes a good hedge or specimen bush.

Blooms: Double
Pink, edged pale pink
Fragrant

Foliage: Dark green

Introduction: 1928

Type: Hybrid Musk

Growth Type: Shrubby

Flowering Period: Repeat flowering

FERDINAND PICHARD

Ferdinand Pichard is one of the best striped roses you can buy as it has a basketful of virtues. The glossy leaves are healthy and abundant, the blooms are large, full of petals and fragrant, and the shrubby bush has an attractive shape. The prime display is in June when the plant is clothed in flowers — regular dead-heading and a sunny location will ensure a succession of flushes until autumn.

Blooms: Double
White, striped pink and red
Fragrant

Foliage: Medium green

Introduction: 1921

Type: Hybrid Perpetual

Growth Type: Bushy

Flowering Period: Repeat flowering

FISHERMAN'S FRIEND

Many English Roses have appeared during the past few decades — this one has not achieved the popularity of its widely-grown relatives such as *Gertrude Jekyll* and *Graham Thomas*. It still has some noteworthy points, such as strong fragrance and showy crimson flowers. These blooms are large and full, but black spot can be a problem. Grow it in a bed or pot — also good as a low hedge.

Blooms: Double
Rich red
Very fragrant

Foliage: Medium green

Introduction: 1987

Type: English

Growth Type: Bushy

Flowering Period: Repeat flowering

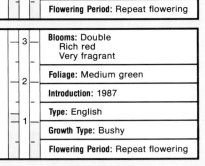

SHRUB ROSES

Blooms:	Double Crimson No fragrance
Foliage:	Light green
Introduction:	1918
Type:	Rugosa
Growth Type:	Bushy
Flowering Period:	Repeat flowering

F.J. GROOTENDORST
Other Name: NELKENROSE

In most ways this Shrub has very little to offer. There is neither fragrance nor hips, and the flowers are small and rather dull. The foliage is pale and small, although it is attractive in the autumn months. The unique feature of *F.J. Grootendorst* is the distinct frill at the edge of the petals, giving a Carnation-like effect. Like all Rugosas, it is reliable under poor conditions.

Blooms:	Single Shell pink Fragrant
Foliage:	Dark green
Introduction:	1914
Type:	Rugosa
Growth Type:	Bushy
Flowering Period:	Repeat flowering

FRAU DAGMAR HARTOPP
Other Name: FRU DAGMAR HASTRUP

Frau Dagmar Hartopp lacks the height of many of the Rugosas, but it is considered by many experts to be one of the best. It has all the good properties of the group — freedom from disease, continuous flowering, blooms which are attractive and scented, and finally hips which are red and large. The bush will grow almost anywhere and is ideal as a low-growing hedge.

Blooms:	Double White No fragrance
Foliage:	Medium green
Introduction:	1901
Type:	Hybrid Perpetual
Growth Type:	Upright
Flowering Period:	Repeat flowering

FRAU KARL DRUSCHKI
Other Name: SNOW QUEEN

Frau Karl Druschki appeared about a century ago, but it is still going strong and is widely offered for sale. Its everlasting appeal is at first surprising — there is no scent and no resistance to mildew. But its virtues can be seen in a large garden — a stately bush covered with masses of pure white blooms opening from red-splashed buds. Prune lightly — peg down long shoots.

Blooms:	Single Orange vermilion Fragrant
Foliage:	Light green
Introduction:	1967
Type:	Modern Shrub
Growth Type:	Upright
Flowering Period:	Repeat flowering

FRED LOADS

This variety has become really popular, even though it has only five petals. The reason is that it makes up for its shortage of petals with bright colouring and huge trusses which can exceed 45 cm across. The flowers are large and unfading, and the bush is well-clothed with leaves. Healthy and vigorous, *Fred Loads* is an excellent choice, although it can look rather top heavy in full flower.

Blooms:	Double Pink Slightly fragrant
Foliage:	Grey-green
Introduction:	1940
Type:	Modern Shrub
Growth Type:	Bushy
Flowering Period:	Midsummer

FRITZ NOBIS

A big and very vigorous shrub which is covered with masses of medium-sized blooms in June. The flowering period is long but there is only one flush. The fragrance is described as spicy. *Fritz Nobis* is recommended as a specimen bush where the large healthy leaves, summer floral display and then the abundant orange hips in autumn can serve as a focal point in a bed or border. It is also a good hedging rose.

Blooms:	Semi-double Yellow Fragrant
Foliage:	Light green
Introduction:	1937
Type:	Scots
Growth Type:	Arching
Flowering Period:	Early summer

FRÜHLINGSGOLD
Other Name: SPRING GOLD

Kordes bred a number of splendid hybrids from *R. pimpinellifolia*, the Scots Briar. *Frühlingsgold* is perhaps the finest — a mature bush in full flower in May is one of the great sights of the rose world. The arching branches are festooned with saucer-sized flowers, and the air is filled with fragrance. The flowering period lasts for only a fortnight, and ample space is essential.

SHRUB ROSES

	Height in m	Width in m

FRÜHLINGSMORGEN
Other Name: SPRING MORNING

Another Kordesii hybrid, smaller and bushier than its yellow sister described on the previous page. The small-leaved Shrub is not particularly attractive, but the flowers are — large, scented and colourful. The pale centre of each pink-edged petal highlights the maroon stamens. The second flush of flowers in September is smaller and not as prolific as the early summer flush.

Blooms: Single
Deep pink, yellow centre
Fragrant
Foliage: Grey-green
Introduction: 1942
Type: Scots
Growth Type: Upright
Flowering Period: June & September

GERTRUDE JEKYLL

This English Rose has become very popular and is listed in many catalogues. The features which have caught the public fancy are the strong old-fashioned perfume, the colourful buds and the clusters of large, rosette-shaped blooms. *Gertrude Jekyll* is indeed an eye-catching rose when in full flower, but the bush can sometimes look gaunt rather than well-rounded. The ideal site is the back of the border.

Blooms: Double
Pink
Very fragrant
Foliage: Dark green
Introduction: 1986
Type: English
Growth Type: Upright
Flowering Period: Repeat flowering

GIPSY BOY
Other Name: ZIGEUNERKNABE

Gipsy Boy received an Award of Garden Merit from the RHS. This large shrub is a fine sight in June when its dark-petalled blooms open to reveal the golden stamens within. The flowers are sweetly perfumed and the plant is both hardy and reliable. The only drawback is that the arching stems may need support when grown as a shrub — can be used as a pillar rose.

Blooms: Double
Crimson purple
Fragrant
Foliage: Medium green
Introduction: 1909
Type: Bourbon
Growth Type: Lax
Flowering Period: Midsummer

GOLDEN WINGS

A popular and highly praised variety, perhaps the best of all the large-flowered yellow Shrub Roses. From June onwards the blooms appear in regular flushes provided the old flowers are dead-headed. The flowers are large and sweet-smelling — light primrose with prominent buff yellow stamens. These blooms are not damaged by rain, but they do fade slightly with age. Disease resistance is good — an excellent choice.

Blooms: Single or semi-double
Pale yellow
Fragrant
Foliage: Light green
Introduction: 1956
Type: Scots
Growth Type: Bushy
Flowering Period: Repeat flowering

GRAHAM THOMAS

This English Rose was named after a leading authority on old-fashioned roses and is one of the best-selling Shrub varieties. Nearly everything about it is unusual. There is the colour — almost unique amongst blooms with an old-fashioned look. Then there is the fragrance — tea-like rather than sweet. Each flower has the form of a Paeony and the flowering season extends from early summer to late autumn.

Blooms: Double
Deep yellow
Fragrant
Foliage: Dark green
Introduction: 1983
Type: English
Growth Type: Arching
Flowering Period: Repeat flowering

HERITAGE

Like *Graham Thomas* this English Rose has *Iceberg* for a parent and so both are robust and free-flowering. They differ somewhat in growth habit — *Heritage* is rather upright whereas *Graham Thomas* is more open and arching. In addition the form of the bloom is not the same — the flowers of *Heritage* are more distinctly cup-shaped. *Heritage* has a good reputation for continuous flowering until autumn.

Blooms: Double
Pale pink
Very fragrant
Foliage: Dark green
Introduction: 1984
Type: English
Growth Type: Upright
Flowering Period: Repeat flowering

SHRUB ROSES

Blooms: Double Pink Fragrant
Foliage: Medium green
Introduction: Before 1832
Type: Damask
Growth Type: Upright
Flowering Period: Midsummer

ISPAHAN
Other Name: POMPON DES PRINCES

Ispahan blooms just once during summer, but the length of the flowering period is outstanding and lasts for many weeks. This old variety is a good choice for the back of the border — both foliage and the red buds are attractive, and the large blooms have a quartered pattern when fully open. *Ispahan* holds the RHS Award of Garden Merit.

Blooms: Semi-double Ivory white Very fragrant
Foliage: Dark green
Introduction: 1989
Type: Modern Shrub
Growth Type: Bushy
Flowering Period: Repeat flowering

JACQUELINE DU PRE

The outstanding feature of this modern variety raised by Harkness is the length of the flowering period. The first buds open to reveal off-white petals and deep orange stamens in late May and flowers continue to appear with little gaps between the flushes until the first frosts of autumn. It is a healthy bush which bears abundant foliage. *Jacqueline du Pré* is regarded as one of the best of the newer Shrub Roses.

Blooms: Double Rose pink Fragrant
Foliage: Medium green
Introduction: 1868
Type: Portland
Growth Type: Upright
Flowering Period: Repeat flowering

JACQUES CARTIER
Other Name: MARQUISE BOCCELLA

This old rose is not as strongly perfumed as its fellow pink Portland *Comte de Chambord* but it is still rated to be one of the best of all Shrub Roses. The flat blooms are made up of numerous short scalloped petals — the buds are red and the shrub is leafy. It is recommended for cutting and for growing in a pot as well as for bed and border.

Blooms: Semi-double Yellow, edged red Slightly fragrant
Foliage: Dark green
Introduction: 1964
Type: Modern Shrub
Growth Type: Open
Flowering Period: Repeat flowering

JOSEPH'S COAT

Seen at its best in June or July, this modern variety bears medium-sized blooms in large trusses. The petals change from yellow to orange and finally to cherry red as they age. This bright but gaudy variety can be trained as a climber, reaching 3 m high, or it can be grown as a hedge or 2 m specimen shrub. It can also be kept pruned as a 1.2 m bush for the small garden, but it is happiest when grown as a shrub.

Blooms: Double Pink Very fragrant
Foliage: Grey-green
Introduction: 1826
Type: Alba
Growth Type: Upright
Flowering Period: Midsummer

KÖNIGIN VON DÄNEMARK
Other Name: QUEEN OF DENMARK

This sweet-smelling Alba is a handsome tall bush which bears medium-sized quartered blooms well above the foliage. When fully open these flowers have a rich pink centre and pale pink outer petals clustered around a green eye. It is thought to have some Damask blood and is highly regarded as a specimen shrub for a mixed border.

Blooms: Single Copper, yellow centre Very fragrant
Foliage: Dark green
Introduction: 1894
Type: Sweet Briar
Growth Type: Open
Flowering Period: Early summer

LADY PENZANCE

R. eglanteria (the Sweet Briar or Eglantine Rose) is a wild English rose with a most unusual property — the foliage emits an apple-like odour after rain. The best hybrid for the ordinary garden is *Lady Penzance* which blooms in early June. The flowers are small and the flowering period lasts for only a week or two — this variety is grown for its fragrant foliage rather than for its blooms. Choose it if novelties appeal to you.

SHRUB ROSES

Height in m Width in m

LA REINE VICTORIA
Other Name: QUEEN VICTORIA

On seeing a photograph of a *La Reine Victoria* bloom you may be tempted to rush out and buy a bush. The flower is a warm pink and deeply cupped, looking like a rose in an old Dutch painting. Before buying one you should consider the drawbacks — this Bourbon Rose needs good soil and has little resistance to black spot. In addition the stems may need support.

Blooms: Double
  Pink
  Very fragrant
Foliage: Medium green
Introduction: 1872
Type: Bourbon
Growth Type: Lax
Flowering Period: Repeat flowering

LA SEVILLANA
Other Name: SEVILLANDA

This Meilland-bred rose is noted for the brightness of its red blooms and the lack of fading during the hot sunny days of summer. The free-flowering bush is quite wide-spreading, sometimes wider than it is tall, with the result that it is sometimes listed as a Ground Cover rather than a Shrub Rose. *La Sevillana* has good disease resistance.

Blooms: Semi-double
  Scarlet
  Slightly fragrant
Foliage: Dark green, tinted red
Introduction: 1982
Type: Modern Shrub
Growth Type: Shrubby
Flowering Period: Repeat flowering

L.D. BRAITHWAITE

L.D. Braithwaite is worth considering if you have room for just one English Rose and want something really eye-catching. The bright red blooms are very large and very full, appearing in large numbers on the spreading bushy plant. The perfume is strong and the flowers are rather flat when fully open. It is a daughter of *Mary Rose*, but the growth habit and flower colour are quite different.

Blooms: Double
  Crimson
  Very fragrant
Foliage: Grey-green
Introduction: 1988
Type: English
Growth Type: Bushy
Flowering Period: Repeat flowering

LITTLE WHITE PET
Other Name: WHITE PET

An old Polyantha Rose — like *The Fairy* it keeps its place in numerous catalogues despite the superior blooms of the modern Floribundas. The flowers are indeed small and pompon-like, but they are borne in huge trusses throughout the summer months. Plant it as a standard or grow the bushes in groups of 3 or 4 in the border. An excellent choice for a small old-world garden.

Blooms: Double
  White
  Slightly fragrant
Foliage: Dark green
Introduction: 1879
Type: Polyantha
Growth Type: Bushy
Flowering Period: Repeat flowering

LOUISE ODIER
Other Name: MADAME DE STELLA

The very full blooms of this Bourbon Rose are often described as Camellia-like, opening when mature to reveal the stamens within. The blooms are large and the trusses bear so many flowers that the stems are often bowed down by their weight. Some support may be necessary, especially in wet weather. *Louise Odier* is sometimes grown as a short Climber.

Blooms: Double
  Rose pink
  Fragrant
Foliage: Medium green
Introduction: 1851
Type: Bourbon
Growth Type: Upright
Flowering Period: Repeat flowering

MADAME HARDY

A lovely old-fashioned rose — full of petals and fragrance. *Madame Hardy* is a Damask Rose, with the non-glossy foliage and lax stems which characterize the group. The green-eyed blooms are borne in large clusters during June or July. Considered by some to be the most beautiful of all white Shrub Rose blooms, they are certainly not the hardiest. Both rain and strong winds damage them and stems may need support.

Blooms: Double
  White
  Fragrant
Foliage: Medium green
Introduction: 1832
Type: Damask
Growth Type: Open
Flowering Period: Midsummer

Height Width
in m in m

Blooms:	Double Deep pink Very fragrant
Foliage:	Medium green
Introduction:	1881
Type:	Bourbon
Growth Type:	Open
Flowering Period:	Repeat flowering

MADAME ISAAC PEREIRE

Pity the poor novice who seeks advice from the experts about this Bourbon Rose. For most of them this old-fashioned variety is a joy — huge flowers with a fragrance which is probably unmatched by any other shrub. To others it is an ugly plant with unattractive foliage and with flowers which are sometimes misshapen... and both sides are telling the truth. The stems need support — it can be grown as a pillar rose.

Blooms:	Double Silver pink, marked red Very fragrant
Foliage:	Medium green
Introduction:	1878
Type:	Bourbon
Growth Type:	Lax
Flowering Period:	Repeat flowering

MADAME PIERRE OGER

The flowers are not large and the growth is not very vigorous, but the cupped, sweet-smelling blooms are borne in attractive clusters. It is a sport of *La Reine Victoria* from which it inherits the shape of the blooms and its fragrance, but it has also the susceptibility to black spot and the weak stems of its parent. It is a good choice if you want to have beautiful old-fashioned blooms, but not if you want a trouble-free shrub.

Blooms:	Double Pale pink Very fragrant
Foliage:	Grey-green
Introduction:	Before 1500
Type:	Alba
Growth Type:	Upright
Flowering Period:	Midsummer

MAIDEN'S BLUSH
Other Name: CUISSE DE NYMPHE

This age-old Alba is a real beauty. There is a single flush of flowers in late June — an eye-catching display of abundant sweet-smelling blooms. It grows strongly and is often tall enough to be regarded as a pillar rose. The attractive foliage has excellent disease resistance. In some catalogues you will find the more compact *Maiden's Blush Small*.

Blooms:	Semi-double Pink, shaded deep pink Slightly fragrant
Foliage:	Medium green
Introduction:	1959
Type:	Modern Shrub
Growth Type:	Arching
Flowering Period:	June & September

MARGUERITE HILLING
Other Name: PINK NEVADA

A sport of the popular shrub *Nevada*. It is identical to its parent in many ways — the same growth habit, foliage and size. It is, however, more free-flowering and the blooms are pale pink overlaid with a deeper shade of pink. The whole base can be covered by the first flush of blooms in June. The leaves are small and dull, and black spot can be a problem.

Blooms:	Single Red, white eye No fragrance
Foliage:	Light green
Introduction:	1978
Type:	Modern Shrub
Growth Type:	Bushy
Flowering Period:	Repeat flowering

MARJORIE FAIR
Other Name: RED BALLERINA

This variety is a hybrid of *Ballerina* and *Baby Faurax*. It inherited its carmine flower colour from neither of its parents, but all its growth characteristics come from *Ballerina*. Here you will find the same large heads of tiny flowers, the mass of glossy leaves and the freedom from disease. It has won awards in several countries, but it is not really a best-seller.

Blooms:	Double Deep pink Fragrant
Foliage:	Medium green
Introduction:	1983
Type:	English
Growth Type:	Bushy
Flowering Period:	Repeat flowering

MARY ROSE

There was a flood of English Roses in the late 1980s and the 1990s, so this 1983 rose is one of the earlier ones. It has still remained popular and you will find it in many catalogues. Its main appeal is the truly old-fashioned look of its flowers — they are large, very full and attractively cupped with pink petals which deepen in colour at the centre. Good for less-than-perfect soil — recommended as a reliable and robust rose.

SHRUB ROSES

Height | Width
in m | in m

MOONLIGHT

This near-white Hybrid Musk was raised by Rev. Pemberton before he got round to introducing the much more popular *Penelope*. *Moonlight* has smaller flowers than its more illustrious sister and there are fewer petals, but it is less prone to mildew. The flowers are borne in large clusters on long reddish stems and at the heart of each bloom is a boss of golden stamens. It will grow in partial shade.

Blooms: Semi-double
Pale yellow
Fragrant

Foliage: Green, tinted red

Introduction: 1913

Type: Hybrid Musk

Growth Type: Bushy

Flowering Period: Repeat flowering

NEVADA

Nevada is one of the great sights of the rose world. In June the whole bush is covered with large creamy white blooms. When mature and well-grown both the small leaves and thornless red stems may be almost completely hidden. Space is essential — trying to keep the bush small by hard pruning leads to disappointing results. If black spot is a problem in your area, regular spraying will be necessary.

Blooms: Semi-double
Creamy white
Slightly fragrant

Foliage: Medium green

Introduction: 1927

Type: Modern Shrub

Growth Type: Arching

Flowering Period: June & September

OLD BLUSH
Other Names: OLD BLUSH CHINA, MONTHLY ROSE

One of the best of the China Roses and the ancestor of many modern varieties. It blooms from June until October and it is claimed that in favourable sites it may be in flower in winter. These blooms are medium-sized and are on stems which are almost thorn-free. One major drawback — it is not fully hardy.

Blooms: Semi-double
Pale pink, flushed crimson
Slightly fragrant

Foliage: Dark green

Introduction: 1789

Type: China

Growth Type: Upright

Flowering Period: Repeat flowering

PENELOPE

Several Hybrid Musks are described in this section, and *Penelope* is easily the most popular. It can be grown in almost every garden. Left unpruned it will produce a large spreading shrub — regularly pruned it can be grown as a 1 m bush. It also makes an excellent hedge. Large clusters of pale flowers cover the bush in June — deadhead regularly to ensure that later blooms will appear in early autumn.

Blooms: Semi-double
Shell pink
Fragrant

Foliage: Green, tinted bronze

Introduction: 1924

Type: Hybrid Musk

Growth Type: Bushy

Flowering Period: Repeat flowering

PERLE D'OR
Other Name: YELLOW CECILE BRUNNER

A close relative of *Cécile Brunner*, hence its age-old alternative name. The tiny buds are pointed and classically shaped, opening into miniature flowers which are apricot at first but turn almost white with age. Excellent for cutting for indoor use — use it outdoors for bedding rather than as a specimen shrub. Growth is more robust than *Cécile Brunner*.

Blooms: Double
Apricot
Fragrant

Foliage: Dark green

Introduction: 1884

Type: China

Growth Type: Open

Flowering Period: Repeat flowering

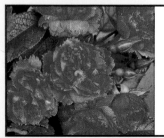

PINK GROOTENDORST

A sport of *F.J. Grootendorst*, with a little more to offer. The novelty of the frilled petals remains, but the colour is much more attractive. The blooms are highly recommended for display as a cut flower. As with its parent, the bush is not attractive but it is tough and hardy. A good choice for hedging in cold and windswept areas — the clusters of small flowers appear throughout summer and autumn.

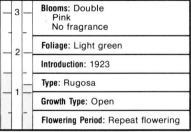

Blooms: Double
Pink
No fragrance

Foliage: Light green

Introduction: 1923

Type: Rugosa

Growth Type: Open

Flowering Period: Repeat flowering

SHRUB ROSES

Blooms:	Double Cream Fragrant
Foliage:	Dark green
Introduction:	1919
Type:	Hybrid Musk
Growth Type:	Bushy
Flowering Period:	Repeat flowering

PROSPERITY

Each individual flower of this Hybrid Musk is not large, but the flower clusters bear so many blooms that the stems bend downwards to give an arching effect when in full flower. Flowering begins rather late in the season, but repeats well until the autumn. The young flowers are beautifully shaped before opening wide when mature to reveal the stamens within. Good for hedging and bedding.

Blooms:	Semi-double Pale crimson Fragrant
Foliage:	Medium green
Introduction:	Before 1300
Type:	Gallica
Growth Type:	Bushy
Flowering Period:	Midsummer

ROSA GALLICA OFFICINALIS
Other Name: APOTHECARY'S ROSE

One of the most ancient roses still grown in our gardens, this original Red Rose of Lancaster is the ancestor of many of today's red H.Ts and Floribundas. In June or July clusters of pale red flowers appear, followed by small round hips. It is available from many rose suppliers, and it can be grown in an average-sized garden. You will have to spray to keep mildew under control.

Blooms:	Single Yellow Slightly fragrant
Foliage:	Grey-green
Introduction:	1899
Type:	Species
Growth Type:	Arching
Flowering Period:	Late spring

ROSA HUGONIS
Other Name: GOLDEN ROSE OF CHINA

A popular wild rose, rather like *Canary Bird* when not in flower. The stems are arching, the leaves are ferny and the bush has a graceful appearance. The flowers appear in May, and have the annoying habit of often remaining half closed. *R. hugonis* is subject to die-back, especially after a hard winter, and so it is better to choose *Canary Bird* or *R. cantabrigiensis*.

Blooms:	Single Scarlet No fragrance
Foliage:	Medium green
Introduction:	1938
Type:	Species
Growth Type:	Arching
Flowering Period:	Early summer

ROSA MOYESII GERANIUM
Other Name: GERANIUM

The wild rose *R. moyesii*, grown for its beautiful red flowers and spectacular hips, is a gaunt giant. It is better to grow the variety *Geranium* — smaller, more compact and with orange red, flagon-shaped hips which are even better than those on the wild variety. The bright red flowers appear among the small leaves in May or June — the 5 cm long hips appear later.

Blooms:	Semi-double Pale pink, striped crimson Slightly fragrant
Foliage:	Medium green
Introduction:	Before 1500
Type:	Gallica
Growth Type:	Upright
Flowering Period:	Midsummer

ROSA MUNDI
Other Name: R. GALLICA VERSICOLOR

By far the most popular of the Gallica Roses, *Rosa Mundi* is a novelty which is more than 400 years old. The small flowers are distinctly striped and they appear on the twiggy, upright bushes for about a month in June or July. Like all Gallicas, this variety will succeed in poor soil but regular spraying against mildew will be necessary. The bushes sucker freely from the base.

Blooms:	Single Pink Slightly fragrant
Foliage:	Grey-green, tinted purple
Introduction:	Before 1830
Type:	Species
Growth Type:	Arching
Flowering Period:	Midsummer

ROSA RUBRIFOLIA
Other Name: R. GLAUCA

A wild rose of central Europe, grown in our gardens for the beauty of its foliage. These leaves have a purplish bloom and the stems are practically free from thorns — a favourite material for flower arrangers. The small flowers are insignificant and short-lived, but the clusters of dark red hips are highly decorative. If space is limited, keep in check by pruning.

SHRUB ROSES

Height in m | Width in m

ROSA RUGOSA ALBA

A typical Rugosa Rose — wrinkled disease-free leaves, fragrant blooms, attractive hips and an iron constitution. *R. rugosa alba* produces large flowers which appear throughout the summer and autumn months, and the orange red tomato-like hips are very large. It forms an attractive hedge, the dense foliage turning gold in the autumn. It can also be grown as a specimen bush, but it must never be hard pruned.

Blooms: Single White Fragrant
Foliage: Light green
Introduction: 1870
Type: Rugosa
Growth Type: Bushy
Flowering Period: Repeat flowering

ROSA RUGOSA SCABROSA
Other Name: SCABROSA

A rival to *Roseraie de L'Haÿ* as the best Rugosa Rose. Both are remarkably healthy, hardy and bear large fragrant flowers. *Scabrosa* scores by producing tomato red hips in the autumn. Flowering begins at the end of spring and continues well into the autumn. Excellent as a hedge or specimen bush — choose it if you do not have the room for its rival.

Blooms: Single Magenta pink Very fragrant
Foliage: Dark green
Introduction: 1950
Type: Rugosa
Growth Type: Bushy
Flowering Period: Repeat flowering

ROSA SERICEA PTERACANTHA
Other Name: WINGED THORN ROSE

A tall impenetrable shrub with a number of unusual features. The small white flowers which appear fleetingly in early June are four-petalled, and the leaves are ferny. The most unusual and decorative features are the thorns on young wood — large and triangular with 2.5 cm red bases. Another unusual feature is the need for regular pruning to ensure a supply of new wood.

Blooms: Single White No fragrance
Foliage: Light green
Introduction: 1890
Type: Species
Growth Type: Bushy
Flowering Period: Early summer

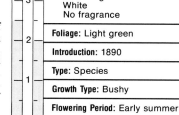
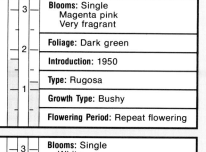

ROSERAIE DE L'HAŸ

One of the best of the Rugosas, and one of the best Shrub Roses for hedging. The plant is densely clothed with tough foliage which remains free from disease. It will grow in poor soil, salt-laden air and in exposed sites. Its toughness, however, is not reflected in its blooms — large, velvety and sweetly scented. Flowering is prolific — its only fault compared with other Rugosas is the lack of hips.

Blooms: Double Wine red Fragrant
Foliage: Dark green
Introduction: 1901
Type: Rugosa
Growth Type: Bushy
Flowering Period: Repeat flowering

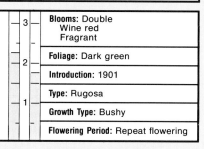

SALLY HOLMES

Two outstanding Shrub Roses (*Sally Holmes* and *Fred Loads*) were raised by the amateur rose breeder R.A. Holmes. This one is quite distinctive — the large open flowers are borne on tall clusters which stand above the foliage. An unusual Delphinium-like effect for a rose, and the catalogue description has made this variety increasingly popular. Take care — it is temperamental and needs wind protection.

Blooms: Single Creamy white, tinged pink Fragrant
Foliage: Dark green
Introduction: 1976
Type: Modern Shrub
Growth Type: Upright
Flowering Period: Repeat flowering

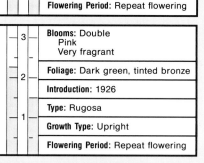

SARAH VAN FLEET

The large cupped flowers are borne in clusters. Like all Rugosa Roses it is recommended for hedging — the flowers are sweetly scented and the foliage is dense. An added advantage is that *Sarah Van Fleet* is one of the earliest roses to flower — a distinct benefit if you like to beat your neighbours. Unlike some other early bloomers, the show goes on — the soft pink flowers appear continuously during summer.

Blooms: Double Pink Very fragrant
Foliage: Dark green, tinted bronze
Introduction: 1926
Type: Rugosa
Growth Type: Upright
Flowering Period: Repeat flowering

SHRUB ROSES

Blooms:	Single
	Red
	Fragrant
Foliage:	Medium green
Introduction:	1952
Type:	Gallica
Growth Type:	Open
Flowering Period:	Midsummer

SCARLET FIRE
Other Name: SCHARLACHGLUT

You won't miss this one when it is in full flower. The massive bush has an open growth habit and the arching stems bear large velvety flowers. The colour is bright red and in the centre of each bloom there are prominent golden stamens. The flask-shaped hips are orange. The floral display is quite prolonged — choose this one only if you have lots of space.

Blooms:	Semi-double
	White
	Slightly fragrant
Foliage:	Dark green
Introduction:	1912
Type:	Rugosa
Growth Type:	Spreading
Flowering Period:	Repeat flowering

SCHNEEZWERG
Other Name: SNOW DWARF

The smallest of the Rugosa Roses, and not the most attractive. The scent is weak, and the foliage is dull and uninteresting. The flowering season, however, is excellent — from late May until the end of autumn the white Anemone-like blooms appear. In autumn new flowers open among the small scarlet hips, but the foliage does not take on the autumn colours of other Rugosas.

Blooms:	Double
	Blush pink
	Fragrant
Foliage:	Medium green
Introduction:	1989
Type:	English
Growth Type:	Upright
Flowering Period:	Repeat flowering

SHARIFA ASMA

There is nothing gaudy about this English Rose. It grows quite strongly but the bush is both short and compact — a good choice where space is limited. The blooms are cupped at first but open to a flat rosette, the pale pink petals fading to almost pure white at the reflexed edges of the flower. The large blooms have many petals and a pleasant fragrance — "all that an Old Rose should be", according to the raiser.

Blooms:	Double
	White, flushed pink
	Very fragrant
Foliage:	Medium green
Introduction:	1843
Type:	Bourbon
Growth Type:	Bushy
Flowering Period:	Repeat flowering

SOUVENIR DE LA MALMAISON

A thing of beauty in the catalogues and quite spectacular in the garden if the conditions are right. The large spicy-scented blooms are full of petals and they are distinctly quartered when fully open. Unfortunately it has its problems. The heavy flowers hang their heads and look bedraggled in wet weather and spraying against mildew is usually necessary. Flowering begins late in the season.

Blooms:	Double
	Pale pink
	Very fragrant
Foliage:	Grey-green
Introduction:	1838
Type:	Scots
Growth Type:	Arching
Flowering Period:	Repeat flowering

STANWELL PERPETUAL

Very prickly, as you would expect from a rose with *Rosa pimpinellifolia* as one of its parents. A large straggly bush, useful as a pillar rose. The leaves are unusually small, numerous and often discoloured — the flowers are medium-sized and fade from pink to white. Nobody is quite sure about its parentage — it appeared in an Essex garden more than 150 years ago. Notable features are the scent and the continuity of flowering.

Blooms:	Double
	Deep red
	Very fragrant
Foliage:	Dark green
Introduction:	1991
Type:	English
Growth Type:	Spreading
Flowering Period:	Repeat flowering

THE DARK LADY

There are a number of English Roses described in this Shrub section — each with its own special character. Perhaps it is this one which illustrates best of all the objective of these old-world lookalikes. The large flat blooms are a rich crimson colour and the petals are loosely arranged — the image is of a flower in an old Dutch painting, but it is a rose of the 1990s. The bush is low and spreading.

SHRUB ROSES

Height in m Width in m

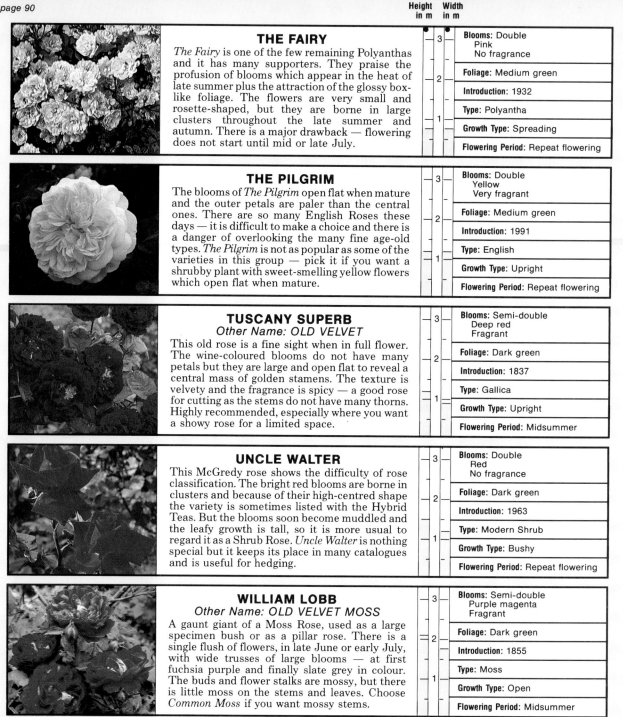

THE FAIRY

The Fairy is one of the few remaining Polyanthas and it has many supporters. They praise the profusion of blooms which appear in the heat of late summer plus the attraction of the glossy box-like foliage. The flowers are very small and rosette-shaped, but they are borne in large clusters throughout the late summer and autumn. There is a major drawback — flowering does not start until mid or late July.

Blooms:	Double Pink No fragrance
Foliage:	Medium green
Introduction:	1932
Type:	Polyantha
Growth Type:	Spreading
Flowering Period:	Repeat flowering

THE PILGRIM

The blooms of *The Pilgrim* open flat when mature and the outer petals are paler than the central ones. There are so many English Roses these days — it is difficult to make a choice and there is a danger of overlooking the many fine age-old types. *The Pilgrim* is not as popular as some of the varieties in this group — pick it if you want a shrubby plant with sweet-smelling yellow flowers which open flat when mature.

Blooms:	Double Yellow Very fragrant
Foliage:	Medium green
Introduction:	1991
Type:	English
Growth Type:	Upright
Flowering Period:	Repeat flowering

TUSCANY SUPERB
Other Name: OLD VELVET

This old rose is a fine sight when in full flower. The wine-coloured blooms do not have many petals but they are large and open flat to reveal a central mass of golden stamens. The texture is velvety and the fragrance is spicy — a good rose for cutting as the stems do not have many thorns. Highly recommended, especially where you want a showy rose for a limited space.

Blooms:	Semi-double Deep red Fragrant
Foliage:	Dark green
Introduction:	1837
Type:	Gallica
Growth Type:	Upright
Flowering Period:	Midsummer

UNCLE WALTER

This McGredy rose shows the difficulty of rose classification. The bright red blooms are borne in clusters and because of their high-centred shape the variety is sometimes listed with the Hybrid Teas. But the blooms soon become muddled and the leafy growth is tall, so it is more usual to regard it as a Shrub Rose. *Uncle Walter* is nothing special but it keeps its place in many catalogues and is useful for hedging.

Blooms:	Double Red No fragrance
Foliage:	Dark green
Introduction:	1963
Type:	Modern Shrub
Growth Type:	Bushy
Flowering Period:	Repeat flowering

WILLIAM LOBB
Other Name: OLD VELVET MOSS

A gaunt giant of a Moss Rose, used as a large specimen bush or as a pillar rose. There is a single flush of flowers, in late June or early July, with wide trusses of large blooms — at first fuchsia purple and finally slate grey in colour. The buds and flower stalks are mossy, but there is little moss on the stems and leaves. Choose *Common Moss* if you want mossy stems.

Blooms:	Semi-double Purple magenta Fragrant
Foliage:	Dark green
Introduction:	1855
Type:	Moss
Growth Type:	Open
Flowering Period:	Midsummer

YESTERDAY
Other Name: TAPIS D'ORIENT

It looks old-fashioned, despite its youth. The small flowers are borne in clusters and the bush is almost continually in bloom throughout the season. Each bloom opens flat, and the colour may range from pale pink to deep mauve. This unusual Shrub is good for cutting and has been given premier awards abroad. A good compact bush which can be trimmed for ground cover.

Blooms:	Semi-double Pink Slightly fragrant
Foliage:	Medium green
Introduction:	1974
Type:	Modern Shrub
Growth Type:	Open
Flowering Period:	Repeat flowering

SHRUB ROSES

CHAPTER 3
CHOOSING &
BUYING ROSES

The secret of success for choosing the right roses is to start early. In summer, look through the selector guides (pages 92–95) and the A—Z sections (pages 12–90). Look through rose catalogues to find larger photographs of your chosen varieties, but never let a pretty picture be your sole guide. Try to see the roses growing in a display garden or nursery — only then will you know if the shape, colour and general form are right for you.

Shop early. If you are buying from a shop or garden centre, the widest selections should be available in autumn. This rule is even more important when shopping by mail order — the grower will substitute a similar variety if the one you have ordered is sold out. If you don't want this to happen, write 'No Substitutes' on your order.

Bargain Offers should be treated with great caution — you really do get what you pay for. Collections are different — they can be a good idea for a beginner but do check on the properties of each variety before buying. Most suppliers offer some form of guarantee system, but do make sure that failure isn't your own fault before claiming.

The type to buy

There are three types of planting material. The **bare-root** bush is lifted at the nursery during the dormant season (October–March) and sold over the counter or by post to the customer. In recent years an increasing number of these bare-root plants have been **prepackaged** for sale through shops, supermarkets and department stores as well as garden centres.

The correct type for some Climbers and Shrubs, most Miniatures and *all* roses during the growing season is the **container-grown** plant.

Bare-root

The traditional type for planting — dug up at the nursery or garden centre and taken home, or put on display with damp peat packed around the roots. Alternatively, the dormant roses are dug up and placed in wax-lined paper containers which are sent by post to the customer. The danger is drying out, see page 103 for instructions on how to deal with this problem.

Prepackaged

Prepackaged roses are bare-root plants with moist peat around the roots and the whole plant housed in a polythene bag and/or a box. There are advantages — reasonable price, ready availability from shops everywhere and coloured pictures plus instructions. But there can be problems — premature growth and shrivelled stems will occur if kept too warm.

Container-grown

Container-grown roses can be bought to provide instant colour, but they are more expensive than bare-root plants and need extra care at planting time. Choose a specimen for its sturdiness and good health — not for the beauty of its few flowers. Make sure that the plant has been grown in the container (container-grown) and not transferred into it from open ground (containerised).

What to look for

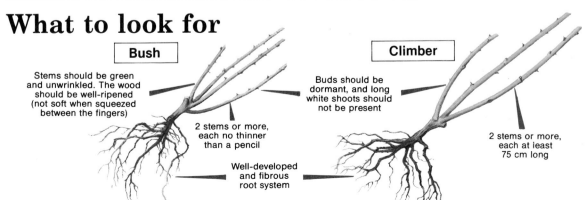

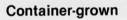

Bush

Stems should be green and unwrinkled. The wood should be well-ripened (not soft when squeezed between the fingers)

2 stems or more, each no thinner than a pencil

Well-developed and fibrous root system

Climber

Buds should be dormant, and long white shoots should not be present

2 stems or more, each at least 75 cm long

HYBRID TEA SELECTOR

Hybrid Teas are chosen for the reasons given on page 12. Now you have chosen this group, it is necessary to pick the varieties which will suit your situation and personal preferences.

Using the keys on these pages you will obtain a short list of roses, selected on the basis of three fundamental features — colour, height and fragrance. Next, look up each variety in the A—Z guide (pages 13–30) to discover its good and bad points. Note carefully that some roses are recommended for producing exhibition blooms and not for garden display — such varieties often produce only a few blooms and may be easily damaged by bad weather.

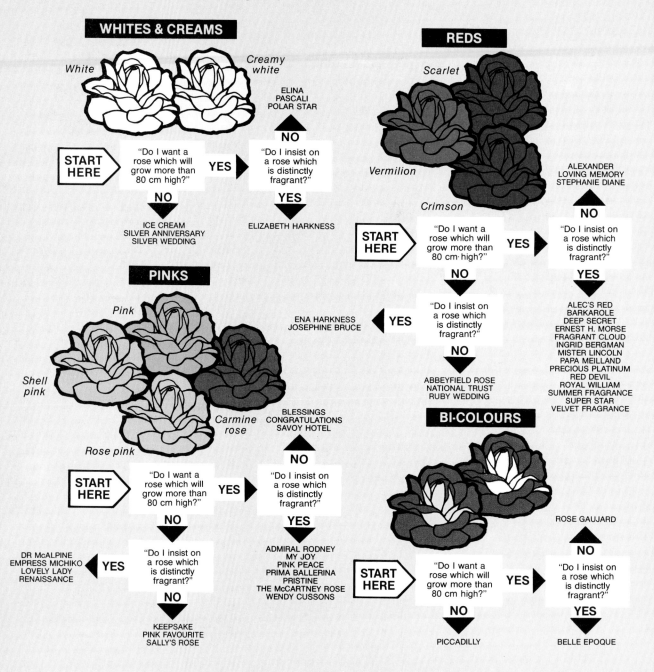

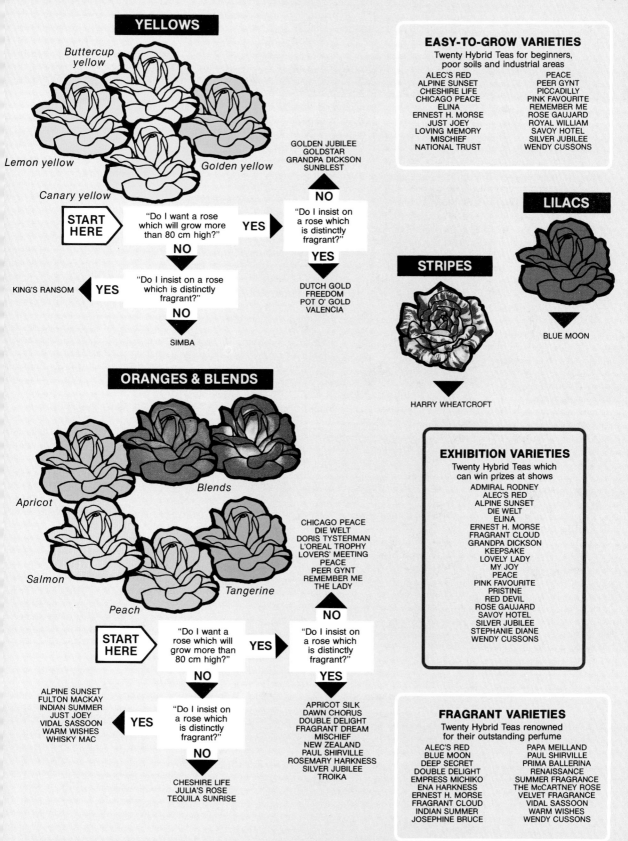

YELLOWS

Buttercup yellow

Lemon yellow

Golden yellow

Canary yellow

START HERE → "Do I want a rose which will grow more than 80 cm high?"

YES → "Do I insist on a rose which is distinctly fragrant?"

NO → GOLDEN JUBILEE / GOLDSTAR / GRANDPA DICKSON / SUNBLEST

YES → DUTCH GOLD / FREEDOM / POT O' GOLD / VALENCIA

NO → "Do I insist on a rose which is distinctly fragrant?"

YES → KING'S RANSOM

NO → SIMBA

ORANGES & BLENDS

Apricot

Blends

Salmon

Peach

Tangerine

START HERE → "Do I want a rose which will grow more than 80 cm high?"

YES → "Do I insist on a rose which is distinctly fragrant?"

NO → CHICAGO PEACE / DIE WELT / DORIS TYSTERMAN / L'OREAL TROPHY / LOVERS' MEETING / PEACE / PEER GYNT / REMEMBER ME / THE LADY

YES → APRICOT SILK / DAWN CHORUS / DOUBLE DELIGHT / FRAGRANT DREAM / MISCHIEF / NEW ZEALAND / PAUL SHIRVILLE / ROSEMARY HARKNESS / SILVER JUBILEE / TROIKA

NO → "Do I insist on a rose which is distinctly fragrant?"

YES → ALPINE SUNSET / FULTON MACKAY / INDIAN SUMMER / JUST JOEY / VIDAL SASSOON / WARM WISHES / WHISKY MAC

NO → CHESHIRE LIFE / JULIA'S ROSE / TEQUILA SUNRISE

STRIPES

HARRY WHEATCROFT

LILACS

BLUE MOON

EASY-TO-GROW VARIETIES

Twenty Hybrid Teas for beginners, poor soils and industrial areas

ALEC'S RED
ALPINE SUNSET
CHESHIRE LIFE
CHICAGO PEACE
ELINA
ERNEST H. MORSE
JUST JOEY
LOVING MEMORY
MISCHIEF
NATIONAL TRUST
PEACE
PEER GYNT
PICCADILLY
PINK FAVOURITE
REMEMBER ME
ROSE GAUJARD
ROYAL WILLIAM
SAVOY HOTEL
SILVER JUBILEE
WENDY CUSSONS

EXHIBITION VARIETIES

Twenty Hybrid Teas which can win prizes at shows

ADMIRAL RODNEY
ALEC'S RED
ALPINE SUNSET
DIE WELT
ELINA
ERNEST H. MORSE
FRAGRANT CLOUD
GRANDPA DICKSON
KEEPSAKE
LOVELY LADY
MY JOY
PEACE
PINK FAVOURITE
PRISTINE
RED DEVIL
ROSE GAUJARD
SAVOY HOTEL
SILVER JUBILEE
STEPHANIE DIANE
WENDY CUSSONS

FRAGRANT VARIETIES

Twenty Hybrid Teas renowned for their outstanding perfume

ALEC'S RED
BLUE MOON
DEEP SECRET
DOUBLE DELIGHT
EMPRESS MICHIKO
ENA HARKNESS
ERNEST H. MORSE
FRAGRANT CLOUD
INDIAN SUMMER
JOSEPHINE BRUCE
PAPA MEILLAND
PAUL SHIRVILLE
PRIMA BALLERINA
RENAISSANCE
SUMMER FRAGRANCE
THE McCARTNEY ROSE
VELVET FRAGRANCE
VIDAL SASSOON
WARM WISHES
WENDY CUSSONS

FLORIBUNDA SELECTOR

Floribundas are chosen in preference to Hybrid Teas where a large splash of garden colour is required, especially where the setting is informal.

The varieties you choose must be right for your garden and right for your personal taste. Use the keys on these pages to obtain a short list, and then look up each variety in the A—Z guide (pages 32–43) for its good and bad points. Check the average height — Floribundas range from 20 cm dwarfs to 150 cm giants, and catalogues are sometimes a little vague about the meaning of 'short' and 'tall'.

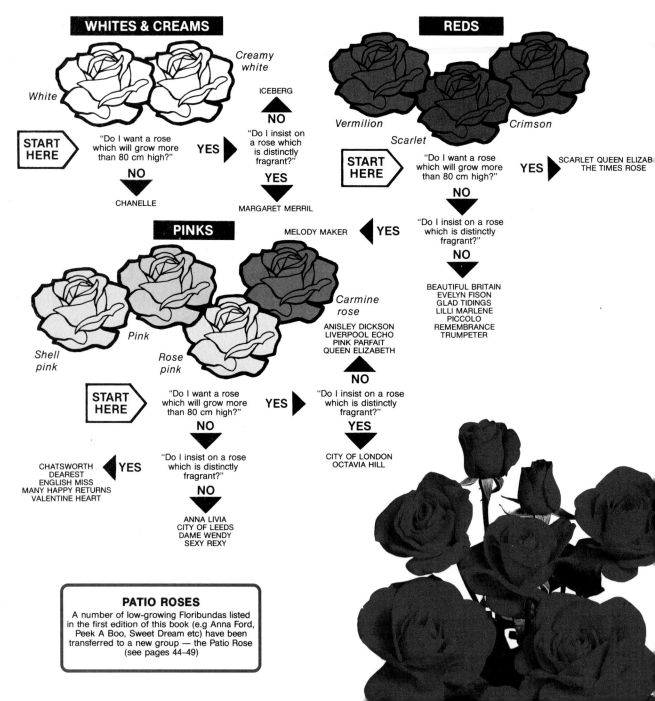

WHITES & CREAMS

White *Creamy white*

ICEBERG
NO

START HERE

"Do I want a rose which will grow more than 80 cm high?" **YES**

"Do I insist on a rose which is distinctly fragrant?" **YES**

NO

CHANELLE

MARGARET MERRIL

REDS

Vermilion *Scarlet* *Crimson*

START HERE

"Do I want a rose which will grow more than 80 cm high?" **YES** SCARLET QUEEN ELIZAB
THE TIMES ROSE

NO

"Do I insist on a rose which is distinctly fragrant?"

NO

BEAUTIFUL BRITAIN
EVELYN FISON
GLAD TIDINGS
LILLI MARLENE
PICCOLO
REMEMBRANCE
TRUMPETER

MELODY MAKER **◀ YES**

PINKS

Shell pink *Pink* *Rose pink*

Carmine rose

ANISLEY DICKSON
LIVERPOOL ECHO
PINK PARFAIT
QUEEN ELIZABETH

CHATSWORTH
DEAREST
ENGLISH MISS
MANY HAPPY RETURNS
VALENTINE HEART **◀ YES**

START HERE

"Do I want a rose which will grow more than 80 cm high?" **YES**

"Do I insist on a rose which is distinctly fragrant?" **NO**

"Do I insist on a rose which is distinctly fragrant?" **YES**

CITY OF LONDON
OCTAVIA HILL

ANNA LIVIA
CITY OF LEEDS
DAME WENDY
SEXY REXY

PATIO ROSES

A number of low-growing Floribundas listed in the first edition of this book (e.g Anna Ford, Peek A Boo, Sweet Dream etc) have been transferred to a new group — the Patio Rose (see pages 44–49)

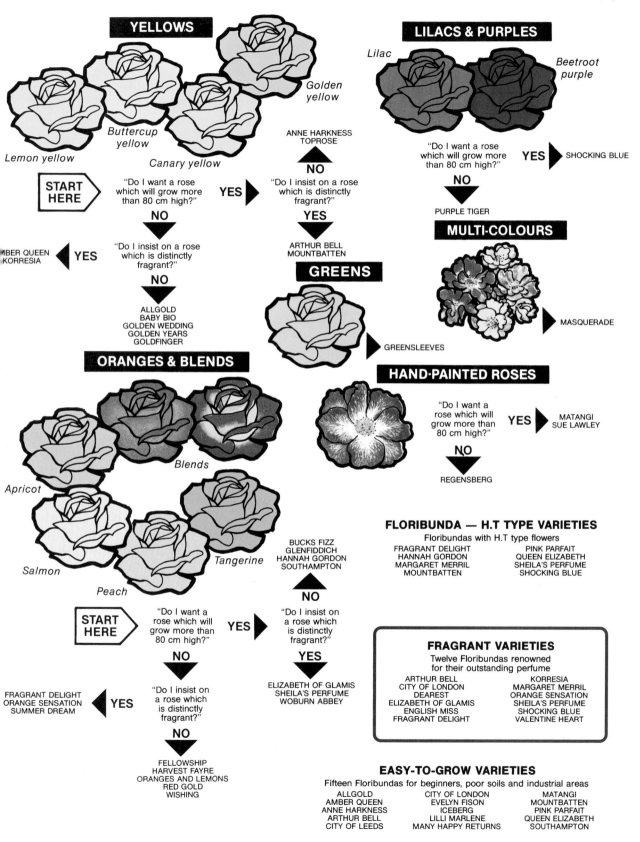

YELLOWS

Golden yellow

Buttercup yellow

Lemon yellow

Canary yellow

ANNE HARKNESS
TOPROSE

START HERE → "Do I want a rose which will grow more than 80 cm high?" → **YES** → "Do I insist on a rose which is distinctly fragrant?" → **NO**

NO

"Do I insist on a rose which is distinctly fragrant?" → **YES**

YES → ...BER QUEEN KORRESIA

ARTHUR BELL
MOUNTBATTEN

NO

ALLGOLD
BABY BIO
GOLDEN WEDDING
GOLDEN YEARS
GOLDFINGER

LILACS & PURPLES

Lilac

Beetroot purple

"Do I want a rose which will grow more than 80 cm high?" → **YES** → SHOCKING BLUE

NO

PURPLE TIGER

MULTI-COLOURS

MASQUERADE

GREENS

GREENSLEEVES

HAND-PAINTED ROSES

"Do I want a rose which will grow more than 80 cm high?" → **YES** → MATANGI
SUE LAWLEY

NO

REGENSBERG

ORANGES & BLENDS

Blends

Apricot

Salmon

Peach

Tangerine

BUCKS FIZZ
GLENFIDDICH
HANNAH GORDON
SOUTHAMPTON

NO

START HERE → "Do I want a rose which will grow more than 80 cm high?" → **YES** → "Do I insist on a rose which is distinctly fragrant?" → **YES**

NO

"Do I insist on a rose which is distinctly fragrant?" → **YES** → FRAGRANT DELIGHT
ORANGE SENSATION
SUMMER DREAM

ELIZABETH OF GLAMIS
SHEILA'S PERFUME
WOBURN ABBEY

NO

FELLOWSHIP
HARVEST FAYRE
ORANGES AND LEMONS
RED GOLD
WISHING

FLORIBUNDA — H.T TYPE VARIETIES
Floribundas with H.T type flowers

FRAGRANT DELIGHT | PINK PARFAIT
HANNAH GORDON | QUEEN ELIZABETH
MARGARET MERRIL | SHEILA'S PERFUME
MOUNTBATTEN | SHOCKING BLUE

FRAGRANT VARIETIES
Twelve Floribundas renowned
for their outstanding perfume

ARTHUR BELL | KORRESIA
CITY OF LONDON | MARGARET MERRIL
DEAREST | ORANGE SENSATION
ELIZABETH OF GLAMIS | SHEILA'S PERFUME
ENGLISH MISS | SHOCKING BLUE
FRAGRANT DELIGHT | VALENTINE HEART

EASY-TO-GROW VARIETIES
Fifteen Floribundas for beginners, poor soils and industrial areas

ALLGOLD | CITY OF LONDON | MATANGI
AMBER QUEEN | EVELYN FISON | MOUNTBATTEN
ANNE HARKNESS | ICEBERG | PINK PARFAIT
ARTHUR BELL | LILLI MARLENE | QUEEN ELIZABETH
CITY OF LEEDS | MANY HAPPY RETURNS | SOUTHAMPTON

CHAPTER 4

USING ROSES

As everybody knows, roses are for growing in beds and borders, growing up walls and growing over arches and screens. But on this page you will find many more uses for the Queen of Flowers. On the appropriate page you will find a list of rules for each of these uses, but do remember that it is *your* garden to use in any way you like ... with one proviso. Make sure that the variety or varieties you choose are suitable for the use you have in mind.

PLANTING IN BEDS page 97

PLANTING IN BORDERS page 98

PLANTING AS SPECIMENS page 99

COVERING SCREENS page 101

GROWING UNDER GLASS page 100

COVERING TREES page 101

PLANTING IN ROCKERIES page 98

COVERING WALLS page 101

USING AS CUT FLOWERS page 132

USING AS HOUSE PLANTS page 133

GROWING IN TUBS page 100

PLANTING AS GROUND COVER page 99

PLANTING AS HEDGES page 99

USING IN BUTTONHOLES page 134

USING IN THE KITCHEN page 134

EXHIBITING page 127

MAKING PERFUME page 133

Planting in Beds

A bed is a planted area which is designed to be viewed from all sides.

FLANKING BED

Many gardens have one or more beds which divide the lawn from a path or driveway. These can be turned into attractive flanking beds by using a single line of roses.

Standards and weeping standards are the most important types for this purpose, and the bed must be wide enough to support them.

Underplanting is essential here. Where roses are used, choose compact varieties which will not compete with the standards. Patio Roses are ideal for this purpose.

Colour

According to some purists, you should only plant one variety per bed. In most gardens this is not practical and would lead to a distinctly dull appearance. It is important to avoid the other extreme — a large bed filled with single plants of many varieties, giving a patchwork quilt effect.

The best plan is to use 3–5 bushes of each variety. You can obtain all sorts of advice from the experts about which colours harmonize and which do not, but the grouping of colour is a matter of taste and you should not worry too much about colour clashes. Reds, however, can be a problem as some shades clash horribly. It is advisable to separate groups of red roses by planting white, cream or pale yellow varieties as dividers between them.

Underplanting

Some rose experts believe that no other plants should be grown in a rose bed. Their reason is usually based on the old tradition that the glory of roses is spoilt by 'inferior' flowers, but there are also sound practical reasons for not underplanting. Mulching is made difficult or impossible, reserves of water and nutrients are depleted and walking between the bushes for maintenance work may become a tricky operation.

If you select the right plants, the drawbacks of underplanting become insignificant and the advantages are important — a colourful display when the roses are leafless or flowerless. The plants chosen must be low-growing and shallow-rooting, and when grown as an edging there is no inconvenience.

Spring bulbs are useful — Crocus, Snowdrop, etc, but avoid bulbs which have to be lifted regularly and avoid the larger bulbs with foliage which looks unsightly after flowering. Other favourites for underplanting are Primula Wanda, Auricula, Primrose, Candytuft, Ageratum, Viola, Aubretia, Alpine Phlox and Arabis.

ISLAND BED

Rose beds first began to appear about 100 years ago, and now they are a basic feature of the British garden. Gravel or crazy-paving is sometimes used to surround them, but grass is the traditional and still the best pathway between beds. Avoid lots of tiny beds — large and few is the general rule.

Beds are usually formal, with the roses planted in a strictly geometric pattern. Hybrid Teas or Floribundas can be used, but it is advisable not to mix the two types. Use Hybrid Teas if the bed is close to the house and where each bloom is to be admired. Choose Floribundas where a large splash of continuous colour is the prime need.

Keep things in proportion — small bushes in small beds. An appearance of flatness is a danger, especially in medium-sized or large beds. This can be avoided by planting a standard or a tall-growing variety in the centre.

Varieties of different heights are not a problem — plant the tall ones in the centre

Keep the shape simple — circular, oval or (best of all) rectangular

Stagger the planting

Keep at least 45 cm between the outermost plants and the edge of the bed

Keep the width 1.5 m or less, or you will have to tread between the plants when pruning, dead-heading, etc

The Ideal Bedding Rose

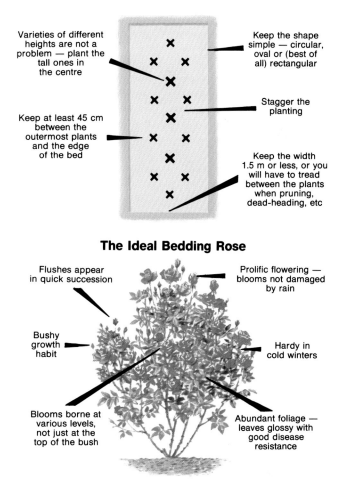

Flushes appear in quick succession

Prolific flowering — blooms not damaged by rain

Bushy growth habit

Hardy in cold winters

Blooms borne at various levels, not just at the top of the bush

Abundant foliage — leaves glossy with good disease resistance

Planting in Borders

**A border is a planted area which is designed to be
viewed from one, two or three sides but not the back.**

In the formal border, the rules on page 97 for the formal rose bed
apply apart from the fact that the tallest-growing varieties are planted
at the back of the border and the shortest at the front. A mass of
colour is all-important and so Floribundas are more widely used than
Hybrid Teas.

It is much more usual for a rose border to be informal, with the plants
grouped and spaced according to their height and width. Here you
can choose from the whole of the rose kingdom. In a large border you
can use Climbers and Ramblers as well as tall Shrubs to make up the
back row — in a smaller garden pillar roses and more modest
Shrubs will be used.

Exploit the wide range of roses to the full — as a rough guide fill about
half the space with Floribundas and a few Hybrid Teas, planting the
rest of the border with roses of other types. Plant *Canary Bird* for
flowers in the spring, and *Rosa rugosa* hybrids for red hips in the
winter.

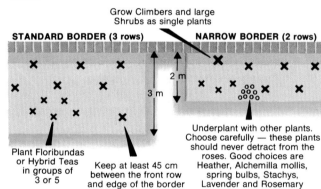

Grow Climbers and large
Shrubs as single plants

STANDARD BORDER (3 rows)   **NARROW BORDER (2 rows)**

3 m

2 m

Plant Floribundas
or Hybrid Teas
in groups of
3 or 5

Keep at least 45 cm
between the front row
and edge of the border

Underplant with other plants.
Choose carefully — these plants
should never detract from the
roses. Good choices are
Heather, Alchemilla mollis,
spring bulbs, Stachys,
Lavender and Rosemary

THE MIXED SHRUB BORDER

A visit to some of the great gardens of Britain will reveal the full
extent of the beauty of a rose border. More modest examples
can be seen in large private gardens throughout the country,
but the simple truth is that for most people there is only room
for one shrub border, and that is made up of Forsythia,
Hydrangea, Ribes, Lilac and the rest.

It is surprising that so many of these shrub borders do not
contain one Shrub Rose — even though it could provide colour
and fragrance in midsummer when so many shrubberies are
short of flowers.

For the rose lover a border of roses interspersed with
approximately the same number of shrubs is an excellent idea.
The roses are helped in three ways:

- Grey-leaved shrubs such as Lavender provide an excellent
  background for the pinks and purples of old-fashioned
  roses when in bloom.
- Evergreens such as Conifers provide a leafy skeleton for
  the border when roses are not in leaf.
- Winter- and early spring-flowering shrubs such as
  Forsythia and Viburnum tinus provide a floral display when
  roses are not in bloom.

THE MIXED HERBACEOUS BORDER

For many people there are rose beds and herbaceous borders,
and never the twain shall meet. In recent years the clear-cut
barriers have started to break down, and many writers now
sing the praises of Floribundas amongst the perennials.

The benefit to the border is obvious — an abundance of flowers
throughout the summer to liven up the large blank spaces
which sometimes occur.

The roses also benefit — bare stem bases can be successfully
hidden and there is surrounding colour before the rose season
begins. Careful selection is obviously important. First of all, get
the height right — tall varieties such as *Queen Elizabeth* or
Alexander are for the back of the border, shorter Floribundas
and Patio Roses for the middle region, and Miniatures for the
front of the border where they make a welcome change from
low-growing perennials.

Colour should also be carefully watched. Brilliant reds can be
too eye-catching — the pinks and creams are especially
suitable. Finally, make sure the bushes are given ample space
— overcrowding can lead to mildew.

Planting in Rockeries

Some years ago it would have been unthinkable to grow roses
in the rockery, but the wide range of Miniatures now available
has changed all that. The taller-growing varieties, such as
Baby Masquerade, can add height when set amongst low
clumps of alpines, in the same way that dwarf Conifers are
used. The smaller varieties, such as *Pour Toi*, can be used to
form 20 cm mounds of green leaves and semi-double
blooms.

Whatever variety is used, Miniature Roses bring the blessing
of midsummer flowers to an area of the garden where spring
colour is abundant but summer colour is scarce. Careful
maintenance is essential. The root run may be restricted, so
watering will be necessary in dry weather. Spray against
mildew and black spot, and keep the plants properly shaped
by pruning with scissors. Do not plant Miniatures amongst
rampant growers.

Planting as Hedges

A hedge is a continuous line of bushes in which the individuality of each plant is lost. Unlike a plant-covered fence (see page 101) a hedge requires little or no support.

The textbooks are right — roses can make a splendid hedge for both large and small gardens. Rose lovers sometimes scorn the all-too-familiar privet and yew, but before digging up your present hedge it would be wise to study the drawbacks of roses used in this way. Firstly, a rose hedge loses its leaves in winter. Next, it is informal and uneven in shape, and must not be chopped into a neat, squared-off outline with shears. Finally, it will not succeed in dense shade.

In the right situation, however, no other living screen will provide such an abundant and continuous display of flowers. Maintenance is simple — just dead-heading in summer and pruning in winter. Pick your variety with care — remember that many shrubs grow more than 1.5 m wide. A hedging variety should be hardy, repeat flowering, abundantly supplied with foliage and it should be healthy — nobody wants to spray a hedge every fortnight!

Rugosa Shrubs (see page 75) are the best of all boundary hedges. The prickly stems are animal- and child-proof, the handsome foliage is mildew-free and many varieties bear attractive hips in winter. *Scabrosa* takes pride of place, closely followed by *Roseraie de l'Hay.* The Hybrid Musks are another popular group with *Penelope* as the favourite. With this group some support may be necessary, and long summer shoots may have to be cut back. The tall-growing Floribunda *Queen Elizabeth* has become a familiar hedge, but it can be disappointing. The secret is to prune the stems to different lengths. In this way leaves and flowers will be borne at varying heights instead of just at the top.

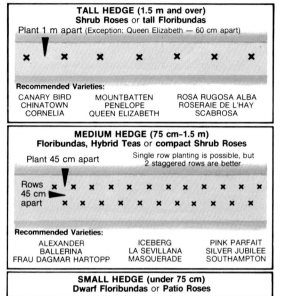

TALL HEDGE (1.5 m and over)
Shrub Roses or **tall Floribundas**
Plant 1 m apart (Exception: Queen Elizabeth — 60 cm apart)

Recommended Varieties:

CANARY BIRD	MOUNTBATTEN	ROSA RUGOSA ALBA
CHINATOWN	PENELOPE	ROSERAIE DE L'HAY
CORNELIA	QUEEN ELIZABETH	SCABROSA

MEDIUM HEDGE (75 cm–1.5 m)
Floribundas, Hybrid Teas or **compact Shrub Roses**
Plant 45 cm apart — Single row planting is possible, but 2 staggered rows are better
Rows 45 cm apart

Recommended Varieties:

ALEXANDER	ICEBERG	PINK PARFAIT
BALLERINA	LA SEVILLANA	SILVER JUBILEE
FRAU DAGMAR HARTOPP	MASQUERADE	SOUTHAMPTON

SMALL HEDGE (under 75 cm)
Dwarf Floribundas or **Patio Roses**

Planting as Specimens

A specimen rose is one which is grown to be admired on its own as distinct from being grouped with other plants.

The faults of a rose in a bed or border are partly hidden by its neighbours. Bare stems can be hidden by low-growing plants in the foreground, and lop-sided growth is often compensated for by the stems of nearby plants.

A specimen rose stands on its own. When well-grown it is a thing of unmatched beauty — when badly grown it can be an eyesore. So for all specimen roses careful selection and proper maintenance are especially important.

The basic rule is to keep the plant in balance with its surroundings. An average-sized Hybrid Tea could look insignificant set as a solitary specimen in a large lawn, in the same way that a giant cascading Shrub has no place in the centre of a tiny front garden. A favourite specimen is the standard rose, grown in a circular bed in the lawn. Weeping, full, half and miniature versions are available (see page 4). In addition, many Shrubs make excellent specimen roses where space is adequate. The catalogues sing the praises of *Nevada*, but there are also *Fred Loads*, *Fruhlingsgold*, *Joseph's Coat* and *Cornelia*.

For the smaller garden, the choice is made from Floribundas and Hybrid Teas. Of course, there are *Iceberg*, *Masquerade*, *Peace*, and *Queen Elizabeth* as a walk along any suburban road will reveal, but there are many others to choose from, such as *Arthur Bell*, *Mountbatten* and *National Trust*.

Planting as Ground Cover

A ground cover rose is a low-growing and spreading plant which forms a dense leafy mat.

Roses as ground cover plants may seem a modern idea, but some wild roses grow this way in their natural habitat. The uses of these prostrate roses in the garden are quite numerous — such as hiding unsightly mounds and manhole covers, edging rose beds and covering steep banks.

Ground Cover Roses are weed suppressors, but never regard them as weed eliminators. Planting in weedy soil will leave you with the hopeless task of trying to pull out grass from a tangled mass of stems.

Numerous varieties are listed in the Ground Cover Roses section (pages 54–59). Some are spreading bushes with arching stems which cover the soil — examples are *Bonica*, *Fiona* and *Rosy Cushion*. Others are prostrate plants with stems which creep across the ground — *Nozomi* and *Max Graf* have been around for years, but are now being challenged by newer ones such as *Grouse* and *Avon*.

If there is a large stretch of land to cover, use one of the wide-spreading 'Game Bird' or 'County' series. Alternatively you can peg down a Rambler such as *Crimson Shower*. Such rampant growers have no place in a bed or border where space is limited — choose *Nozomi*, *Max Graf*, *Pink Bells*, *Bonica* or *Rosy Cushion*.

Growing under Glass

The appearance of the first blooms of the year is eagerly awaited by every rose lover. By growing roses in pots in an unheated greenhouse these first flowers can be obtained in mid April. If the greenhouse is heated, the plants will bloom in March. There are extra benefits — the flowers are perfect, free from wind and rain damage, and delicate varieties such as *Baccara* can be grown.

Planting takes place in October or November. Use a bare-root plant and a 25 cm clay or plastic pot. A clay pot should be soaked in water before use. If a plastic pot is chosen, put a few large pebbles in the bottom to increase stability.

Use John Innes or a peat-based compost. Keep the crown level with the top of the pot and use the end of a blunt stick to firm the compost around the roots. Leave a 5 cm space between the top of the compost and the rim. Finally, water the compost thoroughly.

Stand the pot outdoors on a firm surface (concrete, gravel, ash etc), not in contact with the soil. The site should be unshaded but protected from strong winds and look after it during the spring and summer as if it was an ordinary tub rose (see below). Water in dry weather, spray when necessary and cut off dead flowers. There are one or two differences — remove nearly all flower buds so that only a few blooms appear and feed by spraying the leaves with a foliar feed such as Fillip.

In November or December cut the stems back to 15 cm and move the pots into the greenhouse. Add slow-release fertilizer as recommended on the package to the compost in each pot.

Avoid the various pitfalls which are likely during this forcing stage. Water properly — soak the pot thoroughly and then allow the compost to become partly dry before rewatering. On mild sunny days during spring ventilate the greenhouse adequately to avoid mildew. Paint the glass with Coolglass if the weather remains sunny.

From April onwards, use a liquid feed on a little-but-often basis — make sure the soil is moist before feeding. Once flowering is over, move the pots outdoors again until November, and then begin the sequence all over again. Repot every three years.

Recommended Varieties:

ALEC'S RED	HONEYBUNCH
ALLGOLD	ICEBERG
AMBER QUEEN	JOSEPHINE BRUCE
ANNE HARKNESS	KORRESIA
BABY BIO	MARGARET MERRIL
BEAUTIFUL BRITAIN	NATIONAL TRUST
BLESSINGS	PASCALI
DOUBLE DELIGHT	PEER GYNT
ENA HARKNESS	PICCADILLY
ERNEST H. MORSE	PINK FAVOURITE
FRAGRANT DREAM	RED DEVIL
FULTON MACKAY	SAVOY HOTEL
GINGERNUT	WENDY CUSSONS
GRANDPA DICKSON	WHISKY MAC

The Quick Method

The traditional method outlined on the left results in a gap of 18 months between planting and the appearance of the first greenhouse blooms. A quicker but less satisfactory method is to use a container-grown rose instead of a bare-root plant. Pot up the specimen in a 20 cm pot in October, carefully avoiding root disturbance. Bring the pot indoors in December, and treat according to the general rules. After flowering, stand the pot outdoors and at the end of the summer transplant into a 25 cm pot.

Growing in Tubs

Growing roses in tubs on the terrace is a welcome addition to the plants in the beds and borders of the garden, but for balconies and in some town gardens it is the *only* way to grow roses.

The first step is to choose the right container. Some experts believe that wooden casks make the only truly satisfactory type, but you can choose from a large range of materials — plastic, fibreglass, stone, metal and so on. Much more important than material is size — a good root run is essential which means a depth of 25 cm for Miniatures, 30 cm for Patio Roses (dwarf Floribundas) and 40 cm for average-sized Floribundas and Hybrid Teas.

The tub should be stood on blocks to allow free drainage, and a 2.5-5 cm layer of rubble or crocks placed over the drainage holes. Use a soil-based compost or, if weight is a problem, a peat-based compost.

There is a wide selection of roses to choose from, but reject all varieties which do not have good disease resistance and avoid all varieties which are described as tall and upright. As a general rule the most satisfactory tub roses are the Patio Roses listed on pages 45-49. Standards can be grown, provided firm staking is used.

Edging with spring flowering plants such as Primroses and miniature bulbs or with trailing plants such as Lobelia is a matter of personal taste. The cultural rules, however, must be followed. Place the tub in a sunny spot away from overhanging trees. Water during dry weather but never keep the compost permanently wet. Feed twice a year with a rose fertilizer — first of all when the leaves are beginning to unfold, and again in June or July. Water the compost before feeding — rake in lightly afterwards.

Covering Screens

There are Climber and Rambler varieties, but no rose has a natural climbing habit of growth. They neither twist around supports nor send out tendrils like a vine, so you will need both a sturdy support and some way of attaching the stems to the support.

Fence

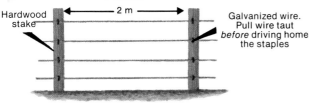

Hardwood stake

2 m

Galvanized wire. Pull wire taut *before* driving home the staples

Trellis

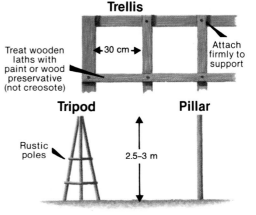

Treat wooden laths with paint or wood preservative (not creosote)

30 cm

Attach firmly to support

Tripod

Rustic poles

Pillar

2.5–3 m

- The basal shoots of climbing roses must be trained as described on page 106. Use plastic-covered wire ties to attach the stems to the support — do not wind the young stems around the straining wires of a fence. Do not twist the wire ties too tightly around the main stems — leave room for the canes to increase in diameter.

- Ensure that all fence posts and pillars are well-anchored. Strong winds can cause havoc when the roses are in full leaf if the underground part of the support is too shallow or rotten.

- Ramblers can be grown on open screens, arches, pergolas, etc where a large area is to be covered. Try to avoid tangling the stems when training. Before choosing a Rambler, read about the drawbacks on page 60.

Recommended Varieties:

Pillars & Fences

ALOHA
ALTISSIMO
BANTRY BAY
BREATH OF LIFE
COMPASSION
DANSE DU FEU
DORTMUND
DUBLIN BAY
EMILY GRAY

GALWAY BAY
GOLDEN SHOWERS
HANDEL
HIGHFIELD
ICEBERG, CLIMBING
LAURA FORD
LEVERKUSEN
MAIGOLD
MASQUERADE, CLIMBING

MORNING JEWEL
NEW DAWN
PARKDIREKTOR RIGGERS
PINK PERPETUE
ROSY MANTLE
SCHOOLGIRL
SWAN LAKE
WHITE COCKADE
ZEPHIRINE DROUHIN

Arches & Pergolas

Ramblers are once flowering, prone to mildew and difficult to prune. For some gardeners, however, the thin pliable stems still make them the first choice for arches and pergolas.

ALBERIC BARBIER
ALBERTINE
CRIMSON SHOWER
EMILY GRAY

EXCELSA
FRANCOIS JURANVILLE
PAUL'S SCARLET CLIMBER
VEILCHENBLAU

Covering Walls

There were roses growing on the walls of British houses before the birth of Hybrid Teas and Floribundas, and they remain an important feature. But they can be more trouble than they are worth if you don't choose wisely and provide a proper support.

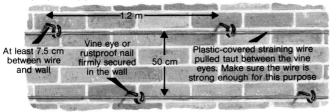

At least 7.5 cm between wire and wall

Vine eye or rustproof nail firmly secured in the wall

1.2 m

50 cm

Plastic-covered straining wire pulled taut between the vine eyes. Make sure the wire is strong enough for this purpose

Recommended Varieties:

Never choose a variety which is particularly prone to mildew, which rules out most Ramblers.

North & East Walls

BANTRY BAY
DANSE DU FEU
GUINEE
LEVERKUSEN
MAIGOLD
MORNING JEWEL
MME ALFRED CARRIERE

South & West Walls

The N&E varieties plus —
CASINO
ENA HARKNESS, CLIMBING
ETOILE DE HOLLANDE, CLIMBING
MERMAID
MRS SAM McGREDY, CLIMBING
ROYAL GOLD

Covering Trees

A dead tree is an eyesore in the garden, and if it is weak or rotten it should be felled. If it is sturdy, however, it can be used as a support for a climbing rose in the same way that some living trees can be employed.

In this role the vigorous Rambler is supreme — this is no job for the compact modern Climber. Plant the rose on the side of the tree from which the prevailing wind blows, and provide some means of attachment to the trunk. The climbing rose will be self-supporting once its canes become entwined among the branches.

Recommended Varieties:

CECILE BRUNNER, CLIMBING
FRANCOIS JURANVILLE
KIFTSGATE
RAMBLING RECTOR
SEAGULL

CHAPTER 5

ROSE PLANTING

The number of new roses planted in Britain each year is staggering — if set out as a single row these plants would girdle the equator! So the chances are that you will be planting new roses this year, and with care you can expect them to last for 20 years or more.

Not all rose planting is successful, because there is more to it than digging a hole, spreading out the roots and then replacing the soil. Before you even lift a spade you should have considered several things. Has the soil already grown roses for many years? Does it need improving? Is the site really suitable for roses? This chapter offers you a step-by-step guide to avoiding all the pitfalls.

PICKING THE RIGHT SPOT

PLENTY OF SUN is required to produce top quality roses, but slight shade during early afternoon is beneficial.
ROSES CANNOT STAND DEEP AND CONTINUOUS SHADE

SHELTER FROM COLD WINDS is helpful. A nearby hedge or fence is useful, but it should not be close enough to shade the bush. Avoid planting in the lowest part of the garden if it is a 'frost pocket'.
ROSES DO NOT THRIVE IN EXPOSED, LOW-LYING SITES

REASONABLY FREE DRAINAGE is essential, so break up the subsoil if necessary.
ROSES CANNOT STAND BEING WATERLOGGED

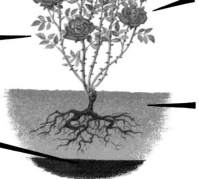

PLENTY OF AIR is required to produce healthy plants. Bush and standard roses do not like being shut in by walls and overhanging plants.
ROSES CANNOT STAND BEING PLANTED UNDER TREES

SUITABLE SOIL is necessary, and fortunately this can be achieved in nearly all gardens. Ideally it should be a medium loam, slightly acid and reasonably rich in plant foods and humus. A high clay content is not necessary, and is actually harmful if not improved by adding humus. A high lime content is harmful. Soil in which roses have grown for more than 10 years is not suitable — see page 103.
ROSES CANNOT THRIVE IF THE SOIL IS POOR

TIMING

Bare-root Plants

PLANTING SEASON

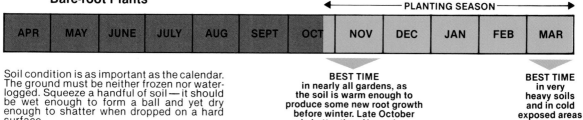

APR	MAY	JUNE	JULY	AUG	SEPT	OCT	NOV	DEC	JAN	FEB	MAR

Soil condition is as important as the calendar. The ground must be neither frozen nor water-logged. Squeeze a handful of soil — it should be wet enough to form a ball and yet dry enough to shatter when dropped on a hard surface.

BEST TIME in nearly all gardens, as the soil is warm enough to produce some new root growth before winter. Late October is better than November in northern counties.

BEST TIME in very heavy soils and in cold exposed areas with high rainfall.

Container-grown Plants

Can be planted at any time of the year, provided the soil condition is suitable. Spring and autumn are preferred.

GETTING THE SOIL READY

The most expensive roses you can buy will grow only as well as the soil allows. Very few soils are naturally ideal, but almost all can be transformed into a satisfactory home for roses with some spadework (especially in clayey gardens) and humus (especially in sandy soils). There is no truth in the old saying that heavy clay is essential for top quality results.

STEP 1

STEP 2

DOUBLE DIGGING is recommended to aerate the top soil and break up the subsoil. The first step is to dig out a trench 45 cm wide and 30 cm deep at one side of the bed or border and transport the soil to the other. Fork over the bottom of the trench to the full length of the prongs, working in garden compost, well-rotted manure, leaf mould or peat. Turn strip A into the trench. Fork over the trench left by the removal of A, again incorporating compost or peat. Turn over strip B and so on, until a final trench is formed which is then filled with the soil from the first one. Do not remove small stones, as they are beneficial in a dry season. Roots of perennial weeds should be removed during digging. To add major and trace elements, fork a rose fertilizer at the recommended rate into the top soil, and then let the ground settle for at least six weeks before planting.

WARNING: SOILS WHICH HAVE GROWN ROSES FOR MORE THAN 10 YEARS
You may wish to replant an old rose bed or just dig up one or two old bushes and replace them with new ones. In either case the soil is likely to be rose-sick (see page 119) if the plants have been growing in the soil for more than 10 years.
The causes of rose sickness are complex and still not yet fully understood, but a well-known effect is for newly-planted bushes and standards to suffer even though the established roses were thriving before their removal.
It is therefore wise to remove the old soil, digging out a hole 60 cm in diameter and 45 cm deep for each new plant. Dig in plenty of organic matter and use a planting mixture made up with soil from a part of the garden which has not grown roses in recent years. The old soil from the rose bed can be safely spread in the vegetable or flower garden.

DRAINAGE is all-important, and double digging will help to prevent waterlogging in wet weather. If top soil is shallow and subsoil composed of heavy clay, the simplest plan is to make raised beds with added top soil, surrounded by paths on hardcore bases which will act as soakaways.

LIMING is not usually necessary because roses prefer slightly acid soil (pH 6.0 to 6.5). Only very acid soils need liming and even then only a light dressing will be required. Avoid overliming, or weak growth will result.

WARNING: CHALK SOILS
If there is less than 45 cm of top soil above the chalk you will have either to add more top soil or excavate a 60 cm hole at each planting site and fill with planting mixture (see page 104). Alternatively, grow chalk-tolerant Shrub Roses — Albas, Damasks and Hybrid Musks.

GETTING THE PLANT READY

IF PLANTING IS TO BE DELAYED FOR LESS THAN 10 DAYS —
Leave the package containing the bush or standard unopened in an unheated but frost-proof cellar, garage or shed.

IF PLANTING IS TO BE DELAYED FOR MORE THAN 10 DAYS —
'Heel-in' the roses by digging a shallow V-shaped trench and then spreading the plants as a single row against one side of it. Cover the roots and lower part of the stems with soil and tread down. Label with some form of permanent tag — paper labels attached by the supplier may rot away.

WHEN YOU ARE READY TO BEGIN PLANTING —
Carefully unpack and place the packing material, sacking, etc. over the roots. Then prepare bush as shown in the adjoining diagram.

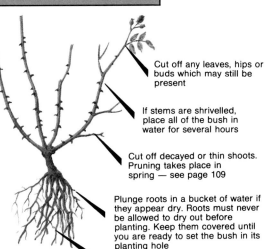

Cut off any leaves, hips or buds which may still be present

If stems are shrivelled, place all of the bush in water for several hours

Cut off decayed or thin shoots. Pruning takes place in spring — see page 109

Plunge roots in a bucket of water if they appear dry. Roots must never be allowed to dry out before planting. Keep them covered until you are ready to set the bush in its planting hole

Cut back any damaged or very long roots to about 30 cm

PLANTING

BUSHES

Bare-root Plants

The first step is to mark out the planting stations with canes to make sure that the bushes will be spaced out as planned. Next the planting hole for each rose must be dug, and the commonest mistake at planting time is to dig a hole which is too deep and too narrow.

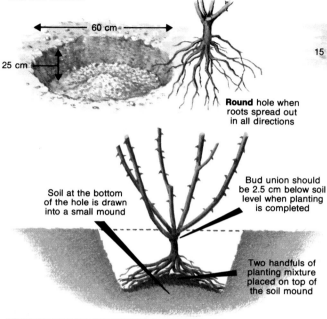

Round hole when roots spread out in all directions

60 cm

25 cm

Fan-shaped hole when roots run in only one direction

30 cm

15 cm

20 cm

Soil at the bottom of the hole is drawn into a small mound

Bud union should be 2.5 cm below soil level when planting is completed

Two handfuls of planting mixture placed on top of the soil mound

Make up the **planting mixture** in a wheelbarrow — 1 part soil, 1 part moist peat and 3 handfuls of Bone Meal per barrow load.

Spread out the roots evenly in the planting hole and work a couple of trowelfuls of the mixture around them. Shake the plant gently up and down and then firm the planting mixture with your fists. Place a cane across the top of the hole to ensure that the bud union is level with the surface.

Half-fill the hole with more of the mixture and firm it down by gentle treading. On no account should you stamp heavily — this would destroy the natural soil structure. Start treading at the outer edge of the planting hole, working gradually towards the centre.

Add more planting mixture until the hole is full, tread down once again and then loosen the surface. Spread a little more soil so that the bud union is about 2–3 cm below the surface and finally attach a weatherproof label bearing the name of the rose. The job is now finished but if frosty weather occurs after planting, refirming may be necessary.

Transplanting Established Bushes

It is occasionally necessary to move a rose bush from one part of the garden to another. Do this job in late autumn or early spring — shorten stems, cut off old leaves and flowers, and then carefully remove the bush from the soil. There are two methods — two people with forks at opposite sides steadily lever up the plant or one person with a spade cuts straight down on all four sides about 25 cm from the centre of the bush and then carefully lifts it on to a wheelbarrow. Plant immediately — keep the soil ball moist and covered if there is to be any delay.

Container-grown Plants

Never regard container-grown plants as an easy way to plant roses. If the environment surrounding the soil ball is not to the plant's liking then the roots will not grow out into the garden soil. This means that it is not enough to dig a hole, take off the container covering, drop in the plant and replace the soil.

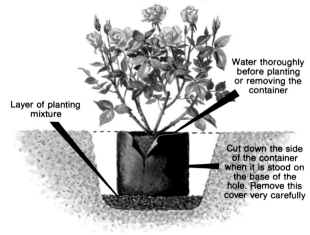

Water thoroughly before planting or removing the container

Layer of planting mixture

Cut down the side of the container when it is stood on the base of the hole. Remove this cover very carefully

Make sure that the soil is moist before digging a planting hole which is large enough and deep enough for the soil ball and a surrounding 7.5–10 cm layer of planting mixture. The cover of the container should be slit and then gently slid off the soil ball. Never lift up the plant to do this and never break up the compost around the roots.

Fill the space between the soil ball and the sides of the hole with planting mixture (see above) and never with ordinary soil — roots may not move from a peat-based compost into ordinary mineral garden soil. Firm down the planting mixture with your fingers or the handle of the trowel. Water regularly during dry weather in spring and summer until the plant is established.

PLANTING continued

STANDARDS

If bushes and standards are to be planted in the same bed, deal with the standards first.

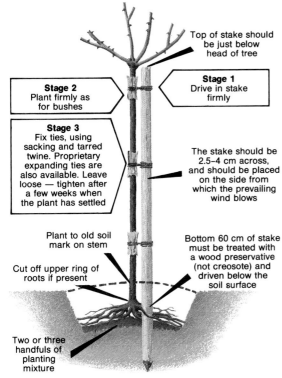

Top of stake should be just below head of tree

Stage 1
Drive in stake firmly

Stage 2
Plant firmly as for bushes

Stage 3
Fix ties, using sacking and tarred twine. Proprietary expanding ties are also available. Leave loose — tighten after a few weeks when the plant has settled

The stake should be 2.5–4 cm across, and should be placed on the side from which the prevailing wind blows

Plant to old soil mark on stem

Cut off upper ring of roots if present

Bottom 60 cm of stake must be treated with a wood preservative (not creosote) and driven below the soil surface

Two or three handfuls of planting mixture

CLIMBERS

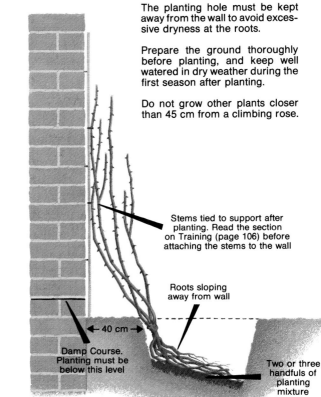

The planting hole must be kept away from the wall to avoid excessive dryness at the roots.

Prepare the ground thoroughly before planting, and keep well watered in dry weather during the first season after planting.

Do not grow other plants closer than 45 cm from a climbing rose.

Stems tied to support after planting. Read the section on Training (page 106) before attaching the stems to the wall

Roots sloping away from wall

← 40 cm →

Damp Course. Planting must be below this level

Two or three handfuls of planting mixture

SPACING

ROSE TYPE	DISTANCE BETWEEN SIMILAR PLANTS
MINIATURE ROSES	30 cm
PATIO ROSES	45 cm
HYBRID TEA & FLORIBUNDA BUSHES Compact varieties	45 cm
HYBRID TEA & FLORIBUNDA BUSHES Average varieties	60 cm
HYBRID TEA & FLORIBUNDA BUSHES Tall varieties	75–100 cm
GROUND COVER ROSES	expected spread
LOW-GROWING SHRUBS	100 cm
STANDARDS	120 cm
SHRUBS	average 150 cm or half of expected height
WEEPING STANDARDS	180 cm
CLIMBERS	200–300 cm

CHAPTER 6
ROSE CARE

The ever-increasing popularity of the Hybrid Tea and Floribunda is no doubt due to the beauty and colours of modern varieties together with their repeat flowering habit. But the simplicity of rose care, compared to the time-consuming job of looking after some other garden favourites is also an important factor.

A number of simple and straightforward tasks have to be carried out during the rose-growing year. Some, such as hoeing and feeding, are generally understood and practised. Others, like mulching and training, are still not widely followed and countless roses suffer as a result. One feature of rose cultivation causes more arguments and concern than all the rest, and that is pruning. Finally, there is one aspect of rose care which does not appear in the textbooks — take time to enjoy your roses by sitting close to them occasionally and doing nothing!

MULCHING

A mulch is a layer of bulky organic material placed on the soil surface around plants. In the rose garden it provides five distinct benefits:

- The soil is kept moist during the dry days of summer.
- Weeds are greatly reduced.
- Soil structure is improved as humus is added to the soil.
- Plant foods are provided by some mulching materials.
- Black spot attacks are reduced.

Suitable materials are moist peat, shredded bark, well-rotted manure, good garden compost and leaf mould. Grass clippings are often recommended and used, but a word of caution is necessary. Do not use them if the lawn contains many weeds or has recently been treated with a weedkiller. If they are used, add only a thin layer at a time and stir occasionally.

The standard time for mulching is late April and early May. Success depends on preparing the soil surface before adding the organic blanket — remove debris, dead leaves and weeds, and then water the surface if it is dry. Apply the spring feed (see page 111) if this has not yet been done, hoe in lightly, and you are ready to apply the mulch. Spread a 5–7 cm layer around the roses, keeping it away from the crown of the plants. Lightly prick this dressing into the top couple of centimetres of soil during October.

Mulching will greatly reduce the need for watering and hoeing, but it cannot replace the need for feeding, as the balance of nutrients in a good rose fertilizer is not generally provided by mulching materials.

Some experts believe that autumn mulching is equal to or even better than late spring mulching, as described above. If you follow this advice, apply the mulch in October before the soil has become cold.

TRAINING

Some shrubs with lax spreading stems may require some form of support after a few years. Use three or more unobtrusive stakes with a secure band or board joining the top of each stake — never rely on a single ugly pole and string.

Climbing roses must be trained from the outset to ensure that they remain attached to their supports and grow in the desired direction. This does not mean that the main stems should be allowed to grow vertically — when this happens the usual result is a mature plant which bears its leaves and flowers at the top.

To prevent this happening, train the main shoots as horizontally as possible. This interruption of the free upward movement of the sap causes lateral branches to appear. It is these laterals which grow upwards to provide both height and cover, and they bear the flowers.

Basal shoots spread out fan-wise to encourage growth of vertical laterals

Fan training is fine for a climbing rose growing against a wall, fence, or screen, but is quite impractical when a pillar or tripod is to be covered. In this case, wind the canes in an ascending spiral around the pole.

The wire ties used to attach the main stems to the supports should not be tied too tightly — these stems thicken with age and a tight tie can strangle growth.

PRUNING

A rose bush, unlike a tree, does not produce shoots which steadily increase in size every year. A rose stem grows actively and bears flowers for only a few years, after which the upper portion becomes exhausted. A new shoot then appears from a bud lower down on the stem, and the part above the new shoot dies.

The result is that a rose bush left unpruned becomes a tangled mass of live and dead wood. The purpose of pruning is to get rid of old exhausted wood every year and to encourage the regular development of strong and healthy stems.

Until recently there was only one basic method of pruning, but in recent years an easy-care or 'rough' technique has evolved. This method has given results which are at least as good as the traditional one but with far less effort.

The tools to use

TWO-BLADED SECATEURS
will cut cleanly for many years with proper care. The cut must be made at the centre of the blades.

or

ONE-BLADED SECATEURS
are easier to use and will cut at the tip of the blade, but tend to wear out more quickly than the two-bladed variety, as the anvil becomes worn.

GLOVES
are necessary to protect your hands from thorns. Buy a stout and flexible pair.

LONG-HANDLED PRUNERS
are essential for tall climbers and shrubs. Many gardeners prefer them to a pruning saw for dealing with thick stems.

KNEELING PAD
will allow you to get close to the bush when the soil is cold and wet at pruning time. Essential for the over-fifties.

PRUNING SAW
if stems over 2 cm diameter have to be cut.

PRUNING KNIFE
if you are experienced in its use.

TRADITIONAL METHOD

All bushes and standards should be tackled in the following way:

STEP 1   Cut out completely all dead wood and all parts of stems which are obviously diseased or damaged. Test: Cut surface should be white. If brown — cut back further.

STEP 2   Cut out completely very thin stems, and remove any branch which rubs against another. Aim to produce an open-centred bush. Remove suckers.

STEP 3   Cut out all unripe stems. Test: Try to snap off several thorns. If they bend or tear off instead of breaking off cleanly, the wood is too soft to be of any use.

STEP 4   Only healthy and ripe stems now remain. Prune these to the length advised on page 109 for the type of rose in question.

The pruning cut

sloping cut

1 cm

CORRECT CUT

outward dormant bud

WRONG CUTS

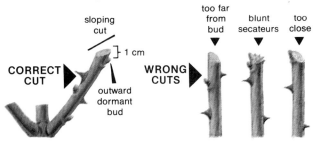

too far from bud   blunt secateurs   too close

All pruning cuts must be clean — pare off any ragged parts. Sharp secateurs are essential — never force them to cut through thick stems, and relegate them to ordinary garden work once the blades are dull.

It is impossible to avoid making some wrong cuts when pruning several bushes on a cold unpleasant day. As a result snags will form above some of the new shoots which develop — merely cut these dead bits off as they appear.

Types of pruning

BEFORE	AFTER	TYPE
		### HARD PRUNING Stems are cut back to three or four buds from the base. This leaves short, sturdy stems about 12–15 cm high. Hard pruning is recommended for newly-planted bush roses and it is often used for established H.Ts grown solely for the production of exhibition blooms. It is no longer recommended for established roses grown for garden display although it is still used for some very weak-growing H.Ts and for rejuvenating neglected roses. Hard pruning should never be used for established Floribundas.
		### MODERATE PRUNING Stems are cut back to about half of their length. Weaker than average stems should be reduced by more than this amount. Moderate pruning is recommended for nearly all established H.Ts growing in ordinary soils. Established Floribundas are pruned using a variation of this system (see page 109). If the roses are well cared for, you can expect exhibition-quality blooms as well as a fine garden display following the use of moderate pruning. Hard pruning is no longer considered to be essential for winning prizes.
		### LIGHT PRUNING Stems are cut back to about two-thirds of their length. This means that after the removal of all unwanted wood, the remaining stems are merely tipped. Light pruning is not generally recommended as it produces tall spindly bushes bearing early but poor quality blooms if used year after year. In special cases, however, light pruning is the only method to use. Very vigorous H.T varieties such as *Peace* should be tackled in this way, and all roses growing in very sandy or smoky areas should be lightly pruned.

When to prune

BUSHES, STANDARDS & CLIMBERS

Early spring pruning is recommended for autumn- and winter-planted roses and for established plants. If the bushes or standards are to be planted in the spring, prune just before planting.

The best time to prune is when growth is just beginning. The uppermost buds will have begun to swell but no leaves will have appeared.

One of the dangers of leaving pruning until spring is the possibility of wind-rock in the winter gales. Avoid this by cutting back long shoots in November.

RAMBLERS

Prune in late summer or autumn once flowering has finished.

Prune at or before the recommended pruning date for your part of the country

EARLY APRIL

LATE MARCH

MID MARCH

Pruning too early may result in buds breaking prematurely in a mild spell, followed by frost injury if freezing weather returns.

Despite this possibility, some rose experts prune regularly during above-freezing weather in January or February and claim they obtain earlier flowering than with the more usual March pruning.

Pruning too late results in the plant being weakened. This is because the sap is flowing freely upwards once the buds are actively growing, and pruning at this stage is bound to cause considerable loss of sap.

Pruning by the traditional method

	NEWLY-PLANTED ROSES (Planted in previous autumn/winter or due to be planted in spring)	**ESTABLISHED ROSES** (Planted at least 12 months ago)
HYBRID TEA BUSHES	**Hard pruning** is required to build up a strong root system and to stimulate the growth of sturdy fresh shoots from close to the base of the bush. Hybrid Teas should be pruned 10–15 cm from the ground — Floribundas and Patio Roses 15 cm. In sandy soils, use moderate pruning at this stage and hard pruning the following year.	**Moderate pruning** is the best method for general garden display. For show blooms hard pruning is sometimes used. In poor sites and for very vigorous varieties light pruning is recommended.
FLORIBUNDA & PATIO ROSE BUSHES		**Moderate pruning** is the basis for dealing with Floribundas, but some old stems are hard pruned to a few centimetres from the ground, whilst new shoots which arose from close to the base last year are only lightly pruned. In this way stems of varying lengths are retained which ensures a long period of continuous flowering.
HYBRID TEA & FLORIBUNDA STANDARDS	**Hard pruning** is recommended, but this should be less drastic than the treatment of newly planted bushes. Cut stems back to about 20 cm from the trunk.	**Moderate pruning** is used to form a properly balanced head which will produce plenty of flowers. Hard pruning should be avoided, otherwise over-vigorous shoot growth will spoil the tree. Make sure that the main branches are of approximately equal length after pruning.
WEEPING STANDARDS	**Hard pruning** is necessary, leaving branches about 15 cm long at the top of the trunk.	In autumn cut out branches which have flowered, leaving the new vigorous shoots which will flower next year. Cut off the tips of these shoots in the following March.
MINIATURE, SHRUB & GROUND COVER BUSHES	No pruning is required.	Very little pruning is required. Remove dead and sickly growth and trim to shape, if necessary. Remove and burn mildewed tips. Use scissors rather than secateurs for Miniatures.
CLIMBERS	Do not prune — merely remove any dead tips which may be present.	The correct pruning method depends upon the variety — see pages 61–71. **Method 1** Cut out dead and exhausted wood. Reduce some of the main stems to where a strong branch arises — shorten the side shoots you can reach by about two-thirds. **Method 2** Cut out dead and exhausted wood. Shorten the side shoots you can reach by about two-thirds. **Method 3** Cut out dead and exhausted wood.

EASY-CARE METHOD

It came as a surprise to many rose experts that the Easy-Care Method of pruning has proved to be so successful. Extensive trials carried out by the Royal National Rose Society and other organisations in the 1990s have shown that this technique is at least equal to the laborious Traditional Method which is recommended in the standard textbooks. The blooms are sometimes larger and more numerous and the bushes are no less healthy than with the standard method.

Nothing could be simpler — the bush is cut to half its height with secateurs or a hedge trimmer. Leave all the weak and twiggy growth — cut out dead wood at the base if you want to. Timing and tools are the same as for the Traditional Method — see pages 107 and 108.

WATERING

One of the blessings of the rose is its deep-rooting habit of growth. This means that watering of established plants is not vital in some seasons.

Unfortunately, this ability of a rose bush to remain fresh and green in summer when shallow-rooted plants have started to wilt leads many people to neglect watering. Trials have shown that during a summer with several dry spells the failure to water leads to impaired growth, small blooms and an early end to flowering even though the leaves may stay firm and green.

Some roses may need watering after only a few days of dry weather — newly-planted roses, climbers growing against walls and bushes planted in sandy soil. All roses will need water, and plenty of it, during a period of drought in late spring or summer.

A watering can is the usual applicator — use about 5 litres for each bush or standard and 15 litres for a climber. Never water little and often. Hold the can close to the ground and water slowly through the spout, not through a rose. Follow the experts by adding a measure of soluble fertilizer to the water.

Trickle irrigation through a perforated hose-pipe laid close to the bushes is perhaps the best method of watering. A quick and easy technique popular in America is to build a ridge of soil around each bush and then fill the basin with a hose-pipe.

HOEING

The main purpose of hoeing is to keep down weeds, such as couch grass, which are not smothered by mulching. For this purpose hoeing must be carried out at regular and frequent intervals so that the underground parts of the weeds will be eventually starved.

Hoeing must not go deeper than 2–3 cm below the surface, or rose roots may be damaged. Do not bother to hoe to keep moisture in the soil — a "dust mulch" is of very little value.

> The garden fork has little place in the established rose garden. A light pricking over in spring and again in autumn can be carried out but deep soil disturbance must always be avoided.

DISBUDDING

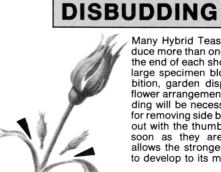

Many Hybrid Teas normally produce more than one flower bud at the end of each shoot. If you want large specimen blooms for exhibition, garden display or indoor flower arrangement, then disbudding will be necessary. This calls for removing side buds by nipping out with the thumb and finger as soon as they are visible. This allows the stronger terminal bud to develop to its maximum size.

CUTTING

The rose is perhaps the most attractive and widely used of all cut flowers for home decoration, and an abundant supply of blooms can be obtained from June onwards from even the smallest rose garden.

A certain amount of care is necessary to avoid weakening the bushes. Do not take more than one-third of the flowering stem with the flower and always cut just above an outward-facing bud.

If the bush is not growing strongly, the flower stems removed should not bear any leaves. Cutting blooms from newly-planted roses is not generally recommended during the first season in the garden, although removal of a few blooms without leaves will do little or no harm.

DEAD-HEADING

The regular removal of dead blooms from Floribundas and Hybrid Teas is an important task. When the flowers have faded remove the whole truss, cutting the stem just above the second or third leaf down. By doing this the plant's energy which would have been lost in forming hips is conserved, and a regular succession of new flowering shoots is ensured. Faded flowers on first year roses should be removed with very little stem.

Do not dead-head once flowering roses nor varieties grown for their decorative hips.

THINNING

Following pruning, it is often found that two or more shoots have developed from a single bud. Only one of these should be retained, the other weaker or inward-facing shoots being gently removed by rubbing out with the fingers.

FEEDING

Hunger signs

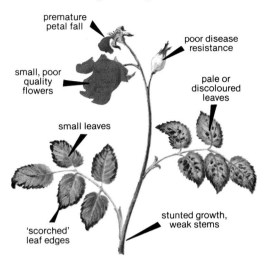

- premature petal fall
- poor disease resistance
- small, poor quality flowers
- pale or discoloured leaves
- small leaves
- 'scorched' leaf edges
- stunted growth, weak stems

Roses, like most other garden plants, make heavy demands on the reserves of plant foods in the soil. If one or more of the vital elements run short, then hunger signs appear on the leaves or flowers and both vigour and display are affected. The answer is to feed your roses every year.

Mulching, as described on page 106, will provide humus and some nutrients. But extra plant foods will be required, and the basic way to provide them is to use a proprietary compound fertilizer containing nitrogen, phosphates and potash.

Powder or granular fertilizer is the usual form, sprinkled around the plants in spring and summer. The most famous powder mixture is Tonks Formula, devised about 100 years ago. A modern version is available as Toprose Fertilizer, which contains magnesium and iron plus gypsum as well as the three major plant foods.

Liquid fertilizers are available in bottles, such as Bio Plant Food, or as boxes of soluble powder, such as Miracle-Gro. An excellent choice for quick and inexpensive treatment — regular repeat treatments are necessary during the season.

Foliar feeding has aroused a great deal of interest and some argument in the rose world. The specially formulated fertilizers are used to supplement and not replace soil feeding, and have the unique advantage of getting into the sap stream only hours after being sprayed on to the leaves. A favourite with exhibitors, as trials have shown that the size of blooms is increased as well as the general health of the plant.

PLANT FOOD TYPE	PLANT FOOD	WHAT IT DOES
MAJOR (required in large amounts)	**NITROGEN (N)**	Nitrogen stimulates the growth of leaves and stems and increases the size of the plant.
	PHOSPHATES (P_2O_5)	Phosphates stimulate the growth of roots and stems and speed up flowering.
	POTASH (K_2O)	Potash stimulates the production of top quality blooms. It also improves drought- and disease-resistance.
INTERMEDIATE (required in moderate amounts)	**CALCIUM (Ca)**	Calcium, magnesium, iron, boron and manganese maintain the normal green colour of the foliage so that growth and appearance are not spoilt by leaf discoloration and premature fall. Boron prevents leaflet distortion, and calcium reduces the incidence of die-back of stems.
	MAGNESIUM (Mg)	
MINOR (required in trace amounts)	**IRON (Fe)**	
	BORON (B)	The minor plant foods, or trace elements, also contribute in some way to disease prevention and the general health of the plant.
	MANGANESE (Mn)	

The Feeding Programme

STANDARD PROGRAMME

Spring treatment before leaves are fully open

Apply approximately one small handful of rose fertilizer around each plant when the soil is moist. Hoe in lightly.

Summer treatment in June or July

Apply approximately one small handful of rose fertilizer around each plant. Do not feed after the end of July or soft, frost-sensitive growth may be produced.

QUICK PROGRAMME

Monthly, from April until the end of July

Useful where a large number of roses have to be fed and where economy is an important factor. Use a diluted liquid or soluble fertilizer and apply through a hose-end dilutor.

EXPERT PROGRAMME

Fortnightly, between the two treatments of the Standard Programme

Many exhibitors and keen rose growers enrich the Standard Programme (see above) by regular foliar feeding. Use Fillip in a sprayer, taking care to wet the leaves thoroughly. Do not spray in bright sunlight.

CHAPTER 7
ROSE TROUBLES

The rose, like any other living thing, is liable to attack by harmful organisms. As a general pattern, the insect pests of spring are followed by the diseases of summer and autumn. Good cultivation is not the whole answer. A well-grown bush is able to withstand the effects of an attack much more successfully than a neglected specimen, but there is no way of completely stopping rose troubles from entering your garden.

Don't immediately assume that every disfigurement is due to an insect pest or a fungus disease — many problems are caused by the weather, lack of nutrients, weedkiller drift and poor management. Fortunately, you are never likely to see more than a few rose troubles in your own garden, and the purpose of this chapter is to show you what the rest look like as well as to list the correct control measures.

Learning to identify the symptoms of rose troubles is, of course, less interesting than learning to recognize rose varieties but it is no less important. This is because most pests and diseases can be checked quite easily if treated promptly, but may be difficult or impossible to control if left to get out of hand due to ignorance or neglect.

How to reduce the risk of troubles in your garden

Buy good plants. Abundant roots and sound stems are essential — see page 91. If you live in a disease-prone area choose varieties which are known to possess good disease resistance — see the A–Z guides on pages 13-49.

Never leave rubbish lying about. Rake up and burn prunings and fallen diseased leaves. Pick off and destroy mildewed shoot tips.

Prepare the ground thoroughly. A rose growing in poorly-drained soil is susceptible to a lot of troubles.

Avoid overcrowding. Do not plant closer together than the recommended spacing — see page 105. Prune to produce an open-centred bush.

Feed the plants properly. Potash is vital here, because it builds up disease resistance and accelerates the ripening of new wood. Phosphates promote a healthy root system.

Avoid overliming. Too much lime in the soil will cause chlorosis — leaf yellowing due to iron and manganese shortage.

Plant in the proper place and in the proper way. This will reduce the risk of problems due to drought, waterlogging, wind rock, frost damage, light deficiency, excessive suckering, etc.

Inspect plants regularly. Catch problems early, when occasional insects can be picked off and diseases kept from spreading by using a fungicide.

Why roses fail to survive

A good quality rose bush planted in the manner described in this book should grow and flourish for many years. Failure to survive will almost certainly be due to one of the following causes:

Loose planting — see page 104. Test: Tug stem gently in spring after planting. If the plant moves easily, tread around the bush

Wind rock especially in exposed sites

Waterlogged soil around the roots because of poor drainage

Severe drought especially in poor soils

Severe frost — see page 113

Use of fresh manure at planting time

Hard pruning every year on Floribundas, and on Hybrid Teas in sandy soils

Dry roots at planting time

Too much lime in the soil

The fatal diseases: rust, canker and honey fungus — see pages 115 and 119

The underground pests: chafer grubs and ants — see page 116

Planting under trees can lead to death from the combined effect of root dryness, dense shade and toxic drip from the leaf canopy

Cultural Problems

NITROGEN SHORTAGE
Young leaves small and pale green. Red spots sometimes develop. Early leaf fall. Stems stunted and weak.

Apply a compound fertilizer.

PHOSPHATE SHORTAGE
Young leaves small and dark green, with purplish tints on underside. Early leaf fall. Stems stunted and weak.

Apply a compound fertilizer.

POTASH SHORTAGE
Young leaves reddish, mature leaves green with brown, brittle margins. Flowers small. Common on sandy soils.

Apply a compound fertilizer.

MAGNESIUM SHORTAGE
Leaves pale at centre, with dead areas close to midrib. Oldest leaves worst affected. Early leaf fall.

Apply a fertilizer containing magnesium (e.g. Toprose).

IRON SHORTAGE
Leaves with large yellow areas. Young leaves worst affected — almost entirely yellow.

Avoid overliming. Apply Toprose Fertilizer. On chalky soils use MultiTonic.

MANGANESE SHORTAGE
Leaves with yellow bands between veins. Oldest leaves worst affected.

Avoid overliming. On chalky soils use MultiTonic at the rate recommended on the box.

FROST DAMAGE

Affected leaves are crinkled and torn with brown markings. Yellow patches sometimes appear. In most areas of Britain this damage is not serious, and the damage to stem tips of even newly-planted roses is not likely to be a problem in an average British winter.

In northern areas where severe and prolonged frosts are frequent, some winter protection may be necessary. Cover the bush with straw and bracken, and then wrap sacking around the covered plant. Remove the protective coating after the worst of the winter frosts have passed and before the growth buds begin to open.

WATERLOGGING

Leaves with large yellow areas. Veins and central area turn yellow first. Prevent by ensuring good drainage and after heavy frosts or gales tread down all plants which have been loosened. No cure — replant in a better prepared site if growth is spindly and flowers are of poor quality.

BALLING

Buds develop normally, but the petals fail to open and then turn brown. It is usually due to the effect of wet weather on varieties with large, thin-petalled blooms. Balling is always worst in a shady spot where the buds are shielded from the drying rays of the sun. It can also be caused by a heavy greenfly attack.

LAWN WEEDKILLER DAMAGE

Leaf stalks twisted spirally, leaves narrow and twisted. Stems distorted and reddish. The cause is lawn weedkiller which has been allowed to drift on to the roses — never treat a lawn on a windy day, and never use a watering can for both weedkilling *and* watering roses. Cut off the affected stems — the bush will recover.

Pest and Disease Control

There are times when pests and diseases will attack, and a spray or dust will be necessary if mildew, black spot or green-fly threaten your roses.

Chemicals used to control garden troubles are called **pesticides** and are safer than the nicotine, arsenic and mercury compounds used in grand-father's day. But they still should be treated with respect and there are a few simple rules to follow.

BEFORE YOU START SPRAYING

- **CHOOSE THE RIGHT PRODUCT.** Insects and other small pests are controlled by **Insecticides** which are used at the first signs of attack. A **Systemic Insecticide** enters the sap stream — in this way new growth will be protected and insects hidden from the spray will be killed. **Fungicides** are designed to prevent (not cure) diseases and so spraying must start before the attack begins and repeat spraying is usually necessary. The **Systemic Fungicides,** such as Systhane, go inside the plant and have some curative effect if a few disease spots have already appeared.
- **READ THE LABEL CAREFULLY.** Follow the instructions — do not make the mixture stronger than recommended. Never use equipment which has contained weedkillers.

SPRAYER TYPES

For a minor attack on a few bushes use a trigger sprayer. Ready-to-use ones are available but you pay more for the convenience. If an aerosol is used, keep the recommended distance away from the foliage. For larger quantities a compression sprayer will be required — choose a 5 litre size for general use. Hose-end dilutors are an alternative way to apply pesticides and liquid feeds.

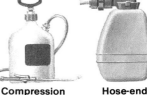

Ready-to-use trigger sprayer **Refillable trigger sprayer** **Compression sprayer** **Hose-end dilutor**

SPRAYING

The weather must be neither sunny nor windy

During the flowering season spray in the evening, when bees will have stopped working

Leaves should be dry

Use a fine forceful spray. It is wise to keep all sprays off the skin. Wash off any splashes

Spray the top and underside of the foliage thoroughly until the liquid starts to run off the leaves

THE ROSE-AID KIT

Nobody wants a garage filled with a large collection of bottles, boxes and assorted brews. It is, however, a good idea to keep a small rose-aid kit for sudden emergencies — derris for greenfly and caterpillars and Systhane or carbendazim for the common diseases. Alternatively you can buy Multirose for combined pest and disease control.

'COCKTAIL' SPRAYS

Because roses are attacked by a range of pests and diseases it is often necessary to apply a combined spray. Do not mix different chemicals together unless recommended by the manufacturer. Some sprays, such as Multirose, are already formulated to control both pests and diseases. More than one fungicide is included to improve the level of disease control. The inclusion of a foliar feed in the mixture helps recovery from pest and disease attack.

EXPERT ROSE CARE PROGRAMME

It is, of course, possible to keep a regular watch on your roses and then spray with the appropriate pesticide when each insect appears or each disease threatens. Some keen rose growers prefer to follow a routine programme each year, and just add extra treatments as the needs arise.

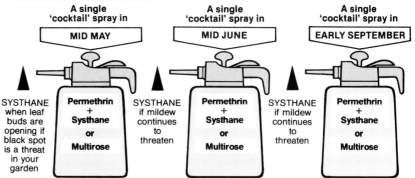

A single 'cocktail' spray in **MID MAY**

A single 'cocktail' spray in **MID JUNE**

A single 'cocktail' spray in **EARLY SEPTEMBER**

SYSTHANE when leaf buds are opening if black spot is a threat in your garden

Permethrin + Systhane or Multirose

SYSTHANE if mildew continues to threaten

Permethrin + Systhane or Multirose

SYSTHANE if mildew continues to threaten

Permethrin + Systhane or Multirose

AFTER YOU HAVE FINISHED SPRAYING

- **Wash out equipment thoroughly.** Wash your hands and face if the label tells you to do so.
- **Do not keep the spray solution.** Make up a fresh batch of spray each time you wish to treat your roses.
- **Store packs in a safe place.** Never transfer chemicals into a beer bottle or any unlabelled container and never keep old illegible boxes and bottles. Throw them in the dustbin after you have emptied the contents down an outside drain.

Diseases

The most serious fungal diseases are mildew, black spot and rust. Some varieties are described as 'resistant to disease', which means that the bush will remain free from attack under ordinary conditions. But under epidemic conditions preventive spraying will be necessary, because these varieties are resistant, not immune.

RUST

Not common, but it is often fatal when it strikes. Rust-prone area is S.W. England. Orange swellings, which turn black in August, appear on underside of leaves. New shoots turn reddish and shrivel. Usual time for attack — July.

It is encouraged by potash shortage and by a cold spring following a dry summer and hard winter.

Spray with Systhane.

PURPLE SPOTTING

Not to be confused with black spot. The markings are smaller, more irregular and without a fringe. It is caused by poor growing conditions, not a fungus. It can also be caused by using a copper-based spray. It is not nearly as serious as black spot.

Improve drainage. Apply a peat mulch and a compound fertilizer.

CANKER

Usually appears as a distinct brown and sunken area close to the base of a stem. The edge of the canker may be swollen and the bark cracked.

The canker fungus enters the stem through a wound caused by insect or disease attack or mechanical damage. Be careful when hoeing!

If the canker enlarges and encircles the stem, the whole of the growth above the diseased area will be killed.

Cut out and burn all of the diseased wood. Paint large cuts with Arbrex. Dip the secateur blades in methylated spirits after use. Apply a balanced compound fertilizer, such as Toprose.

MILDEW

The most widespread rose disease. White powdery mould on leaves and buds — leaf cockling and premature fall take place. Usual time for attack — summer or early autumn.

It is encouraged by closed-in conditions, dryness at the roots, poor feeding and by hot days followed by cold nights.

Spray with Multirose or Systhane at the first signs of disease. Repeat one week later and apply further sprays if the spots reappear.

BLACK SPOT

S.W. England and S. Wales are worst affected areas. Less common in industrial areas. Black spots with yellow fringes spread rapidly, causing leaves to fall. Starts early; becomes clearly visible in July/August. Heavy infections spread to leaf buds and later to stems which die back. Severe defoliation may take place.

It is encouraged by potash shortage and warm, wet weather in summer.

Difficult to control. Always remove and burn fallen leaves which are diseased. Use two sprays of Multirose or Systhane a week apart when leaf buds begin to open. Spray again in summer as soon as the first spots appear. Repeat as necessary.

DIE-BACK

Shoots may die back, beginning at the tip and progressing steadily downwards, for a number of reasons. Die-back is not a specific disease. It can be caused by frost damage, canker at the base of the stem, waterlogging, mildew or black spot. Yellow and orange varieties are more susceptible than others.

A common cause is a deficiency in potash, calcium, phosphates and boron. Feeding is essential in spring if die-back is a problem.

Do not feed in autumn as this leads to the production of unripe and frost-sensitive wood.

Cut off the affected shoot at a bud below the dead area.

Pests on the stem

Peach-potato aphid   Rose aphid

GREENFLY (Aphid)

The commonest and most serious of all rose pests. They can be orange, reddish and black as well as green. The first clusters of these insects can be found feeding on the sap of tender new shoots in the spring, and vigour is seriously reduced.

Growth may be stopped or distorted, and infested buds sometimes fail to open. A sticky substance (honeydew) produced by these pests is soon covered by a black fungus (sooty mould).

The best way to tackle aphids is to use a systemic spray such as permethrin. This goes inside the plant, so foliage missed by the spray is protected, as are the leaves formed after treatment. Protection is not removed by rain.

Alternatively you can spray with a contact insecticide, which kills the aphids it touches. Choose from Malathion, Fenitrothion, Liquid Derris, Sprayday or Multirose.

FROGHOPPER (Cuckoo-spit)

White frothy spittle on shoots in May and June. Inside this froth lives the small yellow froghopper. Affected shoots are distorted and leaves may wilt.

If only a few shoots are affected, wipe off with finger and thumb. Froghopper is susceptible to Derris, Malathion etc, but before using an insecticide, spray forcibly with water to clear away froth.

ROSE SCALE

Small scurfy scales form a crust on old and neglected stems. Unsightly, and growth is weakened.

Small outbreaks can be controlled by painting affected areas with methylated spirits. Large areas will require spraying — use Malathion. Apply a forceful spray to drench the scales.

SHOOT BORER SAWFLY

A green maggot within the pith of the affected shoot. Outward symptom is withering of the tip.

Cut off and burn the branch bearing the maggot. A spray of Fenitrothion in May will prevent this damage.

Underground Pests

ANTS

Soil around the roots is loosened and plants may wilt and die. A pest of sandy areas.

Sprinkle Anti-Ant dust along the runs, or use a few drops of Nippon.

CHAFER GRUB

Fat, curved grub, over 2.5 cm long. A serious root pest which can cause death or weakening of bushes.

Kill any found during soil preparation.

Galls

"ROBIN'S PINCUSHION"

Spongy moss-covered gall on leaves, caused by the gall wasp.

It does no detectable harm, and can be retained as a curiosity. Otherwise cut off and burn.

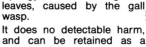

CROWN GALL

Very large, brown and warty outgrowth close to the base of a stem. Causes little or no harm, but can be cut off and the wound painted with Arbrex in autumn.

Crown gall is a much more serious problem when it occurs on the roots.

Pests on the leaf

COCKCHAFER (May bug)
Irregular-shaped holes in leaves in May or June may be due to this large, reddish-brown beetle.

Pick off and destroy beetles. Spray with Fenitrothion.

LEAF-MINER
White blisters on leaves, containing a grub.
Hand-pick affected leaves and burn. Malathion is the recommended spray.

ROSE SLUGWORM
Skeletonised areas on leaves, as only internal tissues but not veins are eaten. Affected areas turn brown.

Greenish-yellow grub may be seen on surface. Spray with Liquid Derris.

RED SPIDER
Bronzed patches on upper surface of leaves, minute yellowish 'insects' and fine webbing on underside.

Attacks occur in hot, dry weather. Spray with Malathion.

CATERPILLAR
Irregular-shaped holes in leaves may be due to caterpillars —

Vapourer moth   Winter moth   Yellow tail moth   Buff-tip moth

Pick off by hand if not too numerous. All of these pests can be very simply controlled by spraying with Fenitrothion or Multirose.

LEAFHOPPER
Pale mottled patches on leaves. Small yellowish insects or their empty white skins may be found on underside.

Growth is checked. Leaf fall occurs after a bad attack. Spray with Sprayday.

LEAF-CUTTER BEE
Regular-shaped holes at sides of leaves.
Control measures are not usually necessary, but destroy nests if found.

Flower Pests

CHAFER BEETLE
Petals and anthers eaten. One-sided blooms sometimes result.

Rose chafer   Garden chafer

Pick off and destroy beetles.

TORTRIX MOTH
Buds holed; brown rose maggot may be found inside, or within a characteristically curled leaf (see page 118).
Spray with Fenitrothion or Multirose.

THRIPS
Petal edges blackened, flowers and leaves mottled and malformed.

Minute 4-winged flies, known as thunderflies, may become serious in a hot summer.

Spray with Liquid Derris or Malathion.

CAPSID
Young buds dead and withered. Small brown spots on young leaves, which become distorted. Bright green insects — which move rapidly when disturbed.

Spray plants and soil with Fenitrothion.

Hide-away Leaf Pests

TORTRIX MOTH

Irregular-shaped holes in leaves. Leaflets spun together by fine silken threads. Brown or green caterpillars (rose maggots) may be found.

Pick and destroy rolled leaves. Spray with Fenitrothion or Multirose in May.

LEAF-ROLLING SAWFLY

Leaflets tightly rolled. Greyish-green grub inside. Affected leaves may shrivel and die. Can be serious if roses are grown near trees.

Squeeze rolled leaflets tightly between thumb and finger and then pick off and burn. To prevent damage, spray with Fenitrothion in May.

LACKEY MOTH

Irregular-shaped holes in leaves. The white, orange and grey caterpillars can cause complete defoliation.

Easy to recognize because of the 'tents' of fine white threads which they spin.

Destroy 'tents'. Spray with Fenitrothion or Multirose.

Virus Diseases

Fortunately, virus diseases have not become a serious problem in Britain. No drastic measures are required, but infected plants should not be used for propagation.

VEIN BANDING ROSE MOSAIC

Pale yellow or cream veining, distinct in late spring but much less so in summer. No serious effect — some regard it as decorative. Feed generously, as recommended on page 111.

LINE PATTERN ROSE MOSAIC

Yellow lines on leaf surface, sometimes forming an oak leaf pattern. Distinct in late spring, much less so in summer. Effect much more serious than vein banding rose mosaic — feed generously.

Blindness

Empty wheat-like husk instead of a flower bud on top of a mature stem. Blind shoots can occur with nearly all varieties, but some are particularly prone — *Peace* and *Red Devil* are examples.

Causes are many and varied — frost damage, lack of food and shortage of light have been blamed. If you are sure the shoot is blind, and not merely slow in flowering, cut it back to half its length to a healthy bud. This will then produce a shoot which should flower normally.

Weeds

It is surprising that weed control is ignored by so many books on rose growing, because weeds are certainly a major problem for millions of gardeners.

There is no single miracle cure for the weed problem — there are a number of interlinked tasks you will have to carry out. You probably already know that some weeds are annuals, and these generally can be kept in check quite easily by hoeing, mulching and spraying. The real problems are the perennial weeds — couch grass, bindweed, docks, thistles, ground elder etc which will come up year after year if left unchecked.

At soil preparation time remove all the roots of perennial weeds that you can find. If the site is a sea of couch grass then you have a real problem. The age-old way of preparing such soil is to treat with Sodium Chlorate, but this will mean waiting for up to two years before planting. A better way is to spray with glyphosate before planting — follow the instructions carefully.

To keep weeds down among growing plants there are several chemical techniques. You can use simazine or dichlobenil — if applied to weed-free soil in spring they will stop most annual weeds from germinating. Alternatively you can use Weedol later in the season as a chemical hoe to burn off all weed growth. Make sure you keep the weedkiller away from the rose leaves. If perennial broad-leaved weeds are present, paint the foliage with glyphosate.

Weedkillers, provided they carry a specific recommendation for roses, are valuable aids but the mainstay of weed control remains hand weeding and hoeing. Pull out or dig out perennial weeds, cut off annual weeds just below the surface, and apply an annual mulch as described on page 106.

Green slime and moss usually indicate poor drainage, surface compaction or fertilizer deficiency. Hoe regularly, and feed twice a year.

Suckers

Suckers are shoots which grow from the rootstock rather than from the named variety which has been grafted on to it. If nothing is done to check this growth then suckers may take over the plant completely and the bush will have reverted.

Suckering is encouraged by loose planting, severe frosts, root damage by hoeing, incorrect removal of previous suckers or the use of *R. rugosa* as a rootstock. You can easily recognize a sucker from a desirable stem by its origin below the bud union and by its different leaflet form and colour. Do not rely on the number of leaflets per leaf as your guide.

Tackle each sucker as soon as it is seen — removal is then a simple job. Trace it back to the point of origin on the root — some soil removal will be necessary. Then pull it off and replace the soil. With a recently planted rose, keep the plant firmly in place with your foot as you pull off the sucker. Snipping off suckers at ground level will only lead to an increase in sucker production.

With standards, rub off sucker growths on the stem as soon as they are seen.

Honey Fungus

A harmless-looking group of toadstools may appear next to a bush in autumn — in fact these toadstools are deadly to roses if they are the honey fungus (armillaria root rot) illustrated above.

On the roots of attacked plants you will find black 'bootlaces' produced by the fungus. Remove and burn dead and dying plants with as much of their roots as possible in order to prevent the disease from spreading. Before replanting, using Armillatox might be a wise precaution.

Soil Sickness

So many books assume that you will always be planting in virgin soil which has never grown roses before. Unfortunately this is not always so, and if the site has grown roses for more than ten years then it is liable to be rose-sick.

Oddly, the old roses may have shown little or no ill-effect as they have adapted to the conditions. But planting a new rose in such soil can lead to poor growth ('replant disease') and for this reason the top soil should be changed. If it is not practical to change all the soil then you can help matters by adding a liberal amount of compost or well-rotted manure plus a dressing of a fish, blood and bone fertilizer to the remaining soil before planting. This treatment will reduce the effect of replant disease (see page 103) but there is still some risk.

CHAPTER 8

GROWING ROSES AS A HOBBY

Most people who grow roses would not describe rose growing as their hobby. To them the queen of flowers is just a beautiful part of the overall garden picture.

For the rest rose growing is something more — the enjoyment of visiting rose shows and gardens, winning (or trying to win) prizes, propagating their own plants and keeping up with the latest trends and varieties. For them the study and practice of rose growing is an absorbing hobby.

Growing roses as a hobby dates from Victorian times, and one of its fascinating aspects is the way it has always cut across the various classes in our society. The workers of the Industrial Revolution were still farm hands at heart, and it was these people who set up the first flower shows. The legend is that it was a visit to a Nottingham miners' rose show which inspired Dean Hole to found the National Rose Society in 1876.

And so it is today, with people from all walks of life enjoying and succeeding in the hobby of rose growing. A rose in the buttonhole was once a badge of office for the man who was something in the City and for the man who looked after the local railway station. The ordinary gardener with a few roses has so much to learn from the hallowed names of the rose world, but it was still possible even in the 1970s for an engine driver with a tiny greenhouse to raise a new rose capable of winning the Gold Medal at Rome.

Learning more about roses

There is always something new happening in the rose world. Each year brings forth a crop of new varieties, and one or more of these may mark another step forward in the quest for perfection. *Peace*, *Super Star* and *Queen Elizabeth* stand out like milestones along the way, and no one can say what the next advance will be.

Will the Floribundas become more and more like Hybrid Teas in shape? Will the boom in Patio Roses continue? Will there be a new way of feeding next year? Nobody can begin to know everything about roses, and even if one did then some of the information would be out of date in a year or two. There are seven basic ways of learning more about roses. Use them all and you will surely become an expert.

Read books and journals on roses

Books and journals perform different jobs. A textbook sets out to give you a sound background to the basic facts about the history, cultivation and selection of roses. The articles in gardening magazines and newspapers are usually concerned with new developments — the latest varieties as well as the experiences of the writer or readers which would be out of place in a textbook.

Study the latest catalogues

The catalogues of our leading rose growers are mines of information. Here you will find coloured illustrations of new varieties as well as old favourites. Essential reading for the enthusiast, but do not expect to find all the faults listed.

Visit nurseries in summer

An excellent way of seeing a multitude of varieties in flower — a great aid in making the right selection. In many ways a nursery visit can give the opposite view to looking through catalogues. The catalogue may give a picture that you might never achieve in your garden —the roses in the nursery are young stock which will be taller and more showy after a few years in your rose bed.

Visit the great Rose Gardens

See pages 123–126

Join your local Horticultural Society

Here you will be able to attend talks and meet fellow rose growers. Undoubtedly the greatest benefit is that you will be able to compare experiences with people who have to contend with similar conditions to your own — the same soil type, weather and air pollution. The knowledge of the long-standing members is especially helpful if you are new to rose growing or to the district.

Visit the Shows

The shows are the highlights of the year. You can see for yourself the beauty of the new varieties, and what experts judge to be perfect form. At the stands you can discuss your problems with a variety of knowledgeable growers and suppliers. Leading shows include:

Spring Competition, London	May
Chelsea Flower Show, London	May
National Southern Show, Shepperton	June
British Rose Festival, London	July
National Northern Show, Middlesborough	July
Shrewsbury Show, Shropshire	August
Great Autumn Show, Harrogate	September

Join the Royal National Rose Society

See page 121

The Royal National Rose Society

In 1876 a group of rose enthusiasts met in London to consider "what could be done to advance the interest of the rose, for in truth the Queen of Flowers has fallen on evil days." The National Rose Society was born. Its first show was held a year later — there were no Hybrid Teas, no Floribundas and very little public interest.

From these modest beginnings, with a deficit of £300 after the first year, one of the world's most important Horticultural Societies developed. In 1961 the Society moved its headquarters to Chiswell Green near St Albans and the heyday of the RNRS was reached in the 1970s. Membership passed the 100,000 mark, making it the largest specialist Society in the world of horticulture, and the prefix 'Royal' was added by command of H.M. Queen Elizabeth II.

Its awards are eagerly sought by rose breeders everywhere and its publications are important reference books. The gardens are unrivalled in Britain (see page 123) and many overseas Rose Societies have based their organization and rules on the successful British model.

The Society caters for all rose growers — the gardener with a few roses as well as the dedicated rosarian. Unfortunately the 1990s has seen a decline in membership as the cost of subscription has risen, but even at these membership rates you receive many benefits and privileges for the price you would have to pay for just a few rose bushes. Application forms are available from The Secretary General, The Royal National Rose Society, Chiswell Green, St Albans, Herts AL2 3NR.

Royal National Rose Society,
Chiswell Green,
St Albans,
Hertfordshire

N TO: ST ALBANS ▲

The Three Hammers Inn
CHISWELL GREEN
B4630 A405
The Noke Inn
A405

▼ TO: WATFORD

BRGA

The British Rose Growers Association publishes an excellent booklet (*Find that Rose!*) which is invaluable for locating sources of unusual varieties. For details write with a stamped addressed envelope to The Editor, 303 Mile End Road, Colchester, Essex CO4 5EA.

Benefits of Membership

FREE PUBLICATIONS

• THE ROSE Sent to all members four times each year — the Society's magazine filled with down-to-earth articles and items of news from the world of roses.
• HOW TO GROW ROSES Sent to new members on joining — a non-technical handbook containing up-to-date information on planting, pruning, problems etc.
• ROSES TO ENJOY Sent to new members on joining — a list of over 1000 varieties available in Britain, together with basic details such as height, colour, fragrance etc.

FREE ROSE

A plant of a selected award-winning rose can be chosen by every new member as a free gift in place of the publications listed above.

FREE SHOWS

Your membership card admits you to many rose shows and to the British Rose Festival at the Hampton Court Palace Flower Show at a discount. This is the U.K's major rose event and has become a mecca to rose enthusiasts from all over the world. There are displays, living catalogues plus live exhibits and competitions.

FREE GARDEN VISITS

The Gardens of the Rose and Trial Ground at St Albans are yours to enjoy throughout the season — there is free admission for yourself and a friend. Here you can see one of the finest collections of roses in the world.

FREE ADVICE

As a member you are entitled to receive advice from the experts on all aspects of rose growing, so useful when you can't find the answer to an out-of-the-way problem. You can also use the reference library if you need more information than is available in your local library.

Awards

An award for a new variety is obviously highly desirable for both the raiser and the gardener. For the rose breeder who raised it there is valuable publicity and acclaim — for the gardener who chooses it there is the knowledge that the variety has proved its reliability for ordinary garden use to a panel of impartial experts. However, winning a high award is not a guarantee of public acceptance. Among the bi-colour Hybrid Tea group it was *Westminster* which won the Gold Medal, not *Piccadilly*. And *Whisky Mac*, one of the most popular of all Hybrid Teas, received no award at all.

The granting of an award is not an infallible guide to excellence and the absence of an award does not necessarily mean that the variety is a poor one. There are four reasons for this:

- There was no National Rose Society trials scheme before 1928, so an old variety could not possibly have received an NRS award.
- Not all new varieties are submitted for trials.
- An award-winning variety can deteriorate after a number of years.
- Foreign awards may be granted to a variety which might fail miserably under damp British conditions.

BRITISH AWARDS

A new variety sent to the Royal National Rose Society for testing is grown for three years in the Trial Ground at St Albans and it is assessed regularly throughout the summer by a panel of experts.

This group look for something more than a pretty flower. They consider many qualities including vigour, growth habit, freedom from disease, fragrance, and freedom and continuity of flowering. If the panel feel that the rose has merit then it can qualify for an award. The highest award they can give is a **Gold Medal** (GM) if the rose has 'some novel or outstanding quality or supersedes a similar variety which has declined'. It is more usual for a **Certificate of Merit** (CM) to be awarded in recognition of outstanding quality. Below that there is the **Trial Ground Certificate** (TGC) if the panel feel the rose should do reasonably well under most gardening conditions — an award for reliability rather than excellence.

At the top of the award ladder is the **President's International Trophy** (PIT), awarded to a variety which has received a Gold Medal and is judged to be the best new rose of the year. There is also a fragrance award — the **Edland Medal for Fragrance** (EM) which is granted to the best scented new seedling of the year.

The **James Mason Memorial Award** (JM) is made to a variety which has given 'particular pleasure to rose lovers over the past 20 years'.

The Royal Horticultural Society grants an **Award of Garden Merit** (AGM) to plants of 'outstanding excellence for garden decoration or use'.

President's International Trophy · Gold Medal · Certificate of Merit · Trial Ground Certificate · Edland Medal for Fragrance

Breeders Choice · Award of Garden Merit · Rose of the Year · James Mason Award · Gold Medal, Glasgow

The British Rose Growers Association and the British Association Representing Breeders enter their new seedlings each year to be judged by an independent panel. From these entries **The Rose of the Year** is chosen and from the rest one or more **Breeders Choice** selections based on 'health, quality and novelty' are made.

The RNRS Rose Analysis

The RNRS Rose Analysis is a useful guide to performance in gardens rather than trial grounds, and is published each year in *The Rose*.

OVERSEAS AWARDS

New roses are tested in trial grounds in many parts of the world and awards are granted on the basis of their reliability or excellence over two or more years. This method of testing roses, rather than judging them on a single day, began in the Bagatelle Gardens in Paris and was not adopted in Britain until many years later. Important European trial grounds are situated in Paris, Lyons, Geneva, Dublin, Belfast, Rome, Madrid and The Hague.

In the vastness of the United States it would not be practical to rely on a single trial site — more than a score of test gardens are used to gain an overall view of the variety under widely differing climatic conditions. Roses must score highly on all features of performance for two years in order to gain the **All-American Rose Selection** (AARS) award.

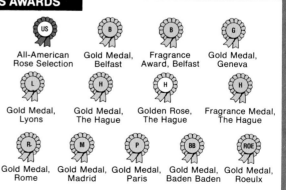

All-American Rose Selection · Gold Medal, Belfast · Fragrance Award, Belfast · Gold Medal, Geneva

Gold Medal, Lyons · Gold Medal, The Hague · Golden Rose, The Hague · Fragrance Medal, The Hague

Gold Medal, Rome · Gold Medal, Madrid · Gold Medal, Paris · Gold Medal, Baden Baden · Gold Medal, Roeulx

Great Rose Gardens of Britain

QUEEN MARY'S GARDEN, Regent's Park, London

Britain's favourite rose garden, as it is only a few minutes' walk from Baker Street tube station. The main circular garden is surrounded by a ring of pillars which are festooned with Ramblers and Climbers. There are large formal beds as well as small secluded beds to house the 40,000 plants grown here. Queen Mary's Garden is not to be missed by any rose lover, for here you will see all types and classes — Climbers scrambling through trees, enormous Shrubs in informal borders, formal beds of modern roses and many good examples of mixed plantings.

ROYAL HORTICULTURAL SOCIETY GARDENS

Wisley (Surrey) is a mecca for all gardeners. These gardens are the showpiece for the RHS and here you will see a wide diversity of rose plantings. In the main gardens there are many rose beds and borders filled with old favourites, but there are also plots with new varieties to show you how they have fared under ordinary garden conditions. Other displays include Ground Cover Roses, rope swags festooned with Climbers and also vigorous varieties growing through trees. At **Hyde Hall** (Essex) there is an extensive collection of 5000 roses which was built up by Dr & Mrs Robinson long before the gardens were acquired by the RHS, and at **Rosemoor Gardens** (Devon) an extensive display of both old and new varieties has been created.

RNRS GARDENS OF THE ROSE, St Albans, Herts

From mid June until mid October these 20 acres of gardens are open to the public for seven days a week. This display is one of the largest living catalogues in the world — you can admire the first Hybrid Tea or an old Shrub Rose and then move to the Trial Ground where you will see varieties still unnamed but which may become tomorrow's favourites. But the St Albans gardens are much more than just an impressive display of 30,000 plants covering 1650 different species and varieties. Here you will find many separate gardens — sunken beds of Miniatures, large beds cut in lawns, small pillars and stately pergolas ... and much, much more.

HELMINGHAM HALL, Helmingham, Suffolk

Helmingham, like Mannington, is an East Anglian moated stately home which has been in the same family for hundreds of years. Lady Tollemache and her mother-in-law before her have created a splendid garden in which Old Garden Roses are the stars. You will find all sorts of different types — Gallicas, Bourbons, Centifolias, Damasks, Moss Roses, China Roses and so on, but pride of place goes to the Hybrid Musks.

ROYAL BOTANIC GARDENS, Kew, London

Roses of all types feature in our national botanical garden, but the collection is not particularly large and the displays are scattered throughout the gardens. The formal beds close to the Palm House are worth a visit, and there is also a comprehensive collection of Shrub Roses. One of the exhibits is a border which has been planted to provide an insight into the history of the rose.

CITY OF BELFAST ROSE GARDEN, Belfast, N. Ireland

In 1964 the first roses were planted in the new Trials Grounds created in the beautiful Sir Thomas and Lady Dixon Park on the outskirts of Belfast. In 1992 the gardens were largely redesigned to coincide with the World Rose Conference held in the city and now provide an outstanding display of both old and new varieties. Here you can see beds of age-old roses close to plantings of seedlings which do not yet have a name.

MOTTISFONT ABBEY, Romsey, Hampshire

Many of the gardens described on these pages are designed to give the visitor an insight into newer varieties, so that he or she will not have to rely on catalogue photographs and descriptions. As a backcloth to these modern Hybrid Teas and Floribundas there are Shrubs, Ramblers and Climbers. Mottisfont Abbey is different — it houses the National Collection of Old Garden (pre 1900) Roses. This rose garden was designed by Graham Thomas for the National Trust and since its creation in 1972 has become popular with people who wish to see Damasks, Centifolias, Gallicas, Hybrid Perpetuals and other Old Garden Roses which were so admired by the Victorians.

PROVINCIAL DISPLAY GARDENS

Award-winning roses can be seen at the RNRS Display Gardens and Trial Ground at St Albans, but for many rose enthusiasts there is no way that they can make an annual pilgrimage to see these new varieties. To overcome this difficulty Display Gardens have been created in provincial parks so that local residents can see the award-winning varieties and information can be gained about their performance away from St Albans. Of course, these Provincial Display Gardens usually have impressive rose displays in addition to the RNRS award winners.

SAUGHTON PARK, Edinburgh, Lothian
QUEEN'S PARK, Colwyn Bay, Clwyd
VIVARY PARK, Taunton, Somerset
ROATH PARK, Cardiff, S. Glamorgan
HARLOW CAR, Harrogate, N. Yorkshire
THE ARBORETUM, Nottingham, Nottinghamshire
HEIGHAM PARK, Norwich, Norfolk
BOROUGH PARK, Redcar, Cleveland
POLLOK PARK, Glasgow, Strathclyde

MANNINGTON HALL, Saxthorpe, Norfolk

At the heart of this lovely garden is the walled Heritage Rose Garden. Along its paths you will find a living history of both roses and rose garden styles, and beyond the walls there is a wide assortment of modern and not-so-modern varieties — this joint project of the Walpole family and the nearby Peter Beales Nursery has resulted in one of the best rose gardens in the country.

GRAND GARDENS

Hidcote Manor

Virtually all of the stately homes and botanical gardens of Britain contain roses, and some list a rose garden as one of their features. Examples are listed below, but you should remember that the size and range of varieties within these rose gardens vary widely.

ANGLESEY ABBEY, Lode, Cambridgeshire
BIRMINGHAM BOTANICAL GARDENS, Midlands (West)
BLENHEIM PALACE, Woodstock, Oxfordshire
BODNANT GARDENS, Conwy, Gwynedd
CAMBRIDGE BOTANIC GARDENS, Cambridgeshire
CAPEL MANOR, Waltham Cross, Hertfordshire
CASTLE HOWARD, York, N. Yorkshire
CLIVEDEN, Maidenhead, Berkshire
CRANBORNE MANOR, Cranborne, Dorset
CRATHES CASTLE, Aberdeen, Grampian
HAMPTON COURT PALACE, Greater London
HATFIELD HOUSE, Hatfield, Hertfordshire
HIDCOTE MANOR, Chipping Campden, Gloucestershire
KIFTSGATE COURT, Chipping Campden, Gloucestershire
LUTON HOO, Luton, Bedfordshire
NESS GARDENS, South Wirral, Merseyside
NYMANS, Handcross, W. Sussex
OXFORD BOTANIC GARDENS, Oxfordshire
SAVILL GARDENS, Englefield Green, Surrey
SISSINGHURST CASTLE, Cranbrook, Kent
STRATFIELD SAYE HOUSE, Reading, Berkshire
TATTON PARK, Knutsford, Cheshire
THE ROSARIUM, Claydon, Suffolk

NURSERY DISPLAY GARDENS

Your local garden centre or nursery will have maiden plants in bloom during the summer months, and some nurseries have special Display Gardens where beds and borders of mature roses can be seen. Notable examples include

C & K JONES, Chester, Cheshire
FRYERS NURSERY, Knutsford, Cheshire
HARKNESS ROSE GARDENS, Hitchin, Hertfordshire
LeGRICE ROSES, North Walsham, Norfolk
PETER BEALES ROSES, Attleborough, Norfolk
MATTOCK'S NURSERY, Nuneham Courtney, Oxfordshire
DAVID AUSTIN ROSES, Albrighton, Staffordshire
NOTCUTT'S NURSERIES, Woodbridge, Suffolk
DICKSON ROSES, Newtownards, N. Ireland
COCKER ROSES, Aberdeen, Scotland

Great Rose Gardens Overseas

IRELAND

ST ANNE'S PARK, Dublin

The landscaped rose garden was created in the 1970s, and both the wide range of varieties and the beautiful aspect have received international acclaim. There is a trial ground here, and the Miniature Rose display garden was one of the first in Europe.

SWITZERLAND

PARC DE LA GRANGE, Geneva

Perhaps the loveliest rose garden of all, admired for its architecture as well as its roses. It consists of three terraces with pools and fountains. Each level is graced with many types of roses, and the whole area is floodlit during the summer months. Geneva Rose Week is the time of the International Rose Judging, and it is also the time when an open-air ballet is performed amid the 12,000 floodlit roses.

ITALY

MUNICIPAL ROSE GARDEN, Rome

This garden has the finest setting of all — a natural amphitheatre on the slopes of the Aventine Hill. In front of it are the ruins of the Palace of the Caesars. Around its edge runs a gallery of 200 climbing varieties and the central area contains Species Roses, early hybrids and popular modern varieties. An important International Rose Competition is held here each year.

SPAIN

PARQUE DEL OESTE, Madrid

A favourite argument amongst well-travelled rosarians is whether Geneva or Madrid boasts the loveliest rose garden in Europe. If variety is what you like then the Parque del Oeste would probably be your choice. Miniature Roses hugging the ground near Climbers as tall as houses — statuary, fountains, cypress trees and flower-decked tunnels as well as an impressive collection of 30,000 roses.

U.S.A.

HERSHEY ROSE GARDEN, Pennsylvania

If you had to pick just one of the countless American rose gardens to visit, then you would have to choose between the Hershey and the Park of Roses in Columbus. In the Hershey Rose Garden all rose tastes are catered for — there are thousands of modern Hybrid Teas and Floribundas as well as many hundreds of Shrub Rose varieties.

PARK OF ROSES, Columbus, Ohio

This 14 acre garden was once the home of the American Rose Society, and today it is a mecca for people who want to learn about as well as just enjoy roses. There are regular demonstrations throughout the year and the collection of over 30,000 roses covers all the various classes and types.

AMERICAN ROSE CENTER, Shreveport, Louisiana

In the 1970s work began on the creation of a rose garden around the new headquarters of The American Rose Society following its move from Columbus, Ohio. The approach has been different to the A–Z living dictionary style found in so many rose gardens. Here display is the paramount feature, with the beds and borders showing ways in which the plants can be grouped together for maximum effect.

HUNTINGDON BOTANICAL GARDENS, San Marino, California

This fascinating horticultural park has many features for the keen gardener and two special items for the rosarian. There is the world's largest collection of Tea Roses and also a Rose History Walk studded with about 1000 old varieties.

CANADA

ROYAL BOTANICAL GARDENS, Hamilton, Ontario

Canada's best known rose garden is part of the Royal Botanical Gardens complex in Ontario. In 1967 a Centennial Rose Garden was created and there are about 3000 Floribundas and Hybrid Tea varieties on display. Among and around these beds of modern roses there are collections of old varieties. Other notable Canadian rose gardens include the **Floralies Rose Garden** (Montreal), **Canadian Horticultural Society Rose Garden** (Niagara) and the **Dominion Botanic Gardens** (Ottawa).

NEW ZEALAND

ROGERS ROSE GARDEN, Hamilton

This modern rose garden is not the largest but is probably the most attractive of all the New Zealand rose displays. There are only a few acres and a few thousand plants but the informal planting is attractive and a change from the geometric beds found in the majority of rose gardens. **Parnell Rose Garden** (Auckland) is larger and for people interested in tomorrow's varieties there is the **N.Z National Rose Society Trial Ground** at Palmeston North.

page 126

FRANCE

LA ROSERAIE DE L'HAY LES ROSES, Paris

Not a vast collection of plants, but undoubtedly one of the most comprehensive outdoor rose museums in the world. Here you will find beds displaying the history of the rose, beds containing the varieties grown at Malmaison and even a Theatre of the Rose.

BAGATELLE, Paris

The Roseraie at the Bagatelle contains many thousands of rose plants, and one of its great attractions is the multitude of neat geometric beds bearing the latest varieties. The first International Rose Competition was held at the Bagatelle, and the Gold Medal of the Concours International des Roses Nouvelles is still one of the rose world's top honours.

PARC DE LA TETE D'OR, Lyons

One of the world's great rose gardens was opened in 1964 at the birthplace of the modern rose. There are 100,000 plants in 14 acres of Display Garden — Miniatures in rockeries, Climbers on pergolas, vast seas of bushes in beds, hundreds of Shrub varieties and the trial grounds for new French seedlings.

GERMANY

WESTFALENPARK, Dortmund

The original German Rosarium was created at Sangerhausen. This great rose garden was not easily accessible after World War II as it was situated in the German Democratic Republic, and so in 1969 a new German National Rosarium was started. The varieties are arranged geographically in the 25 acre site, and each recognized breeder has his own plot. Apart from these modern roses there is a large collection of old-fashioned varieties and you will also find small greenhouses filled with tender roses.

INSEL MAINAU, Lake Constance

This garden on an island in Lake Constance has a beauty which differs from all the others described on these pages. Here the old varieties are grown as shrubs among semi-tropical plants in an Italianate setting. There are also massed plantings of newer varieties — a great treat for all lovers of roses.

ZWEIBRUCKEN ROSARIUM, near Saarbrucken

Insel Mainau is the place to go to if you want to see roses in a semi-tropical setting, but Zweibrucken Rosarium is the garden to visit to see roses set among water features such as fountains, lakes and pools. There are about 60,000 roses planted here set in a wide variety of designs and with a wide range of plants grown as companions. It has been described as one of the loveliest gardens in Europe.

SANGERHAUSEN ROSARIUM, near Leipzig

In 1903 this 30 acre display garden opened and soon became the largest collection of old varieties in the world. Just one hedge contains about 800 Species Roses and there are thousands upon thousands of different Old Garden Roses. The grounds suffered in the years before the reunification of Germany, but Sangerhausen is the place to go if you want to see old varieties you will have never seen before.

DENMARK

VALBYPARKEN, Copenhagen

Opened in 1963, this large rose garden is only a few minutes away from the centre of Copenhagen. There is an extensive collection — about 20,000 plants in beds arranged in the shape of a horseshoe. Danish rose breeders carry out their National Trials in Valbyparken.

HOLLAND

WESTBROEKPARK, The Hague

The rose garden in this public park was created after the war, and it has now become the largest and most important collection in the Benelux countries. More than 20,000 plants are set out in the multitude of 16 sq. metre beds which make up the main display area of the rose garden.

Exhibiting your roses

Decorative Classes
The roses are judged on the basis of the overall effect of the blooms together with the leaves and stems in a bowl or vase. Artistry and peak condition are much more important here than flowers which are above average in size

Specimen Classes
The roses are mainly judged as individual blooms. The usual container is the display box (see page 128) and the quest here is for blooms which are as near perfect as possible in shape and colour and which are significantly larger than average.

You do not have to exhibit your blooms in order to be a rose lover or a rose expert. But the show-bench has a definite place in teaching you how to grow better roses, because it introduces the spirit of competition and makes you pay more attention to detail. Blooms which once were thought to be perfectly satisfactory may suddenly become second-rate when seen through the eyes of the exhibitor. The joy, of course, is in receiving an award rather than in the prize money . . . which is hardly likely to cover your expenses.

Start with your local horticultural show and don't go in for too many classes — you will soon learn that staging your exhibits takes far longer than you think. Begin by looking around this year's show — note the classes, write down the winning varieties and try to see why the winners received their awards. All of this will prepare you for your entry in next year's show. You may be puzzled by the poor standard of the First Prize display, but remember that you are seeing the exhibits *after* the judging — and judges make their awards for appearance at the time of their inspection.

If you want to take up rose showing seriously then you *must* become a member of the Royal National Rose Society. From them you will receive lists of varieties, judging standards etc., and also the right to exhibit in the RNRS classes at the shows.

HOW ROSES ARE JUDGED

Points gained

Blooms: Decorative classes — good average size for the variety.
Specimen classes — larger than average size for the variety.
Hybrid Teas — half to three-quarters open with a circular outline and well-formed centre.
Floribundas — fully open.

Petals: Bright, firm, clean and free from blemish.

Leaves: Clean and undamaged. Adequate in quantity and size.

Stems: Straight and in proportion to flower size.

Presentation: Graceful balance, artistically arranged. Flowers neither crushed together nor too widely spaced.

Points lost

Blooms: Fewer than the average number of petals for the variety.
Size not typical. Immature or blown blooms.
Hybrid Teas — blooms with split or confused centres. Obvious removal of petals or obvious overdressing (see page 128).

Petals: Faded, drooping, soiled or diseased.

Leaves: Diseased or damaged. Inadequate in quantity and size.

Stems: Weak, bent, diseased or twisted.

Presentation: Untidy or lop-sided. Poor colour arrangement or an excessive display of stems and/or leaves.

GROWING PRIZE ROSES

Pick your varieties carefully
The judges will be looking for large blooms with many petals and high centres. On page 93 there is a list of H.T varieties which frequently win prizes at local and national rose shows. Some of these are not recommended for general garden display but others, such as *Alec's Red* and *Pink Favourite* will give you a fine garden display as well as prizes at the show.

Keep records
Most keen rose exhibitors keep a detailed diary. In this they note the time of pruning, feeding dates and other comments so that they will know for next year what they did right ... and wrong.

Get the timing right
One of the skills of successful showing is learning how to get a flush of blooms in peak condition just in time for the show. On average it takes about twelve weeks from pruning to the perfect bloom stage, but this can be as little as ten and as much as sixteen weeks. There is one basic way of making sure you don't miss having blooms on the vital day — try to grow as many plants as possible and prune them on different dates.

Follow the basic rules of rose care
Follow the principles of rose cultivation and soil preparation laid down in Chapters 5 and 6. Many rose exhibitors insist on hard pruning (see page 108) but this is not really necessary. Regular feeding is recommended — supplement the basic spring top-dressing with regular applications of liquid fertilizer or foliar feed (see page 111). Watering in dry weather and timely pest and disease control are vital.

GETTING READY FOR THE SHOW

About three or four days before the show you will start to get ready in earnest — at this stage you will look for blooms and stems which will be at their best on the big day. But there are several jobs, such as disbudding and covering, which will have taken place a week or two before selection, and even earlier you will have carried out one of the most important tasks of all — studying the show schedule.

Judges may mark you down or disqualify you for a minor breach of the rules — it does not have to be important. Select the class you wish to enter and make sure your exhibit will meet *all* the requirements. Does the specified number refer to blooms or stems? Is wiring allowed? Are vases and bowls supplied? Clear up these and any other points well before the show.

DISBUDDING This should be carried out as soon as the side buds are big enough to handle — see page 110 for instructions. Stake the stem if the site is exposed or if the bloom is to be covered (see below).

In the case of Floribundas, some disbudding should be done about two weeks before the show. Remove the large central bud and one or two of the smallest ones from each truss, so that there will be many open and equal-sized blooms on the day of the show.

COVERING A conical protector on a wooden stake above each bloom is a useful aid for the serious exhibitor. Rain is prevented from spotting delicate petals, which is vital in the more important classes.

Put the cover in position about ten to fourteen days before the show. It must be firm enough to avoid rocking against the bloom in windy weather, and it must be at the correct height to protect the bloom without shading it unduly. It must also be large enough to prevent rain from dripping down on to the petals.

TYING Many exhibitors loosely tie the centres of selected blooms with wool about three days before the show. The purpose is to lengthen the petals.

Choose half open (never fully open) blooms and use wool which is uncoloured, soft and thick. The petals must be dry at the time of tying. Secure the wool with a couple of twists and loosen slightly each day. This technique is best avoided by the novice as blooms can be damaged in unskilled hands.

CUTTING If you are exhibiting locally it is possible to cut in the early morning of the day of the show so that you can make a last-minute selection. If the selected stems have to travel some distance then cutting the night before will be necessary and many experienced exhibitors believe that cutting the previous night is the right time even for the local show. You will then have time to prepare and grade the stems properly — there will be very little time on the morning of the show.

As soon as the blooms are cut, remove the lower leaves and thorns and immerse in water to at least half the stem length. Keep in a cool and dark place.

ON THE DAY OF THE SHOW

Leave in good time and take everything you will need with you. Make a check-list — there may be a surprising number of items to carry. A typical list will contain pens, labels, scissors, secateurs, notebook, schedule, rushes, knife, camel-hair brush, house plant watering can, florist's wire and cotton wool.

TRAVELLING Cut and take double the number of blooms called for in the schedule. There are many methods of transporting them in a car, and each exhibitor has his or her favourite way. The rules are to keep the bottom of the stems wet, the blooms dry (wrap in soft paper) and the stems quite tightly packed together. If you use a bucket, put in a top layer of balls of newspaper to prevent undue splashing. If several buckets are to be carried, place them in a crate with packing material between each one.

LABELLING Do write the name of the rose or roses neatly on a card and place it alongside your display. If you do not know the name of the variety, state "variety unknown". A clearly-labelled exhibit does impress the judges.

DRESSING This is the final arrangement of the petals to secure maximum beauty. Use either your finger or a camel-hair brush to open the outside petals and partially open the second row. Never "overdress" or disturb the natural arrangement.

If an outer petal has been damaged, carefully remove it and gently press down the one above to take its place.

WIRING This is useful for roses to be arranged in vases, provided that it is not forbidden in the rules.

Push one end of the wire (obtainable from florists) into the swollen receptacle below the petals and twist the lower half around the stem. The flower can be easily broken off the stalk if this job is done clumsily, so practise on ordinary flowers from the garden before the big day.

STAGING THE EXHIBIT

3 bloom display

6 bloom display

Vases
Obtain vase from the Show Secretary on arrival. Pack with rushes before inserting the stems — make sure that lower leaves and thorns have been removed. Blooms should be close but not touching. Place the largest bloom at the base of the display. After arranging, fill the vase with water.

Bowls
Each bloom must be clear of its neighbour, but large bare gaps must be avoided. In a bowl of mixed varieties, do not have any two similarly coloured blooms next to each other. Use bright colours separated by pastel shades. If you have to supply your own bowl, make sure that it is simple in shape and neutral in colour.

Boxes
Box classes have declined in popularity. You will have to make or purchase your own specimen box for six or twelve blooms — they are not supplied by the organisers. Blooms should not touch — place the largest flowers in the back tubes which should be raised for extra display. Fill the space between the blooms with fresh green moss and label the display.

Increasing your stock

There are four ways of propagating roses — seed-sowing, layering, budding and taking cuttings. All of these methods are described in this section, but they are certainly not of equal importance. Seed-sowing and layering are rarely-used techniques for a limited number of varieties. Your basic choice, therefore, is between budding and taking cuttings.

Each of these two methods has its advantages and drawbacks. Most commercially-grown roses are raised by **budding**, which involves the insertion of a bud or "eye" of the selected variety into a T-shaped cut in the stem of a rootstock — close to the ground for a bush or some distance up the stem for a standard. It is suitable for all modern varieties, and the new plant has ready-made roots which results in quick development. But there are some disadvantages for the ordinary gardener — it calls for obtaining rootstocks and acquiring new skills.

Taking cuttings is the more popular method for the amateur — it really does mean getting new roses for nothing. The technique is child's play, but there are drawbacks. Not all roses can be propagated in this way and the new plants will take about three years before they are fully established in the garden.

BUDDING

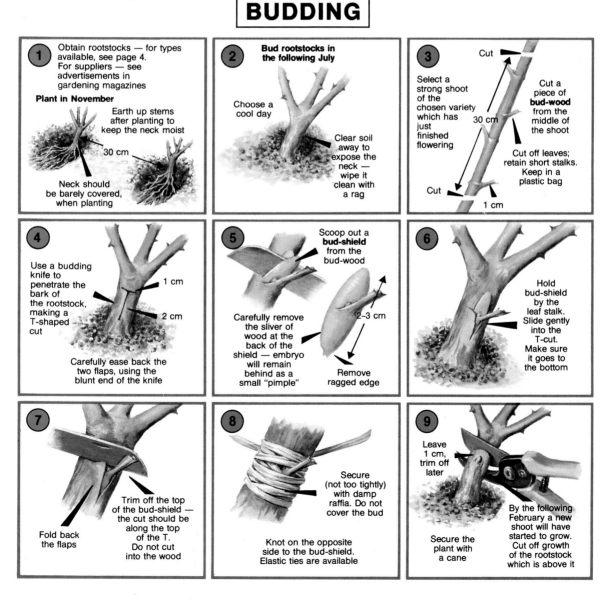

1 Obtain rootstocks — for types available, see page 4. For suppliers — see advertisements in gardening magazines

Plant in November

Earth up stems after planting to keep the neck moist

30 cm

Neck should be barely covered, when planting

2 **Bud rootstocks in the following July**

Choose a cool day

Clear soil away to expose the neck — wipe it clean with a rag

3 Select a strong shoot of the chosen variety which has just finished flowering

Cut

Cut a piece of **bud-wood** from the middle of the shoot

30 cm

Cut off leaves; retain short stalks. Keep in a plastic bag

Cut

1 cm

4 Use a budding knife to penetrate the bark of the rootstock, making a T-shaped cut

1 cm

2 cm

Carefully ease back the two flaps, using the blunt end of the knife

5 Scoop out a **bud-shield** from the bud-wood

Carefully remove the sliver of wood at the back of the shield — embryo will remain behind as a small "pimple"

2-3 cm

Remove ragged edge

6 Hold bud-shield by the leaf stalk. Slide gently into the T-cut. Make sure it goes to the bottom

7 Fold back the flaps

Trim off the top of the bud-shield — the cut should be along the top of the T. Do not cut into the wood

8 Secure (not too tightly) with damp raffia. Do not cover the bud

Knot on the opposite side to the bud-shield. Elastic ties are available

9 Leave 1 cm, trim off later

Secure the plant with a cane

By the following February a new shoot will have started to grow. Cut off growth of the rootstock which is above it

TAKING CUTTINGS

This method is not recommended for many Hybrid Teas, especially the yellow varieties, as the root system may be too weak to transplant satisfactorily, but you can expect to succeed with Ramblers, vigorous Climbers, vigorous Floribundas and most Shrub Roses. An advantage of a rooted cutting compared to a budded rootstock is the absence of suckers — all shoots belong to the variety being grown.

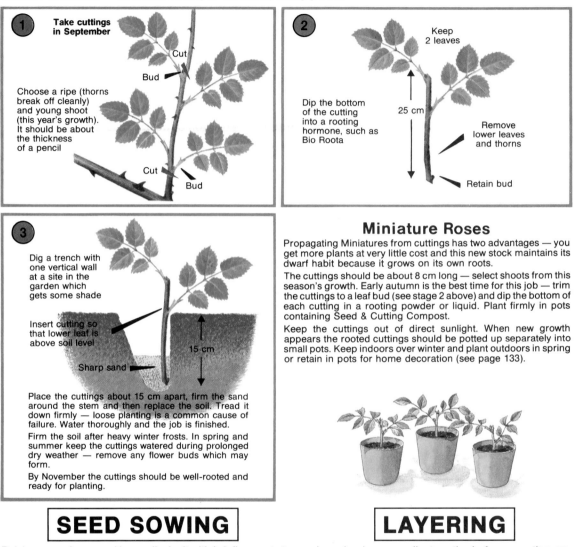

1 **Take cuttings in September**

Cut
Bud

Choose a ripe (thorns break off cleanly) and young shoot (this year's growth). It should be about the thickness of a pencil

Cut
Bud

2 Keep 2 leaves

Dip the bottom of the cutting into a rooting hormone, such as Bio Roota

25 cm

Remove lower leaves and thorns

Retain bud

3 Dig a trench with one vertical wall at a site in the garden which gets some shade

Insert cutting so that lower leaf is above soil level

15 cm

Sharp sand

Place the cuttings about 15 cm apart, firm the sand around the stem and then replace the soil. Tread it down firmly — loose planting is a common cause of failure. Water thoroughly and the job is finished.

Firm the soil after heavy winter frosts. In spring and summer keep the cuttings watered during prolonged dry weather — remove any flower buds which may form.

By November the cuttings should be well-rooted and ready for planting.

Miniature Roses

Propagating Miniatures from cuttings has two advantages — you get more plants at very little cost and this new stock maintains its dwarf habit because it grows on its own roots.

The cuttings should be about 8 cm long — select shoots from this season's growth. Early autumn is the best time for this job — trim the cuttings to a leaf bud (see stage 2 above) and dip the bottom of each cutting in a rooting powder or liquid. Plant firmly in pots containing Seed & Cutting Compost.

Keep the cuttings out of direct sunlight. When new growth appears the rooted cuttings should be potted up separately into small pots. Keep indoors over winter and plant outdoors in spring or retain in pots for home decoration (see page 133).

SEED SOWING

Raising roses from seed is usually dealt with briefly or not at all in the textbooks. There is no point in trying to raise a hybrid in this way — it will not breed true. The Species Roses will be true to type when grown from seed, but they will take years to reach a reasonable size and are much more easily raised from cuttings.

Miniature Roses are different — it is worthwhile growing them from seed and you can buy packets of various mixtures from several seedsmen. No long delays are involved — seeds sown in gentle heat in spring may be in flower by summer. Sow indoors in April in Seed & Cutting Compost. Germination is rather slow and erratic so try to sow a reasonable quantity of seeds. Prick out the best seedlings into small pots and make your selection in summer. Some of the young plants are bound to be poor and spindly — throw them away and just keep the most attractive. Repot as necessary and overwinter the plants in a cold greenhouse or on the windowsill of an unheated room.

LAYERING

Layering is an excellent method of propagating any rose which bears long and flexible stems. It is ideal for many Shrubs and Climbers.

In July or August work some peat into the area where the layering is to take place. Choose a stem which is mature but still flexible, and make a cut about 8 cm long on the side of the stem which will be buried in the prepared area. Place a twig in this cut and then bury this section in the ground. It should be pegged down with a forked stick.

The tip of the shoot should be secured in an upright position by tying it to a cane, and the ground should be kept watered in dry weather. Rooting will have taken place by the following March, and the new plant can be separated from the parent by cutting through the section of stem between them. Transplant the new rose — do not allow it to flower during its first season.

Breeding a new rose

SEED PARENT
The plant which serves as the female. It is fertilized to produce the seeds.

POLLEN PARENT
The plant which serves as the male. It is used to provide pollen for the seed parent.

Breeding roses at home is like buying a national lottery ticket — it is easy to enter but almost impossible to come up with a winner. To raise a new rose is simple — you just transfer the pollen of one variety to the stigmas of another and then sow the seeds which result. Each seedling will be unique, but the chance of one being a significant advance in the rose world is almost nil.

Professional breeders often talk about the large element of luck in the discovery of a winner, but for them it is much more than a lottery. Great care goes into the selection of parents, hundreds of thousands of seedlings are raised and a high degree of skill goes into the detection of desirable characteristics at an early stage.

None of this need worry the novice. Home-bred plants need not be world-beaters — there is great satisfaction in having a variety, however flawed, which doesn't exist anywhere else!

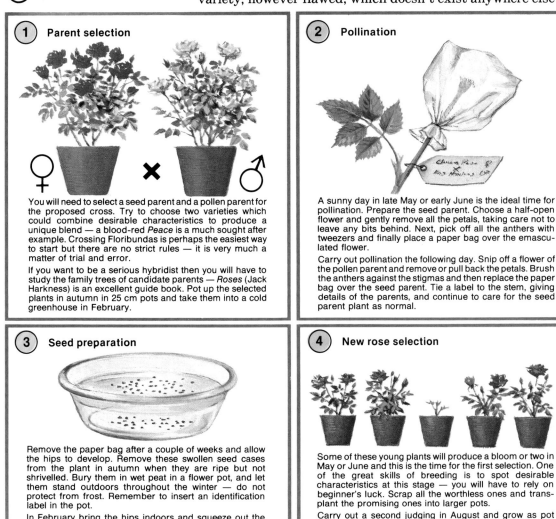

1 Parent selection

You will need to select a seed parent and a pollen parent for the proposed cross. Try to choose two varieties which could combine desirable characteristics to produce a unique blend — a blood-red *Peace* is a much sought after example. Crossing Floribundas is perhaps the easiest way to start but there are no strict rules — it is very much a matter of trial and error.

If you want to be a serious hybridist then you will have to study the family trees of candidate parents — *Roses* (Jack Harkness) is an excellent guide book. Pot up the selected plants in autumn in 25 cm pots and take them into a cold greenhouse in February.

2 Pollination

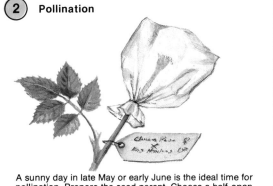

A sunny day in late May or early June is the ideal time for pollination. Prepare the seed parent. Choose a half-open flower and gently remove all the petals, taking care not to leave any bits behind. Next, pick off all the anthers with tweezers and finally place a paper bag over the emasculated flower.

Carry out pollination the following day. Snip off a flower of the pollen parent and remove or pull back the petals. Brush the anthers against the stigmas and then replace the paper bag over the seed parent. Tie a label to the stem, giving details of the parents, and continue to care for the seed parent plant as normal.

3 Seed preparation

Remove the paper bag after a couple of weeks and allow the hips to develop. Remove these swollen seed cases from the plant in autumn when they are ripe but not shrivelled. Bury them in wet peat in a flower pot, and let them stand outdoors throughout the winter — do not protect from frost. Remember to insert an identification label in the pot.

In February bring the hips indoors and squeeze out the seeds into a bowl of water. The floaters are infertile — sow the ones which have sunk to the bottom. Use Seed & Cutting Compost and when the first true rose leaves appear transplant the seedlings into small pots.

4 New rose selection

Some of these young plants will produce a bloom or two in May or June and this is the time for the first selection. One of the great skills of breeding is to spot desirable characteristics at this stage — you will have to rely on beginner's luck. Scrap all the worthless ones and transplant the promising ones into larger pots.

Carry out a second judging in August and grow as pot roses for a second season the few you wish to retain. If one shows promise you can plant it outdoors on its own roots or bud it on to a rootstock in July. You now have your very own rose variety growing in the garden.

CHAPTER 9
ROSES IN THE HOME

The use of cut roses for flower arranging is universal — apart from countless garden blooms employed for this purpose, scores of millions of florist roses are sold every year. Any of your roses can be used for cutting but some last longer than others — see the Recommended List below for varieties which have a longer-than-average vase life.

There are many other uses for roses indoors, but the part they play in the home has declined in the sophisticated world of today. In the homes of Ancient Rome, in the refectories of mediaeval monasteries and in the kitchens of large Victorian villas you could find rose wine, rose perfumes, rose jams and so on. These are now rarities, but there is no reason why you should not try some of the old recipes which appear in this chapter.

THE ROSE AS A CUT FLOWER

It is not surprising that the favourite garden flower should be so popular for cutting. Unfortunately, as poets throughout the ages have pointed out, rose blooms are short-lived. Although you cannot expect cut roses to last as long as carnations, anemones or chrysanthemums, their life can be considerably extended if you follow a few simple rules when cutting, conditioning and arranging.

1 CUTTING

Choose a variety recommended for cutting. See list below and check in the A–Z guides (pages 13–43)

Blooms cut too early or too late will disappoint. Hybrid Teas: Sepals opened out; petals in the bud showing colour. Floribundas: Most of the flowers in the truss half-open

Cut in the evening if you can — otherwise cut in the morning

Cut just above a leaf. See page 110

Put cut blooms in a bucket of tepid water immediately

2 CONDITIONING

Remove lower leaves and thorns. Slit the bottom of each stem upwards for about 2–3 cm. Stems should be stood up to their necks in water

Keep the bucket of roses in a cool dark place overnight

Bucket filled with water containing a dessertspoonful of sugar

If the leaves have wilted in the morning, stand ends of stems in 2–3 cm of very hot water for a few minutes before arranging

3 ARRANGING

Arrangement can be a single flower or a massed display. Roses can be grouped alone or mixed with other flowers

Keep the arrangement in good light but out of direct sunlight

Fill with tepid water — add a preservative to extend life of blooms and keep water fresh

If plastic foam is used as the base, soak throughly before use and fix in position before inserting stems

Drying Roses

Dried roses will last almost indefinitely if you handle and arrange them with care. Choose semi-double blooms — cut off the stems and when quite dry lay the flowers face upwards on a layer of oven-dry fine sand in a biscuit tin. Leave about 2–3 cm between the blooms. Slowly add more dry sand so that all parts of the flowers are covered — avoid air pockets. Finally, cover the blooms with a 3–5 cm layer of sand and replace the lid. Seal with adhesive tape.

Store in a warm dry place for three weeks. Remove blooms gently — they should be dry and crisp. Turn each one upside down and shake out the sand — remove any remaining grains with a fine brush. Insert a piece of stout florist wire in the base of each bloom and cover with green florist tape.

RECOMMENDED VARIETIES

Hybrid Teas	Floribundas
ALEXANDER	AMBER QUEEN
ALPINE SUNSET	ANISLEY DICKSON
APRICOT SILK	ANNA FORD
BARKAROLE	ANNE HARKNESS
BLUE MOON	ARTHUR BELL
DUTCH GOLD	BUCKS FIZZ
ELIZABETH HARKNESS	CHANELLE
FULTON MACKAY	CITY OF LONDON
JULIA'S ROSE	DEAREST
JUST JOEY	ELIZABETH OF GLAMIS
LOVERS' MEETING	ENGLISH MISS
MISCHIEF	GLENFIDDICH
NATIONAL TRUST	GREENSLEEVES
PASCALI	ICEBERG
PEACE	LIVERPOOL ECHO
PRECIOUS PLATINUM	MARGARET MERRIL
ROYAL WILLIAM	MELODY MAKER
RUBY WEDDING	ORANGES & LEMONS
SAVOY HOTEL	PINK PARFAIT
SILVER JUBILEE	QUEEN ELIZABETH
SILVER WEDDING	RED GOLD
SUNBLEST	REMEMBRANCE
TROIKA	SEXY REXY
VALENCIA	SHEILA'S PERFUME
WENDY CUSSONS	SOUTHAMPTON

THE ROSE AS A HOUSE PLANT

The more books you read on growing roses indoors, the more confused you will become. At one end of the scale are the British authorities who claim that the Miniature Rose is not a house plant at all. It is a garden plant, to be brought indoors when the buds start to colour and then taken out again as soon as the flowers have faded.

At the other end of the scale there are the U.S enthusiasts who scoff at such an idea — for them the Miniature Rose is a true indoor plant, providing regular flushes of blooms every two months throughout the year.

Surprisingly, both these opposed views are correct — it depends on the care provided. If all you want to do is put the pot on the sideboard and water it occasionally then it is right to keep the plant indoors for as short a time as possible. If however you can provide fluorescent lighting above the pots and a humid atmosphere around them, then it is perfectly feasible to achieve the American all-the-year-round result.

The best compromise for most rose growers is to use the Pebble Tray technique. By this method you can have Miniature Roses in bloom by early spring in the living room, and there they can stay, producing regular flushes of flowers until late summer or early autumn.

The secret is to ensure that the plants receive **maximum light** and **adequate humidity** whilst they are indoors — see the diagram below for details.

Use rooted cuttings rather than Miniatures which have been budded on to rootstocks. In autumn transfer the pots outdoors and bring them in again in January. Prune to about half their present height and stand the pots in an unheated room for about two weeks before placing them in the heated room where they are to bloom. Avoid temperatures above 22°C. Keep a careful watch for red spider mite.

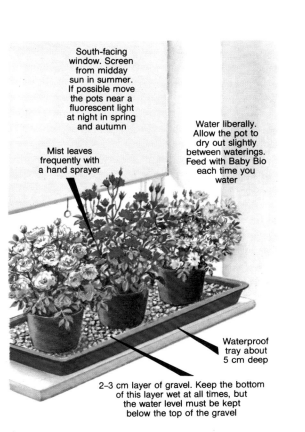

South-facing window. Screen from midday sun in summer. If possible move the pots near a fluorescent light at night in spring and autumn

Mist leaves frequently with a hand sprayer

Water liberally. Allow the pot to dry out slightly between waterings. Feed with Baby Bio each time you water

Waterproof tray about 5 cm deep

2–3 cm layer of gravel. Keep the bottom of this layer wet at all times, but the water level must be kept below the top of the gravel

THE ROSE IN PERFUME-MAKING

Pot-pourri

Pot-pourri is a mixture of dried flower petals and sweet-smelling oils, spices and fixatives. When the mixture has matured, it is placed in open bowls or pomanders to scent the room or placed in sachets in drawers to scent the linen.

Choose fragrant roses when they are at their prime. Cut them when the petals are dry. Spread a thin layer of petals on newspapers and place in a warm, dry room — an airing cupboard is ideal. Stir occasionally and when the petals are cornflake crisp after one or two weeks, place them in a polythene bag. Add the following mixture to the bag:

For each quart of dried petals —

    30 gm dried orris root (to 'fix' the scents)

    ½ teaspoon allspice

    ½ teaspoon cinnamon

    A few drops of rose oil

Shake thoroughly and leave the bag closed for about three weeks — then place the pot-pourri in any attractive container.

This is the basic rose pot-pourri. To vary the scent add dried orange and lemon peel, or dried aromatic leaves such as scented geranium, mint, rosemary, etc.

Rose Water

You can buy rose water from your local chemist, but if you have a plentiful supply of fragrant blooms you can try to make your own in the following age-old way:

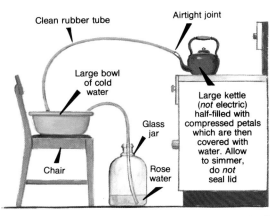

Clean rubber tube

Airtight joint

Large bowl of cold water

Large kettle (not electric) half-filled with compressed petals which are then covered with water. Allow to simmer, do not seal lid

Glass jar

Chair

Rose water

When the kettle is nearly (but not completely) dry, switch off the heat. Carefully drain the contents of the tube into the glass jar.

Rose Oil

You will not be able to obtain concentrated rose essence from your roses (it takes about 5 tonnes of fragrant petals to produce just half a kilogram of attar of roses) but you can make a simple rose oil if you have an abundance of petals and time.

Place half a litre of olive oil in a large bowl and add as many fragrant petals as the container will hold. Leave them to soak in the oil for two days and then squeeze through a fine strainer. Press the petals against the inside of the sieve to ensure that all the oils are squeezed out.

Repeat the process about ten times with fresh petals. Finally, decant the oil into a container with an airtight screw lid. Use the oil as a perfume or for making pot-pourri.

THE ROSE IN THE KITCHEN

The rose is not a vegetable — it is a plant to be admired for its beauty in the garden outdoors or in a vase or pot indoors. But there are recipes which call for roses, and one or two of them can be tried by the adventurous cook. If you intend to follow any of these recipes, make sure that the petals or hips are fresh and disease-free, and they should not have been recently sprayed or dusted. Petals and hips can be used in many ways, but never use rose leaves.

Rose Hip Jam

Wash and 'tail' the rose hips. Place in a large pan with an equal volume of water and cook until tender — about 15 minutes. Push the pulp through a fine strainer and to each cup of pulped hips add half a cup of sugar. Cook and stir until the mixture thickens to a jam-like consistency and then pour into sterilized jars and seal.

Rose Vinegar

Fill a large glass or glazed earthenware jar with red fragrant petals. Press them down and cover with wine vinegar. Cover the jar and leave for several weeks; then filter into screw-topped bottles.

Crystallised Rose Petals

Prepare a bowl containing beaten egg whites and another containing granulated sugar. Remove the petals gently from a dry bloom and using tweezers dip each one first into the frothy egg whites (avoid any excess on the petals) and then into the granulated sugar. Dry the crystallised petals on a lined baking tray in the airing cupboard. Store between layers of greaseproof paper in an airtight tin.

Rose Honey

Wash and 'tail' 100 gm of rose hips and boil in a cup of water in an enamel saucepan for about 15 minutes. Push the pulp through a fine strainer and add 450 gm of honey. Boil and stir the mixture until it thickens to a jam-like consistency and then pour into sterilized jars and seal.

Rose Wine

Rose wines have been made in Britain for centuries, but the methods used often led to failure. The modern techniques of home wine-making have taken the risks and guesswork out of this absorbing hobby, and both petals and hips can be used to make rose wine. You will need about 2 litres of petals or 1 litre of hips to make 5 litres of wine.

There are more ingredients than just rose petals or hips plus sugar and water. The list is a long one, including yeast, nutrient tablets, Campden tablets, pectin-destroying enzyme and grape tannin. There is also special equipment — fermentation jars, airlocks, filters and the rest. Do not let this list put you off — if you have never tried your hand at wine-making you can begin with roses and a simple guide from your bookshop will give you step-by-step instructions.

If you do not wish to go to the trouble and expense of wine-making it is possible to make 'instant' rose wine. Just mix 250 gm of red fragrant petals with half a litre of hot water and pulp them through a fine sieve. Add more petals until the liquor is a rich red colour and then stir in 450 gm of sugar and ¼ litre of brandy.

THE ROSE AS A BUTTONHOLE FLOWER

Once the buttonhole rose was the badge of nearly every stationmaster and City gentleman, but its popularity has greatly declined. No more will you find it described in the rose books, but some men do still wear a rose in their lapel — the summer-long symbol of their hobby.

Any shapely and compact bloom will do — the ideal is a half-opened bud, pointed and high-centred with a good colour. There are varieties which have earned a high reputation as buttonhole roses (*Cecile Brunner* and *Sweet Dream* are examples) but many other Hybrid Tea and Shrub Roses will do just as well.

Pick your buttonhole rose in the evening and stand its short stem immediately in tepid water. Leave it overnight and then prepare it for your jacket. The fashion in the early years of this century was to insert the stem into a water-filled metal tube worn at the back of the lapel, but these and the glass tubes which replaced them are now gone.

The modern way of preparing a buttonhole rose is shown on the right. As you can see, neither skill nor a special holder is called for.

Silver foil or green florist tape wrapped tightly around both the stem and the cotton wool covering the base

Cotton wool, soaked in water, placed around the cut end of the stem

CHAPTER 10

ROSE CALENDAR

JANUARY

Frosts are likely, so there is usually little to do in the rose garden this month.

Check roses growing on supports to make sure that the ties are strong enough to hold them. Inspect autumn-planted bushes and standards to see if they have been loosened by frosts. Firm if necessary.

Planting can take place if soil is free-draining and not heavy, and if weather is dry and not freezing. Beds to be planted in March should be prepared this month.

Heating of the greenhouse containing pot roses may be required to keep the temperature at 4°–7°C.

FEBRUARY

The soil will almost certainly be wet and cold, but planting can continue in light-soil areas if the temperature is above freezing. In mild districts the pruning of vigorous Floribundas can begin at the end of the month. Stocks budded last year can be cut back.

Pot roses will now be starting to grow, and a temperature of 10°–15°C should be maintained. Spray the shoots with water to create moist conditions. Greenfly and caterpillars can cause serious damage to the new and tender shoots, so keep careful watch for these pests and spray at the first sign of attack.

MARCH

Finish planting this month. In most areas March is the best time to prune bush and standard roses. Burn all prunings.

Fertilizer may be spread around the bushes immediately after pruning and lightly pricked into the surface, but it is generally better to wait until April.

Weed beds thoroughly — apply a simazine-based weedkiller if regular hoeing is not possible.

Pot roses in the greenhouse may now be in bud. A weekly feed with a liquid fertilizer will improve bloom quality. Continue spraying shoots with water. Increase house temperature to 15°–18°C.

APRIL

Pruning must be completed by the beginning of the month, as roses will now be starting to grow actively. Rub out any surplus young shoots.

Apply a fertilizer, such as Toprose, which contains the main and minor plant foods needed by the rose. Keep the powder off new growth, and lightly prick into the soil surface.

Neaten bed edges with a half-moon edging iron. In areas where bad attacks of black spot are common apply two Systhane sprays a week apart as soon as leaf buds open.

Continue feeding and watering pot roses under glass, some of which will bloom this month. Spraying with water should now be directed at the paths, not on the roses. Keep watch for mildew, greenfly and caterpillar. Ideal house temperature is 18°–24°C. Apply Coolglass to the panes if weather is sunny.

MAY

Garden roses will now be growing rapidly, and a mulch should be applied around the stems. Hoeing can be carried out to destroy weeds, but do not dig in the mulching material.

The first of the early-flowering Shrubs (e.g *Canary Bird*) will now be in flower.

Greenfly attacks are likely, and a systemic insecticide which works internally is the best method of control (see page 116). A spray or dust for other insect pests or early disease outbreak may be necessary — watch for first attacks. If you plan to feed using the liquid fertilizer approach then apply the first feed this month when the soil is moist. Apply a foliar feed to backward plants.

Visit the Chelsea Flower Show in London.

Pot roses which have finished flowering should be moved outdoors and stood on concrete, ashes, etc, but not on earth. Water as necessary.

JUNE

Roses are now coming into flower. Hoeing, spraying and watering should continue as necessary.

Mulch with grass clippings if they are free from weedkiller. Cut flowers for indoor decoration from established plants, not from newly-planted bushes.

Disbudding of Hybrid Teas (see page 110) will ensure top-quality blooms. A summer fertilizer dressing with Toprose will keep the plants growing vigorously and help to produce a succession of flower buds. If you plan to enter your roses at a flower show, obtain show schedule as soon as possible. Continue foliar feeding for top-quality blooms.

Apply a mixed systemic insecticide/fungicide spray to keep pests and diseases at bay.

The last of the pot roses should now be moved out from the greenhouse to their outdoor quarters.

JULY

Bushes and standards should now be in full flower — July is usually the best month to enjoy your roses. Dead-head (see page 110) flower stalks when the blooms they carry have finished flowering. Apply a summer dressing of fertilizer if this was not done last month.

Hoe, disbud, mulch and water if necessary as described for June. Keep a special watch for the first signs of black spot and mildew. Spray immediately if seen.

If you are going away on holiday, remove all flowers which have begun to fade so that hips will not form during your absence.

Visit the British Rose Festival which is part of the Hampton Court Palace Flower Show in London. Many local rose shows are held during this month.

Bud rootstocks this month.

AUGUST

The cultural techniques described for July apply this month, with the exception of fertilizer application which should stop at the end of July.

Now is the time to start thinking ahead to next year's varieties for your garden. If you can, visit the nursery of a large specialist rose grower to see the new varieties in bloom. Your local garden centre is well worth a visit. Some nurseries have special Display Gardens (see page 124). Other displays worth visiting are the RNRS Gardens of the Rose at St Albans, the Provincial Display Gardens (see page 124) and the Southport Flower Show.

Send off your rose order as soon as possible, as new introductions and popular varieties are frequently sold out before planting time.

Begin the preparation of new rose beds as described in Chapter 5.

SEPTEMBER

Roses will generally still be flowering freely, and dead-heading now will help to ensure a fine late display.

Vigorous summer-flowering Climbers and weeping standards should have been pruned by now (see page 109). Never leave these plants for pruning in the spring.

Carry on preparing new beds for planting in November and despatch your order to the nursery if this was not done last month.

Continue hoeing and spraying against disease if necessary. September is a good month to take cuttings of Climbers, vigorous Floribundas etc. See page 130 for instructions.

Visit the Great Autumn Show in Harrogate — many local autumn rose shows are held in September.

OCTOBER

This month is the start of the rose grower's year. Tidy up beds. Hoe in the mulching material and collect up and burn leaves.

Finish preparing new beds. Nurseries start sending out their plants in October and planting can start at the end of the month. Trim off leaves and unripe wood as described on page 103 before placing each plant in its new quarters.

Inspect pot roses this month, and repot if necessary. Buy and pot up new plants. Remove shading and clean out green-house. Begin bringing the plants inside at the end of October.

NOVEMBER

Get plants ready for winter. In exposed areas, long stems should be cut back a little to prevent wind rock during winter storms. In cold districts the stems should be earthed-up with about 10 cm of soil (remove in spring) or covered with straw (see page 113):

An excellent time for planting. If the bushes or standards arrive when the weather is unsuitable or before you are ready, leave package unopened or heel-in plants as described on page 103.

All pot roses should be placed in the greenhouse during this month.

DECEMBER

The soil will now generally be colder and wetter than last month so planting should be completed as soon as possible. Never try to plant when the soil is either hard with frost or waterlogged.

There is no work to do in the established rose garden, but work can begin on the preparation of rose beds which are to be planted up in March.

All pot roses will now be housed under glass and the temperature should be kept above freezing point if heat is available. Keep the pots fairly dry for a short time after housing, and prune at the end of the month.

CHAPTER 11

ROSE GROWER'S DICTIONARY

A

ACID SOIL A soil which contains no free lime and has a pH of less than 6.5.

AMERICAN ROSE SOCIETY Started in 1899, the ARS has become one of the most active rose societies in the world. Its members receive a monthly magazine together with the American Rose Annual each year, which features the *Proof of the Pudding* survey. The headquarters are at the American Rose Center where an extensive rose garden is being created. Details of membership can be obtained from the Secretary, American Rose Society, Shreveport, Louisiana, USA.

ANTHER The part of the flower which produces pollen. It is the upper section of the *stamen*.

ARMED Bearing strong thorns.

ATTAR OF ROSES A yellowish oil distilled from rose petals which is used for making perfumes. Its production has been a major industry in the Balkans for centuries.

AUSTIN, DAVID English breeder, who began hybridising in the 1950s. His 'English Roses' (*Graham Thomas*, *Constance Spry* etc) have become popular in Britain and the U.S — see page 74 for further details.

AXIL The angle between the upper surface of the leaf stalk and the stem that carries it.

B

BALLING The clinging together of petals in wet weather so that the bloom fails to open — see page 113.

BARE-ROOT A rose dug up at the nursery and sold with no soil around its roots — see page 91.

BASAL SHOOT A shoot arising from the neck or crown of the plant — see page 4.

BEALES, PETER English grower with the most comprehensive commercial collection in the world — 1200 varieties are offered for sale.

BENNETT, HENRY The father of scientific rose breeding. He was a cattle breeder, and realized the need to control the pollination and keep a careful record of the crosses. In 1879 he introduced his Ten Pedigree Hybrids of the Tea Rose.

BLEEDING The loss of sap from plant tissues due to late pruning.

BLIND SHOOT A mature stem which fails to produce a flower.

BLOWN BLOOM A many-petalled bloom which has opened wide, revealing its stamens.

BLUE ROSE No true-blue rose exists, and it is extremely unlikely that one will ever be raised, because the blue flower pigment (delphinidin) is missing from the rose family. The so called "blue" roses, such as *Blue Moon*, *Mr Bluebird* etc are really lavender, mauve or violet.

BLUEING The transformation of a red or deep pink bloom to mauve or purple as it ages.

BOSS The ring of stamens when it is prominent and decorative.

BOX A container which bears six or twelve tubes for the display of specimen blooms — see page 128.

BRACT A small leaf-like growth on the flower stalk — see page 4.

BREAKING BUD A bud which has started to open.

BRITISH ASSOCIATION REPRESENTING BREEDERS The objects of BARB are to encourage, improve and extend the introduction and growing of new roses under *Plant Breeders' Rights*. About 250 nurseries are registered with BARB, and there is a very simple method of licensing new varieties to these growers.

BRITISH ROSE GROWERS ASSOCIATION The BRGA is an association of the leading rose growers who jointly produce more than three-quarters of the roses sold in this country. They seek publicity for roses and rose growing, and to improve standards they publish information. The BRGA stages a major exhibit at the annual Rose Festival held at Hampton Court.

BUD A flower bud is the unopened bloom. A growth bud or *eye* is a condensed shoot found in the *axil* of a leafstalk.

BUD UNION The point where the bud and the rootstock are united.

BUDDING The grafting of a bud into the neck of a rootstock — see page 129. The standard commercial method of propagating roses.

BURNING The bleaching or scorching of the petals in bright sunshine.

BUSH A growth type — see page 4.

C

CALLUS The scar tissue which forms over a pruning cut or at the base of a cutting.

CALYX The green cover of the flower bud, which opens into five sepals.

CANE A main stem or basal shoot — a term frequently used in the U.S.

CANKER A diseased and discoloured area on the stem — see page 115.

CANTS OF COLCHESTER This distinguished nursery was started by William Cant in 1765. Its best-known success was *Just Joey*, and other well-known introductions include *Goldstar* and *English Miss*.

CHLOROSIS An abnormal yellowing or blanching of the leaves due to lack of chlorophyll. See page 113 for possible causes.

CLIMBING SPORT A mutation of a bush variety which bears longer stems but identical flowers to the parent.

CLUSTER A number of flowers connected by their *footstalks* to a single stem — see page 4.

COCKER, ALEC Scottish breeder, who began to raise roses in 1963 and died in 1977 — shortly before his great achievement *Silver Jubilee* received Britain's highest award. Other successes from the Aberdeen nursery include *Alec's Red*, *Rosy Mantle*, *Toprose*, *Fulton Mackay* and *Remember Me*.

COMPOST Two meanings — either decomposed vegetable or animal matter for incorporation in the soil or a potting/cutting mixture made from peat ('soilless compost') or sterilized soil ('loam compost') plus other materials such as sand, lime and fertilizer.

CONE A conical protector used by exhibitors to prevent rain and bright sunshine from spoiling their show blooms whilst they are still on the plant — see page 128.

CONFUSED CENTRE The centre of a bloom where the petals are disarranged, giving an asymmetrical appearance.

CROCK A piece of broken flower pot used at the bottom of a container to improve drainage.

CROSS The offspring arising from cross-pollination.

CROWN The point where the basal shoots sprout from the rootstock.

CULTIVAR Short for 'cultivated variety' — it is a variety which originated in cultivation and not in the wild. Strictly speaking, all modern varieties are cultivars, but the more familiar term *'variety'* is used in this book.

CUT-BACK A bush which is one or more seasons older than a *maiden*.

CUTTING A piece of stem cut from a plant and used for propagation.

D

DEAD-HEADING The removal of faded flowers — see page 110.

DE-SHOOTING The removal of small shoots to prevent overcrowding. Another term for 'thinning' — see page 110.

DICKSON & SONS LTD The Dickson nurseries in County Down have a long and distinguished history of rose breeding. There were Dickson roses before the 20th century and *Shot Silk* (1924) still appears in the catalogues. More recent successes have been *Grandpa Dickson, Melody Maker, Gentle Touch, Sweet Magic, Beautiful Britain* and *Magic Carpet*.

DIE-BACK The progressive dying back of a shoot from the tip — see page 115.

DISBUDDING The removal of young flower buds to allow the maximum development of the remainder — see page 110.

DOG ROSE The common wild rose found in hedgerows — so called because the Romans used it as a cure for hydrophobia.

DORMANT PERIOD The time when the plant has naturally stopped growing due to low temperature and short day-length.

DOT, PEDRO Spain's greatest hybridist. His work spanned 50 years and although he raised many noteworthy Hybrid Teas he will always be remembered as one of the world's leading breeders of Miniatures. *Josephine Wheatcroft, Pour Toi, Coralin* and *Baby Gold Star* are examples of his introductions.

DOUBLE BLOOM A flower with more than twenty petals — see page 5.

DRESSING The manipulation of an exhibition bloom in order to improve its appearance on the day of the show — see page 128.

E

EARTHING-UP The drawing up of earth around the base of a bush to protect it during a period of abnormally cold weather.

EMASCULATION A technique used in hybridising — the removal of the anthers from the seed parent to prevent self-pollination. See page 131.

EYE Two unrelated meanings — a dormant growth bud or the centre of a single or semi-double bloom where the colour is distinctly different from the rest of the flower.

F

FERTILE HYBRID A hybrid which bears viable seed capable of producing new plants. A sterile hybrid does not produce viable seed.

FERTILIZATION The application of pollen to the stigma to induce the production of seed.

FILAMENT The supporting column of the *anther*. It is the lower part of the *stamen*.

FIXED A vital feature for a new variety — it means that the new colour or growth habit is stable.

FLOWER-SHY A vague term indicating that a variety bears a below-average number of blooms during the flowering season. The opposite condition is *free-flowering*.

FLUSH The period during which the plant bears its normal complement of blooms — there may be more than one such period during the season — see *repeat flowering*.

FOLIAR FEED A fertilizer capable of being sprayed on and absorbed by the leaves — see page 111.

FOOTSTALK The pedicel or flower stalk — see page 4.

FORCING The process of making a plant grow or flower before its natural season.

FOSSIL ROSES Fossilized rose leaves have been found in rocks in Europe, Asia and North America. They are thought to be 7–30 million years old.

FREE-FLOWERING A vague term indicating that a variety bears an above-average number of blooms during the flowering season. The opposite condition is *flower-shy*.

FRYER'S ROSES A number of popular roses including Rose of the Year winners *Sweet Dream* and *Top Marks* have been bred by this Cheshire firm. Others include *Warm Wishes* and *The Lady*.

FUNGICIDE A chemical used to control diseases caused by fungi.

FUNGUS A primitive form of plant life which is the most common cause of infectious disease — mildew, black spot and rust are examples.

G

GARNETTE ROSE A red Floribunda, similar to the variety *Garnette*, grown commercially under glass for sale as a cut flower.

GRAFTING The process of joining a stem or bud of one plant on to the stem of another.

GREGORY, WALTER One of the group of great Nottinghamshire rose growers, who began breeding new varieties in 1952. In the span of nearly 30 years before his death in 1980, he introduced *Blessings, Pink Perpetue* and his crowning glory, *Wendy Cussons*.

GUILLOT, JEAN-BAPTISTE The first of the great rose breeders from Lyons. His creation in 1867, *La France*, was the original Hybrid Tea and started the era of the modern rose. In the following decade he introduced *Ma Paquerette, Gloire des Polyantha* and *Mignonette* — the first of the dwarf Polyanthas which gave rise to the modern Floribundas.

H

HARDY A plant which will withstand overwintering without any protection against frost.

HARKNESS, JACK The family firm was established in Yorkshire over 100 years ago, and in 1892 a branch was set up in Hertfordshire to specialise in roses. It was Jack Harkness who first turned to hybridising and his successes have been outstanding — *Alexander, Mountbatten, Compassion* and *Amber Queen.* His collaboration with Alec Cocker was one of the great success stories in the world of rose breeding. Other Harkness roses include *Savoy Hotel, Octavia Hill, Fellowship* and *Anna Ford.*

HEAD The framework of stems borne at the top of the stem of a standard.

HEADING-BACK The removal of the stems of the rootstock above the union after budding — see page 129.

HEELING IN The temporary planting of a new rose pending suitable weather conditions for permanent planting.

HEP See *hip.*

HILDESHEIM ROSE A specimen of *Dog Rose* growing at Hildesheim Cathedral in Germany. The legend is that it was planted by Charlemagne over 1,000 years ago, but it is probably 300–500 years old. Generally accepted as the oldest living rose.

HILLING U.S term for *earthing-up.*

HIP The fruit of a rose, large and decorative in some varieties — see page 6.

HOLE, REV SAMUEL REYNOLDS Although an active churchman (he became Dean of Rochester), Reverend Hole was the dominant figure in the Victorian rose world. He amassed a collection of 5,000 varieties, arranged the first National Rose Show and was a leading figure in the formation of the National Rose Society in 1876. The Dean Hole Medal is the RNRS's highest award for distinguished service.

HONEYDEW Sticky, sugary secretion deposited on the leaves and stems by such insects as aphid and whitefly.

HURST, CHARLES C. Cambridge scientist who worked out the family history of the modern rose, as outlined on pages 8–9.

HYBRID A rose with parents which are genetically distinct. The parent plants may be different *cultivars, varieties* or *species.*

I

INFLORESCENCE The arrangement of flowers on the stem.

INORGANIC A chemical or fertilizer which is not obtained from a source which is or has been alive.

INSECTICIDE A chemical used to control insect pests.

INTERNODE The part of the stem between one *node* and another.

J

JACKSON & PERKINS Claimed to be the largest rose nursery in the world. At their trial grounds in California many great roses have been raised, first by Eugene Boerner and more recently by William Warriner. Some are readily available in the U.K — examples are *Pristine, Dorothy Perkins* and *Masquerade.*

JOSEPHINE Empress Josephine, wife of Napoleon I, bought *Malmaison* in 1799 and set out to stock it with every variety of rose grown anywhere in the world. Her passion created the world's first rose display ground, and it made the rose a fashionable flower for the wealthy to grow on their estates.

K

KNUCKLE U.S term for *bud union.*

KORDES, WILHELM Wilhelm Kordes, until his death in 1977, ranked along-side *Tantau* as the greatest rose hybridist in Germany. The list of his introductions starts with *Crimson Glory* in 1935. Others include *Iceberg, Ernest H. Morse, Peer Gynt* and *Simba.* One of his most outstanding achievements was the development of the Kordesii climbers, such as *Dortmund* — more recent launches from the company include *Royal William, Grouse, Festival* and *The Times Rose.*

L

LANCASTER ROSE The Red Rose of Lancaster is *Rosa gallica officinalis* (see page 87). The legend is that the first Earl of Lancaster brought it from France to England during the 13th century.

LANKY Spindly growth — a stem with a gaunt and sparse appearance.

LATERAL BRANCH A side branch which arises from a main stem.

LAWRANCE, MARY Authoress of the first book devoted entirely to roses — 'A Collection of Roses from Nature' (1799).

LEACHING The drawing away of chemicals from the soil, caused by rain or watering.

LE GRICE, EDWARD Norfolk breeder who was responsible for one of the best yellow Floribundas — *Allgold.* His career was a long one; in 1938 he received a Certificate of Merit for *Dainty Maid* — in 1970 he was awarded a Gold Medal for *News.* In between these two were *My Choice* and *Lilac Charm.*

LENS, LOUIS The Lens nurseries have been the most successful breeding establishment in Belgium for half a century. Louis entered the firm in 1945 and later succeeded his father, Victor. His most famous introduction was *Pascali,* which remains one of the best white Hybrid Teas.

M

MAIDEN A rose bush in its first year after budding.

MALMAISON A chateau with extensive grounds situated near Paris, famous as the first great rose garden. Empress *Josephine* stocked it with more than 200 different varieties from all over the world and new techniques for breeding and cultivation were developed. Her work at Malmaison began in 1799 — following her divorce in 1809 she moved there permanently.

McGREDY, SAM Sam McGredy IV has a family tradition of rose breeding, and since taking over the nursery in 1952 in N. Ireland and then emigrating to New Zealand in 1972, he has joined the ranks of the world's great hybridists. Even his major achievements are too numerous to list in full — they include *Mischief, Piccadilly, Sexy Rexy, Regensberg, Arthur Bell, Evelyn Fison, Handel, Chanelle* and *Elizabeth of Glamis.*

MEILLAND Francois Meilland raised *Peace* just before World War II and secured an everlasting place in the Gardening Hall of Fame. Other successes included *Baccara,* but perhaps one of his greatest achieve-ments was to secure breeders' rights for new roses. Alain now carries on his father's work — *Papa Meilland, Susan Hampshire, Sweet Promise, Starina* and *Chorus* are a few of the products of the Antibes nursery.

MODERN ROSES The first edition of this rose variety 'bible' appeared in 1930. The latest edition of Modern Roses contains details of many thousands of varieties. It is produced by the *American Rose Society,* which is the international organization for the registration of rose names.

MOORE, RALPH S. Californian breeder who has revolutionised the world of Miniature Roses. He has developed Miniature Moss Roses and Miniature Climbers — his creations include *New Penny, Easter Morning* and *Little Buckaroo.*

MULCH A layer of bulky organic material placed around the stems.

MUTATION A sudden change in the genetic make-up of a plant, leading to a new feature which can be inherited.

N

NECK The part of the plant above the roots and below the stems.

NEUTRAL Neither acid nor alkaline — pH 6.5–7.5.

NODE The point on the stem at which a leaf or bud is attached.

NORMAN, A. An amateur rosarian, famous as the raiser of *Ena Harkness* and *Frensham.*

O

ORGANIC A chemical or fertilizer which is or has been alive.

OVARY The part of the flower which contains the *ovules.*

OVERDRESSED Petals which have been bent back to such an extent on the day of the show that the bloom has an unnatural appearance.

P

PEACE Seedling No. 3-35-40 was raised by Francois Meilland at Lyons before World War II and a few plants were sent out on the last plane to America as France fell. He had named the plant *Mme Antoine Meilland* but it was taken to Germany as *Gloria Dei.* When the War ended the U.S nursery which had raised his stock placed a bunch of the flowers at each seat at the Peace Conference. The rose received its final name — *Peace.*

PEDICEL The flower stalk — see page 4.

PEGGING DOWN The bending over of long shoots and the retention of their tips at ground level by means of pegs.

PERGOLA A long arched structure used to support climbing plants; a rose-covered tunnel.

PERNET-DUCHER, JOSEPH Born in 1858, he earned the title "Wizard of Lyons" by transforming the colour range of modern roses. His early successes included *Mme Caroline Testout,* but he is best remembered for *Soleil d'Or,* introduced in 1900, which brought yellow to bedding roses.

pH A measure of acidity and alkalinity. Below pH 6.5 is acid, above pH 7.5 is alkaline.

PISTIL The female organ of a flower, consisting of the *stigma, style* and *ovule.*

PITH The spongy material at the centre of the stem. An unripe stem is sometimes described as 'pithy'.

PLANT BREEDERS' RIGHTS Until the 1960s a U.K breeder of a new rose received no royalties from the growers who propagated and sold it. The first plant patent was awarded in the U.S — *New Dawn* in 1930. British protection dates from 1964 (the Plant Varieties & Seeds Act). Growers pay a small royalty to the breeder for each patented rose they propagate. The payment of a royalty does not apply if you propagate roses for your own pleasure and not for sale.

POLLEN The yellow dust produced by the *anthers.* It is the male element which fertilizes the *ovule.*

POLLINATION The application of *pollen* to the *stigma* of the flower.

POULSEN The Poulsen family of Denmark have produced many great roses during the past 60 years. Svend Poulsen raised the first Hybrid Polyantha (later called Floribundas) in 1924, and he was responsible for several famous varieties, such as *Else Poulsen.* The company has carried on the tradition with *Troika, White Bells* and *Chinatown.*

PROOF OF THE PUDDING The U.S equivalent of the Royal National Rose Society Analysis (see page 122). The ratings are based on the experience of members of the *American Rose Society* who have grown the roses in question.

PROPAGATION The multiplication of plants — see pages 129–130 for the range of methods.

PRUNING The removal of parts of the plant in order to improve its performance.

R

RECURRENT FLOWERING Same as *repeat flowering.*

REDOUTE, PIERRE JOSEPH French artist commissioned by Empress *Josephine* in 1805 to make a pictorial record of every rose grown at *Malmaison.* The three volumes of Les Roses portray 170 of these roses, and reproductions of these paintings are still immensely popular.

REMONTANT/REMONTANCE Same as *repeat flowering.*

REPEAT FLOWERING The production of two or more *flushes* during the flowering season — see page 6.

REVERSE The side of the petal which faces away from the centre.

REVERSION Two meanings — either a *sport* which goes back to the colour or growth habit of its parent or a cultivated variety which is outgrown by suckers arising from the rootstock.

RIVERS, THOMAS & SON LTD The first nursery in Britain — founded 1725. Their 'Rose Amateurs Guide' first appeared in 1837 and listed 700 varieties for sale.

ROGUE A rose supplied which was not ordered, and which is not close enough to be regarded as a *substitute.*

ROOTSTOCK The host plant on to which a cultivated variety is budded — see page 4.

ROSA The *genus* to which all roses belong. There are about 140 different species.

ROSACEAE The *family* to which roses belong, together with other plants which have rose-like flowers, such as cherry, plum, hawthorn and strawberry.
ROYAL NATIONAL ROSE SOCIETY See page 121.

S

SANGERHAUSEN Founded by the German Rose Society in 1903, this Rosarium is reputed to have the most extensive collection of old roses in the world.

SCION The technical term for the bud which is grafted on to the rootstock.

SEEDLING A young plant raised from seed; in the rose world it also means a mature plant raised by sowing seed rather than by budding or taking cuttings.

SEPAL One of the five green divisions of the *calyx*.

SHOOT A stem or cane. Some rose experts prefer to be more precise — a shoot is used for young growth, a stem describes mature growth.

SHOT A surface which changes colour when viewed from different points.

SIDE SHOOT Same as *lateral branch*.

SNAG A section of stem left above a bud when pruning.

SPECIES Roses which are genetically similar and which reproduce exactly when self-fertilized. The popular meaning is a wild rose or one of its near relatives.

SPIT The depth of the spade blade — usually about 25 cm.

SPLIT CENTRE Irregular arrangement of petals at centre.

SPORT A plant which shows a marked and inheritable change from its parent; a *mutation*.

SPOTTING The appearance of spots and blemishes on the petals during wet weather.

STAMEN The male organ of a flower, consisting of the *anther* and *filament*.

STIGMA The part of the female organ of the flower which catches the *pollen*.

STIPULE The small outgrowth at the base of the leafstalk.

STOCK See *rootstock*.

STRATIFICATION The breaking of seed dormancy by placing hips in a refrigerator or overwintering them outdoors in damp peat before removing seeds for sowing — see page 131.

STRIKE The successful outcome of taking cuttings — cuttings 'strike' whereas grafts *'take'*.

STYLE The part of the female organ of the flower which connects the *stigma* to the *ovule*.

SUBSTITUTE A similar variety sent out by a nurseryman if the ordered variety is not available.

SUCKER A shoot growing from the rootstock — see page 119.

SWIM, HERBERT C. Californian hybridist who has produced more All-American Selection Award winners than any other breeder. His successes include *Sutter's Gold, Summer Sunshine, Mojave, Pink Parfait, Royal Highness* and *Mister Lincoln*.

SYSTEMIC A pesticide which goes inside the plant and travels in the sap stream.

T

TAKE The successful outcome of budding — grafts 'take' whereas cuttings *'strike'*.

TANTAU The father and son partnership of Mathias Tantau and Mathias junior has produced such world-famous roses as *Super Star* and *Fragrant Cloud*. The first Tantau rose from the N. German nursery was *Beauty of Holstein* (1919). Since then the list has been outstanding — *Deep Secret, Whisky Mac, Polar Star, Chatsworth, Glad Tidings, Blue Moon, Prima Ballerina* and many more.

THORN A characteristic spine or prickle, usually found on the stems but occasionally on the backs of leaves and on hips.

TRANSPLANTING Movement of a plant from one site to another.

TREE ROSE U.S term for a standard rose — see page 4.

TRUSS A number of flowers connected by their *footstalks* to a single stem — see page 4.

TUDOR ROSE The royal badge of England, combining the Red Rose of Lancaster with the White Rose of York. It was adopted as our national emblem when Henry Tudor (Henry VII) married Elizabeth of York in 1486.

U

UNDERSTOCK See *rootstock*.

UNION See *bud union*.

V

VARIETY Strictly speaking, a naturally occurring variation of a species (see *cultivar*). The popular meaning in the rose world is any distinct type of rose which bears one or more unique features.

W

WEEPING STANDARD A Rambler budded on to a tall standard stem — see page 4.

WHEATCROFT, HARRY Until his death in 1977, Harry Wheatcroft was 'Mr Rose' to millions of British gardeners. His nursery at Edwalton, Nottinghamshire, produced two million plants a year, but he will be best remembered for his personal appearances and his introduction to Britain of such great roses as *Super Star, Peace, Fragrant Cloud* and *Queen Elizabeth*.

WILD ROSES Rose species which are native to a particular country. The British wild roses include *R. arvensis (Field Rose), R. canina (Dog Rose), R. pimpinellifolia (Burnet Rose),* and *R. eglanteria (Sweet Briar)*.

WILLMOTT, ELLEN Authoress of 'Genus Rosa' published between 1910 and 1914 with illustrations painted by Alfred Parsons. This book is regarded as one of the milestones in rose literature, rivalling the work of *Redoute*.

WORLD FEDERATION OF ROSE SOCIETIES The rose societies of 17 nations belong to this worldwide organization which held its first meeting in New Zealand in 1971. It meets every few years, and its objects include establishing common standards for judging and classification, granting international awards, avoiding confusion over the naming of new roses and encouraging research.

WORLD'S FAVOURITE ROSE Competition run by the *World Federation of Rose Societies* in which each member society votes. Winners have included *Peace, Queen Elizabeth, Fragrant Cloud, Iceberg* and *Double Delight*.

Y

YORK ROSE The identity of the White Rose of York is not known for certain. It was probably *Rosa alba semi-plena*, but it may have been *R. arvensis*.

CHAPTER 12

ROSE INDEX

Acknowledgements

The author wishes to acknowledge the painstaking work of Gill Jackson, Paul Norris, Linda Fensom and Angelina Gibbs. Grateful acknowledgement is also made for the help or photographs received from Peter Harkness, Angela Pawsey (Cants of Colchester and BRGA), Tony Slack (BARB), Lt-Col Ken Grapes (RNRS), Robert Wharton (Whartons Nurseries Ltd), David Clark (Notcutts Nurseries), Chris Styles (L W van Geest Farms Ltd), Rosemary Gandy (Gandy's Roses Ltd), Gareth Fryer (Fryers Nurseries Ltd), Pat Dickson (Dickson Nurseries Ltd), Alec Cocker (James Cocker & Sons), Peter Beales (Peter Beales Roses), David Austin (David Austin Roses Ltd), Chris Wheatcroft (Wheatcroft Roses Ltd), Keith Jones (C & K Jones), Selection Meilland UK Ltd, Dick Balfour, Joan Hessayon, Colin Bailey, Barry Highland (Spot On Repro Ltd), Harry Smith Horticultural Photographic Collection, The Lord & Lady Tollemache, Pat Brindley, Mary Evans Picture Library, Sotheby's Picture Library, Rex Butcher/ The Garden Picture Library, David Askham/The Garden Picture Library, Bob Challinor/The Garden Picture Library, J Sira/The Garden Picture Library, Brigitte Thomas/The Garden Picture Library, Len Wood and Jerry Harpur.

Artwork for this book was produced by the late John Woodbridge, Henry Barnett, Norman Barber and John Dye.